IMAGES
of America

HENDRICKS COUNTY

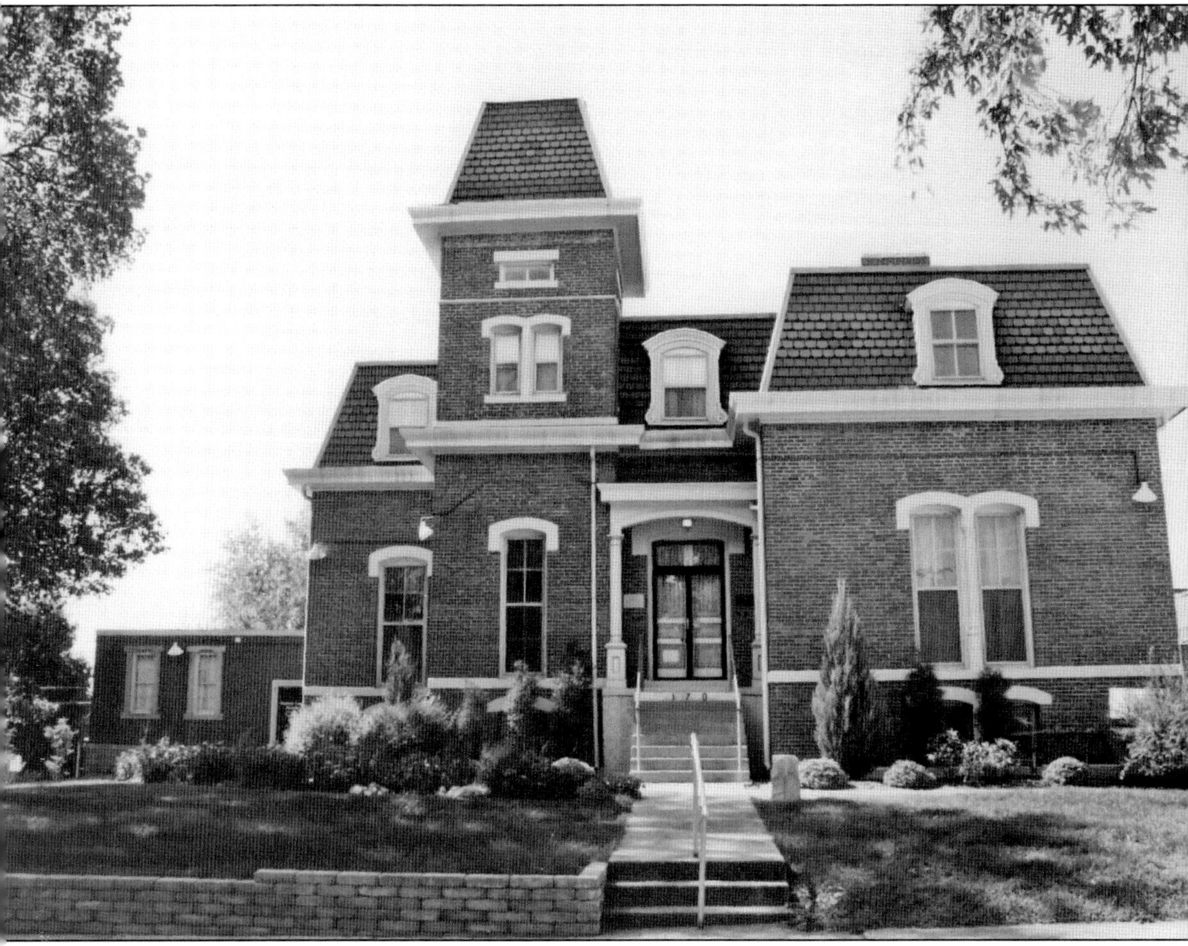

The Second Empire–style structure at 170 South Washington Street in Danville was built in 1866 as the jail and residence for the sheriff and his family. Plumbing and electricity were added when the utilities became available. In 1974, the county built a new jail, and this building was turned over to the Hendricks County Museum. (Phyllis Parsons.)

On the Cover: The All-County Orchestra is gathered together on April 13, 1928, as they prepare for a performance. They are on the lawn of Central Normal College. In the background is the former Danville Regular Baptist Church. (Guilford Township Collection–Plainfield Library.)

IMAGES
of America

Hendricks County

Gail M. Tharp and Phyllis West Parsons

ARCADIA
PUBLISHING

ISBN 978-0-7385-9897-0

Published by Arcadia Publishing
Charleston, South Carolina

Printed in the United States of America

Library of Congress Control Number: 2012953405

For all general information, please contact Arcadia Publishing:
Telephone 843-853-2070
Fax 843-853-0044
E-mail sales@arcadiapublishing.com
For customer service and orders:
Toll-Free 1-888-313-2665

Visit us on the Internet at www.arcadiapublishing.com

Dedicated to Don and John, our husbands, for their support and encouragement through this exciting project.

Contents

Acknowledgments

The following people have graciously assisted us with their time and knowledge pertaining to Hendricks County: Beverly Riggen and Susan Truax of Avon–Washington Township Library, Larry Whitmore and Wanda Pearson of Brownsburg–Middle Township Library, Ann Cummings of Clayton–Liberty Township Library, Cheryl Myers Steinborn of Coatesville–Clay Township Library, and Cindy Rutledge and Rose Ann Sigborn of Danville–Center Township Library.

Special thanks go to Steven Smith of the Danville Public Library and Reann Poray of the Plainfield Public Library for their assistance with the photographs and to Phyllis Walters for her editing expertise.

A thank-you goes to John Parsons, our Hendricks County historian, for sharing his knowledge of Hendricks County.

Thanks also go to the many individuals who allowed us to use their photographs and postcards. Individual acknowledgments can be found at the end of each caption.

Introduction

From the 1816 treaty between the government and the Indian tribes, 30 counties were created in central Indiana, and Hendricks County had the honor of comprising the land first surveyed along the second principal meridian in 1819.

This area was laid off into congressional townships, which are 14, 15, 16, and 17 North and Ranges 1 and 2 East and West.

Nine civil townships were laid out in July 1824 in William Ballard's log cabin in Liberty Township. They were Brown, Centre, Eel River, Franklin, Guilford, Liberty, Marion, Middle, and Washington. They were very nearly the same size. Later were added Clay, Lincoln, and Union Townships, and some land from Morgan County was added to Liberty and Franklin Townships. By 1868, our county consisted of the present 12 civil townships in size and shape.

Most county business is conducted by using civil townships, as we know them. However, several areas still require knowledge of congressional townships, such as legal descriptions of one's property.

In 1824, when the county was formed, there were only four townships with enough people to form a local township government. They were Centre, Guilford, Liberty, and Washington. The spelling of Centre was later changed to Center.

Farmers largely settled Hendricks County, and today, it is still an agricultural county. But we would like to show in this book how creative the population was. If there was a need, someone would fill it. So among the fertile fields sprang up mills, buggy shops, blacksmith shops, tanners, hardware stores, and businesses that sold implements. Coupled with this ever-increasing need, general merchandise stores abounded. Sugar camps were made, followed by sorghum mills and those who would butcher animals for you. Eventually, tile and brick factories were abundant along with a stave factory. Wagons, buggies, carriages, and sleighs were manufactured in almost every village and town in the county. At the turn of the century, bicycles were sold by a host of salesmen.

Water mills devoted to grinding grain, preparing ginseng, carding wool, and sawing lumber were all over the county. Where waterpower was not available, they used horses to power the mills. By the end of the Civil War, most mills were powered by steam.

Hendricks County people were very patriotic and resourceful. They could make a good living off this land. And their children were raised in a place that valued education and church going.

The majority of our early settlers came from North Carolina, but a quick glance at the records from our 1850 census reveals that numerous families traced their ancestry from other states and countries.

An 1866 list of men's names of Hendricks County has been found. After their names, their occupations are listed. The following are some of the different occupations listed: ex-sheriff, editor, nurseryman, farmer, stock raiser, common pleas court judge, dentist, carpenter, druggist, furniture manufacturer, sewing machine agent, plasterer, life insurance agent, hardware store proprietor, dry goods clerk, dry goods merchant, wagon maker, blacksmith, photographer, grocer, music teacher, soldier, undertaker, brick mason, carriage maker, railway station agent, tile maker, mechanic, and harness maker.

As times have changed, Hendricks County has developed a split personality. The eastern portion of the county, which includes Avon, Brownsburg, and Plainfield, has evolved into a suburb of Indianapolis containing the most populated portion of the county. It has become the shopping center with major restaurants and many company distribution centers, which provide a large employment base. The western and northern portions, which include Amo, Belleville, Cartersburg, Clayton, Coatesville, Hazelwood, Lizton, New Winchester, North Salem, Pittsboro, and Stilesville, remain rural and are a reminder of the quieter days of the past. Danville sits in the center of the county as the county seat, the home of the county museum and many small-town shops.

Please excuse our mistakes. Our hearts were right in what we wanted to say and do, but errors do creep in, and we hope you understand.

We want to help you relive yesterday. We would like for you to say, "I remember that," or "My Grandpa told me about that," or even, "Well, I didn't know that."

Welcome to Hendricks County, and we hope you enjoy your time with us.

One

Early Hendricks County

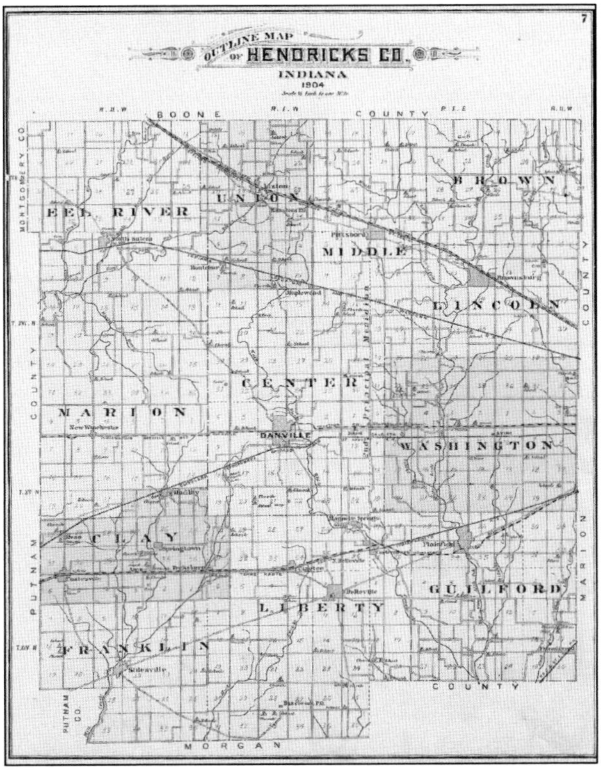

This 1904 map of Hendricks County shows life as it was 100 years ago. There were many small communities, country schools, and two-lane dirt or gravel roads. In general, Hendricks County was a quiet, rural area. Many of the towns have since disappeared and are featured in the Communities Remembered chapter at the end of this book. (Hendricks County government website.)

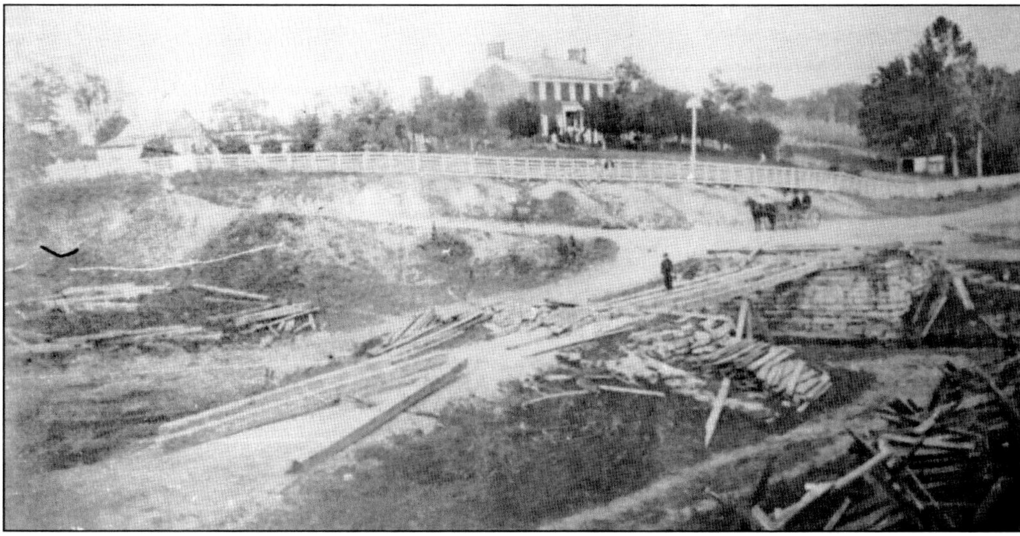

Judge Alexander Little built this large brick home in the 1830s. It was on the Old National Road and served as an inn and tavern. It sat near the Cartersburg Road. The area just east of here was platted in 1827 as the town of Union by Thomas Irons and James Downard. Union had a post office from 1828 to 1831. The area pictured became known as Spring Hill. (Guilford Township Collection–Plainfield Library.)

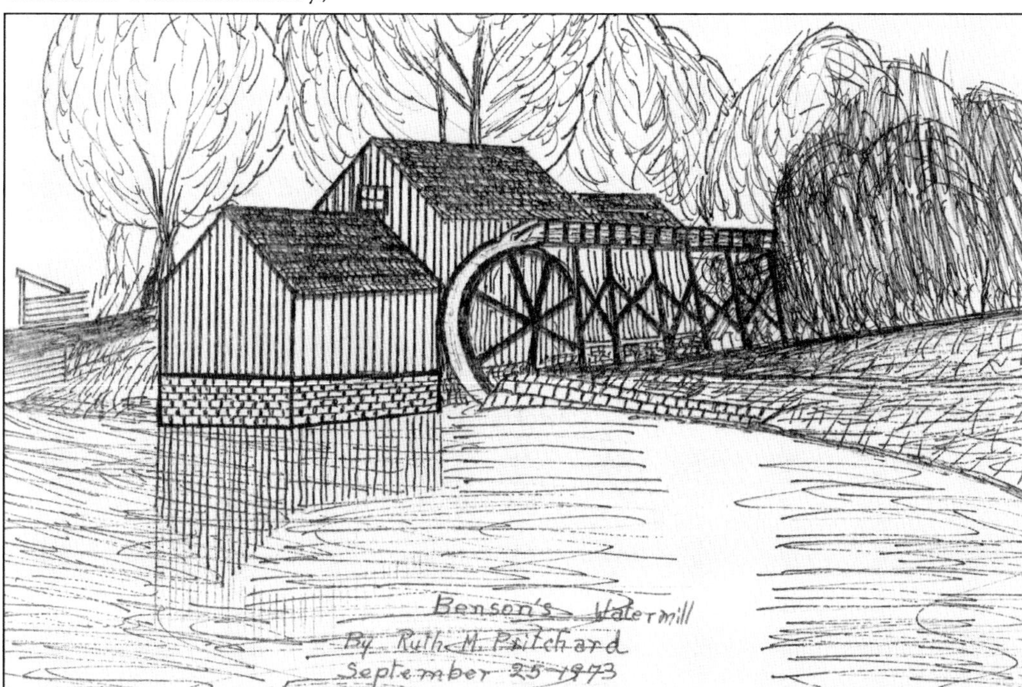

John P. Benson built the first water mill in the county on Rock Branch in Eel River Township in 1826. It was described as a very patient and industrious mill but "rather slow." The Benson Mill soon disappeared when, in 1829, Jacob Crum built a mill not far from the location of the Benson Mill. Ruth Mitchell Pritchard made this drawing in 1973 of how the mill may have looked. (Guilford Township Collection–Plainfield Library.)

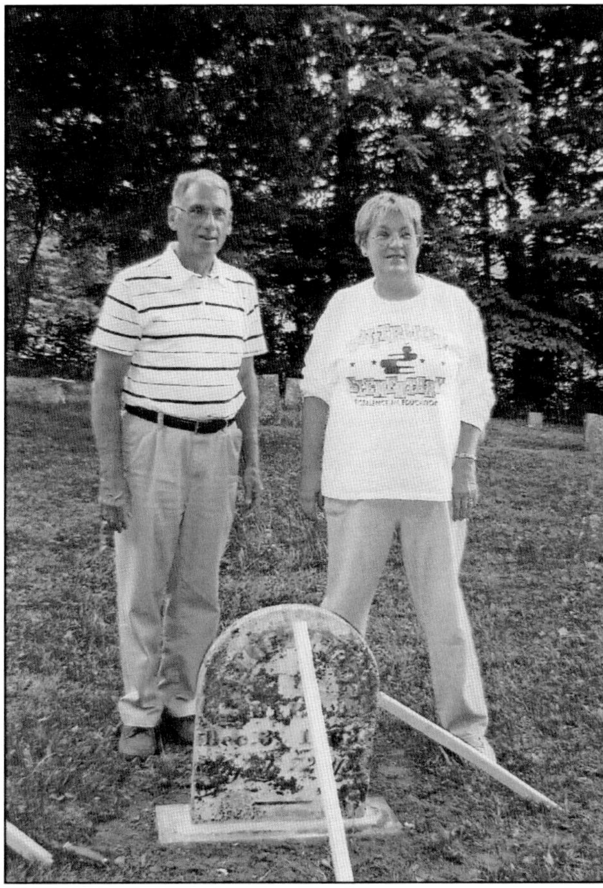

Nancy Hughes and Donald Tharp stand next to the grave of their pioneer ancestor Ezekiel Moore. Ezekiel and his father, George, were two members of the first settlement in the county in 1820. They came from North Carolina into Kentucky and then to Indiana. Nancy and Don recently restored Ezekiel's original stone at Abner Creek Cemetery and added a historical marker. (Both, Gail Tharp.)

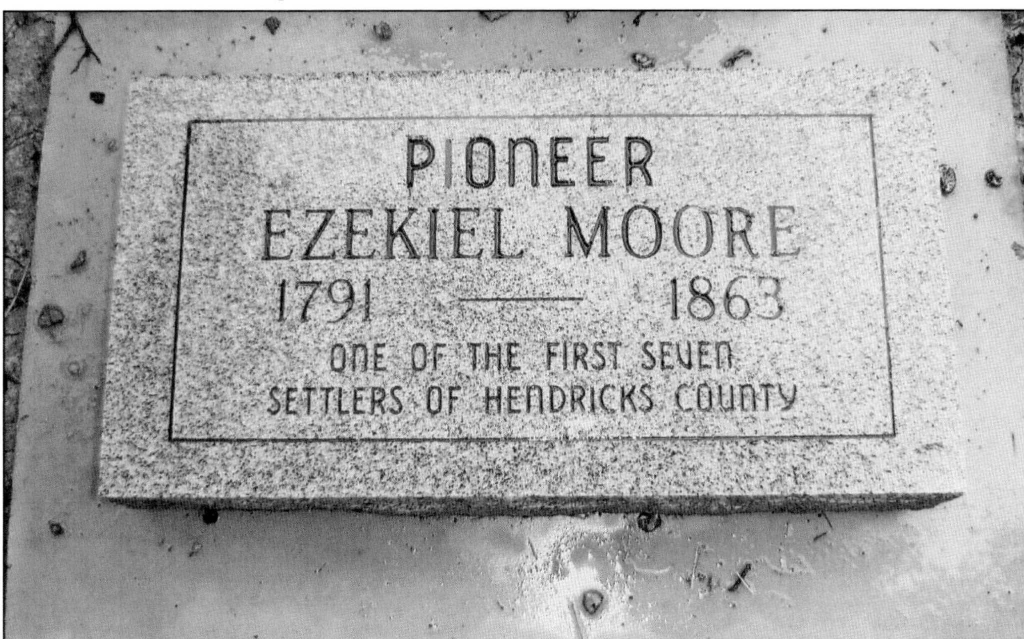

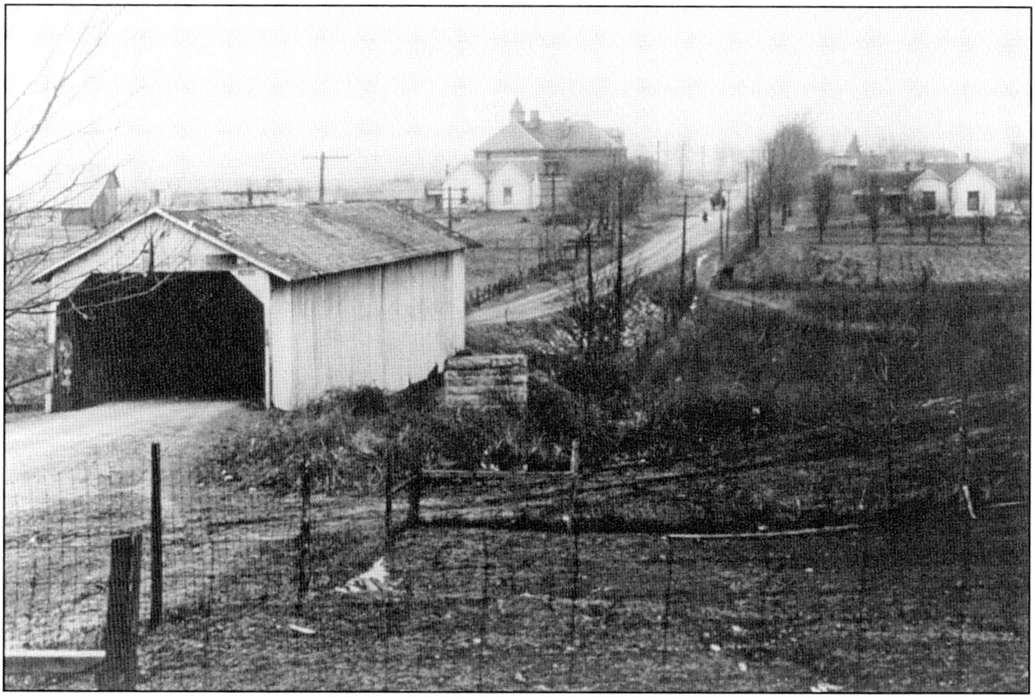

In years past, Hendricks County had several covered bridges. The bridge in these two pictures was located over White Lick Creek on the Crawfordsville Road (now US 136), near Brownsburg. It was built in 1861 by P.O. "Tobe" Walters, a Pittsboro carpenter, and was taken down in 1927 and replaced by an iron bridge. The building in the upper portion of the picture above is the West Point School. The picture below shows the same bridge in a picturesque winter scene. (Both, Brownsburg Public Library.)

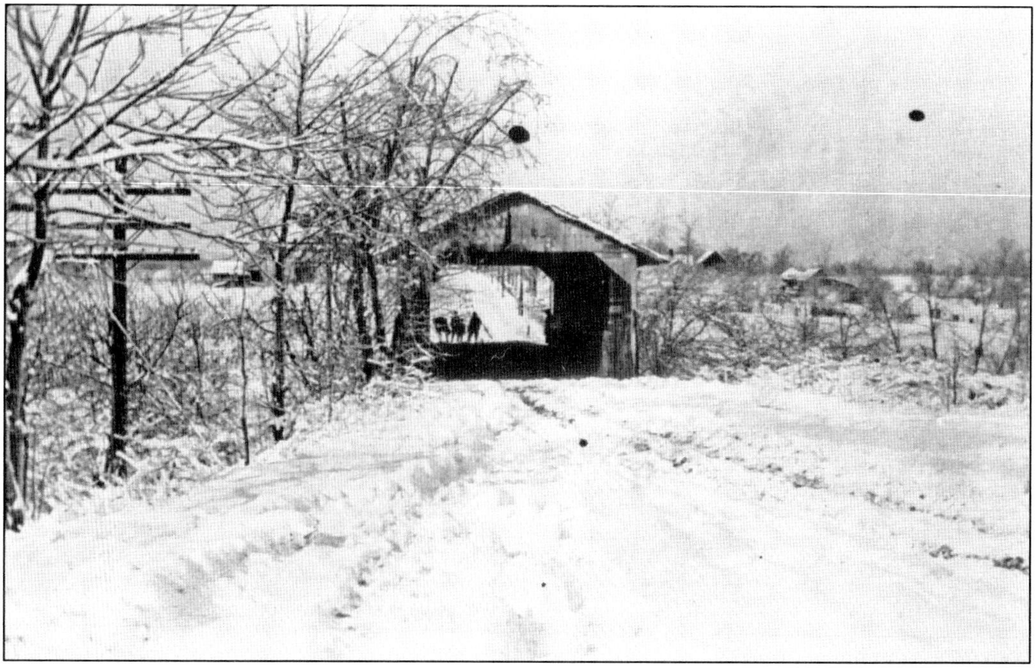

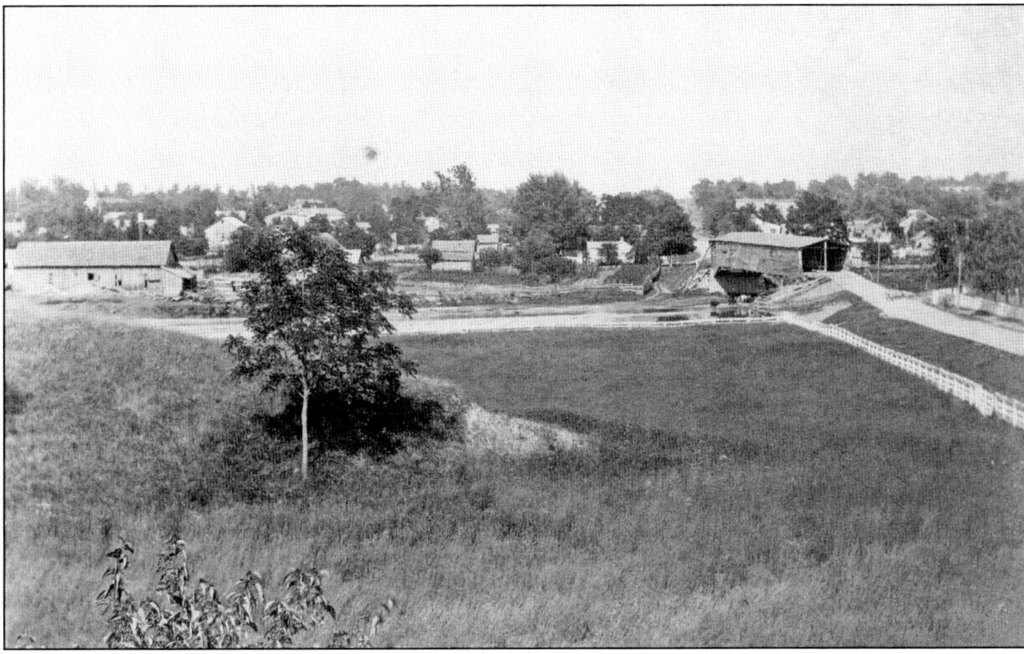

J.P. Calvert took the above picture on the west side of Plainfield in the 1870s. Calvert was a photographer whose brother, William, was the Hendricks County sheriff from 1868 to 1872. The covered bridge is over White Lick Creek. It is thought to have been finished in 1833 and served the public for about 50 years. The two-lane iron bridge, shown below, replaced the covered bridge in about 1883. Today, the same route is a four-lane bridge on US 40. (Both, Guilford Township Collection–Plainfield Library.)

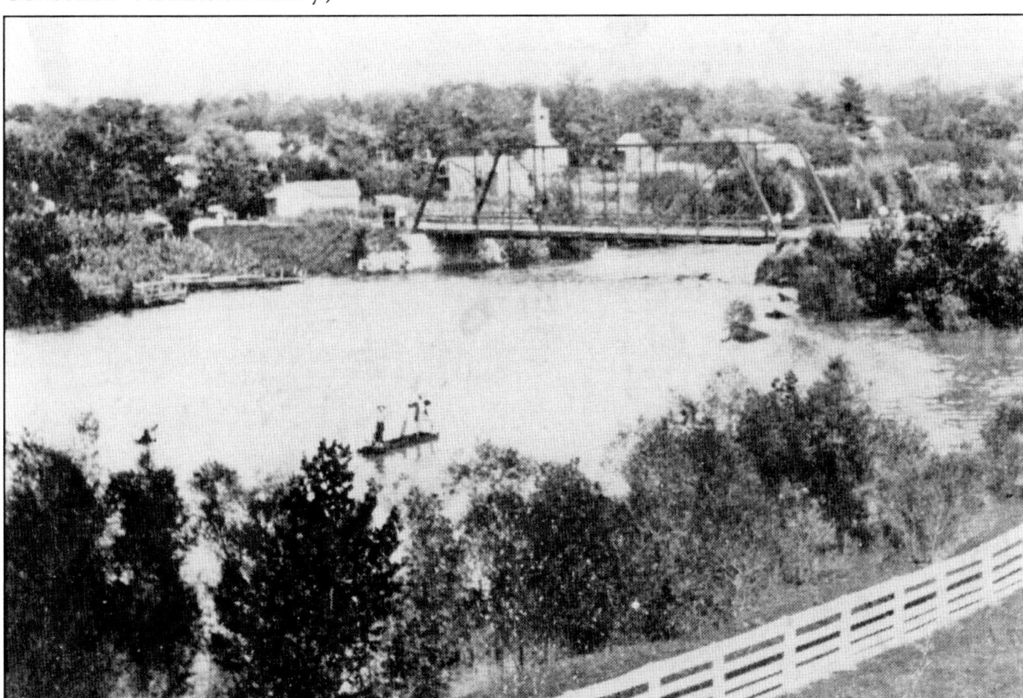

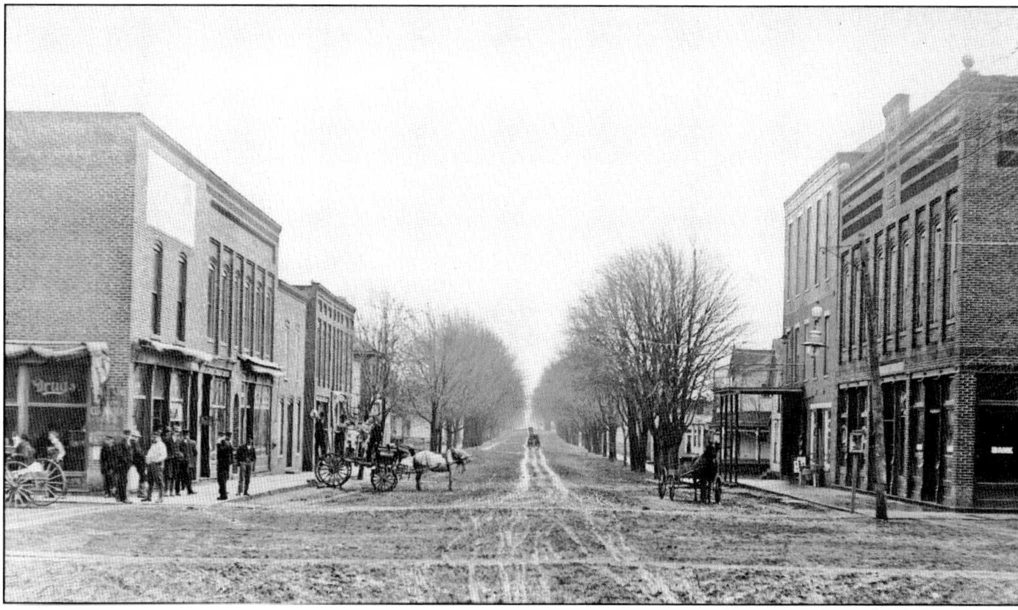

A century or so ago, the town of Brownsburg looked much quieter. In this picture, a man drives his wagon east down the dirt Main Street, while several community people gather in front of the drugstore at the northeast corner of Main and Green Streets. (Guilford Township Collection–Plainfield Library.)

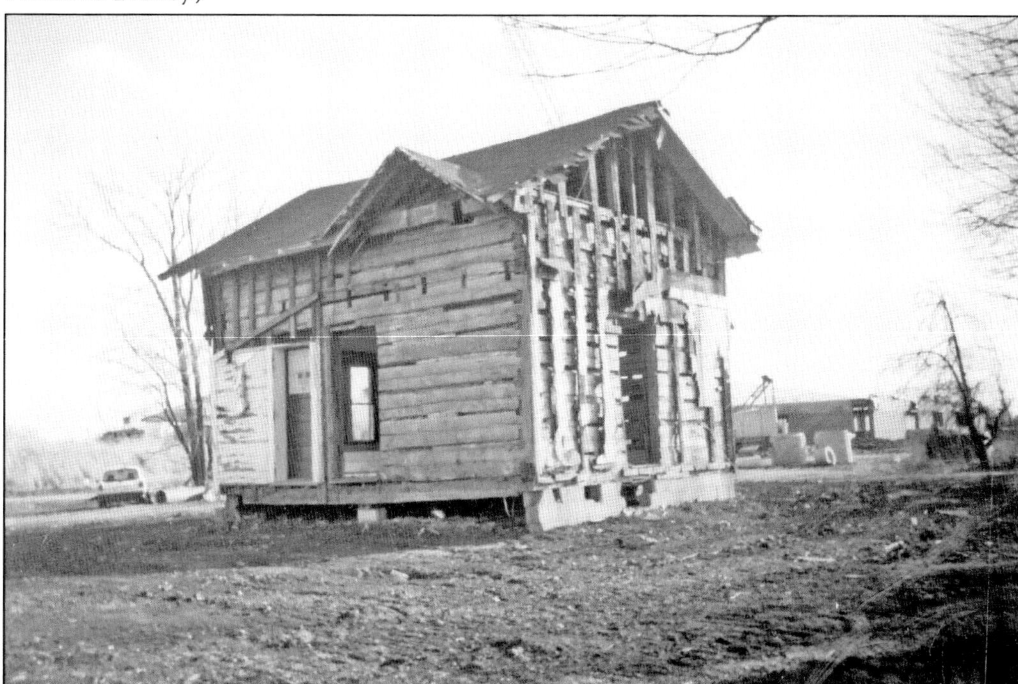

The past came to life a few years ago when a log cabin was discovered during the dismantling of the Keifer home for the construction of the new Danville South Elementary School. The home had been built around the cabin. The cabin was moved to the back of the property and later sold and moved to another location. (Hendricks County Museum.)

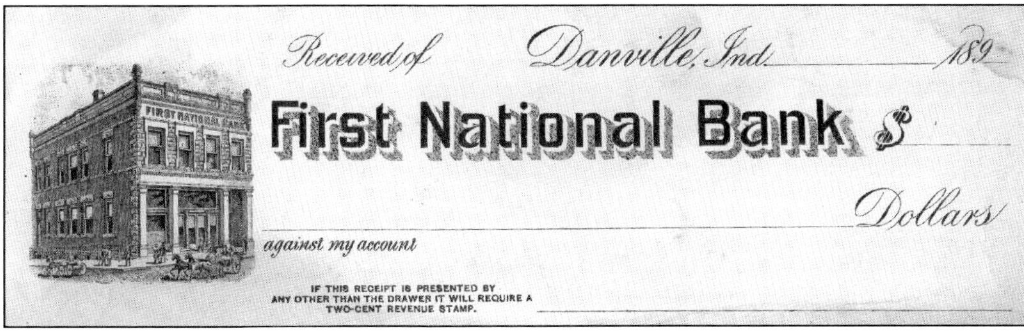
Received of Danville, Ind. 189

First National Bank $

Dollars

against my account

IF THIS RECEIPT IS PRESENTED BY ANY OTHER THAN THE DRAWER IT WILL REQUIRE A TWO-CENT REVENUE STAMP.

The First National Bank of Danville was established in the 1860s. It was located on the east side of the courthouse square. An illustration of their beautiful building appears on this statement from the 1890s. The building is still standing but is no longer a bank. (Hendricks County Museum.)

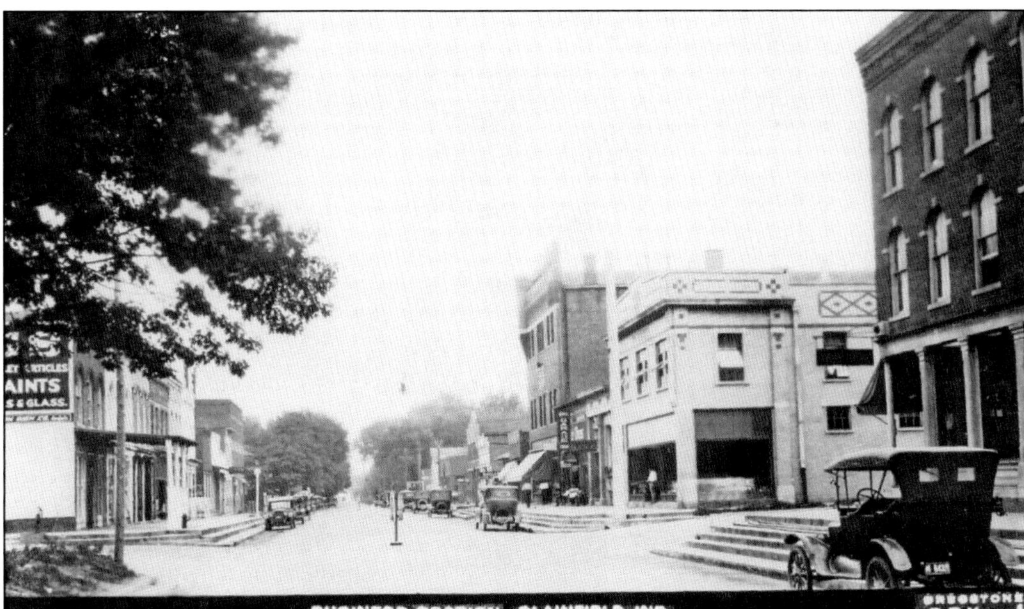

It is interesting how many changes have been made in towns over the past 100 years, and yet, with the help of some buildings, the towns can still be recognized. Plainfield's sidewalks no longer have steps down to the street, but some of these buildings are still there and look much the same. (Joseph Seiter.)

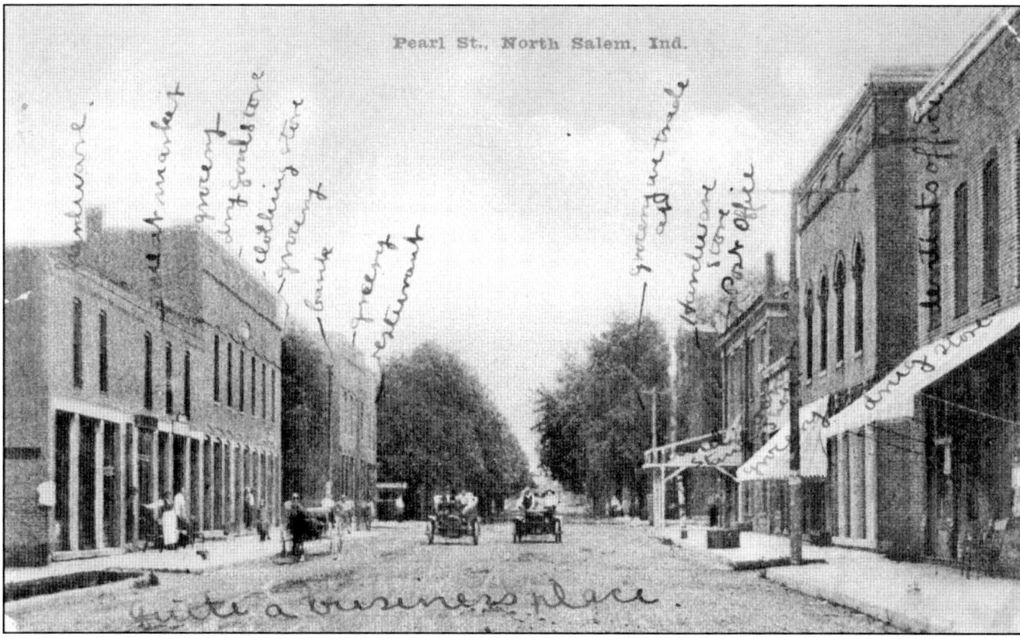

This North Salem postcard has been labeled with the types of businesses that were there. The post office is in the same location today as it was in this picture. Note that in the center of the picture, the two automobiles appear to be coming down the street in the same direction. (Bonnie Eggers.)

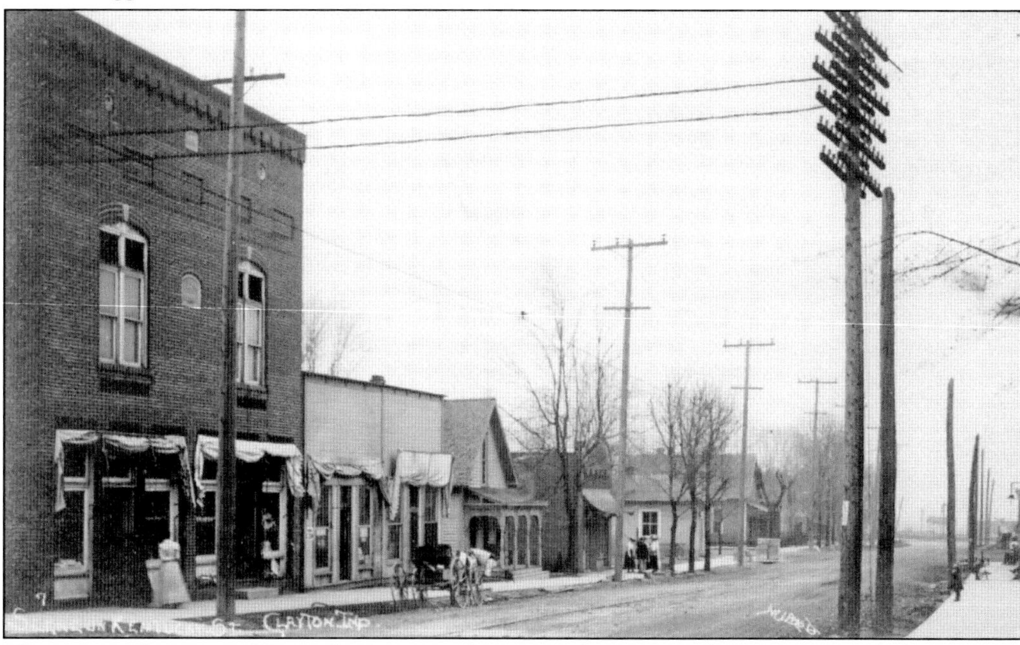

This is an early scene of Kentucky Street in the town of Clayton. Clayton was founded about 1852 after the railroad was put through the area. By 1858, it had a hotel, a carriage and wagon maker, a steam sawmill and steam gristmill, a lawyer, harness maker, stove and tin dealer, dressmaker, tailor, blacksmith, watch maker, and jeweler, as well as other businesses. (Guilford Township Collection–Plainfield Library.)

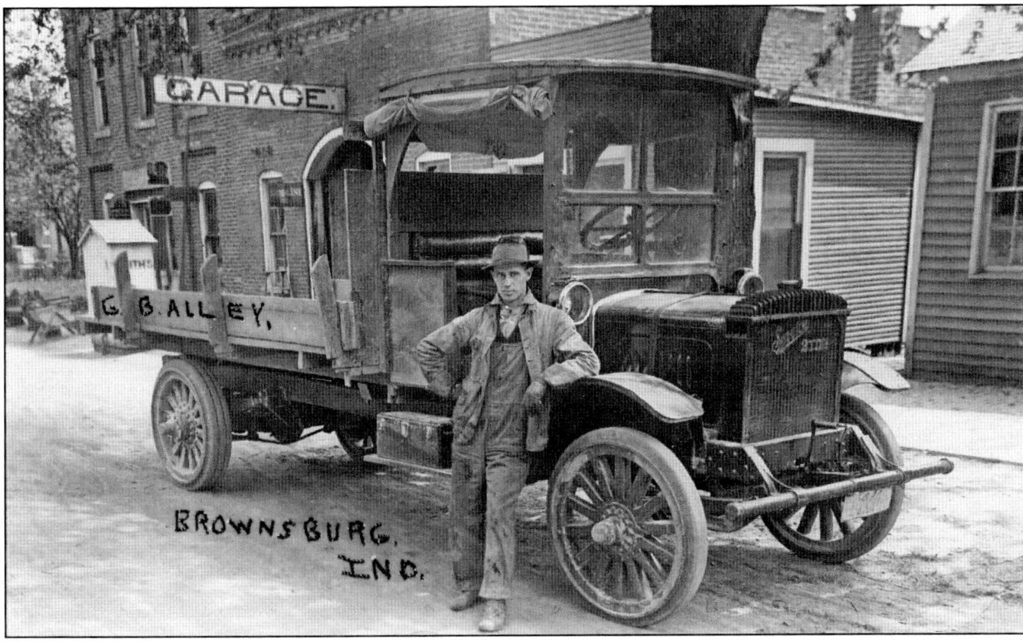

This gentleman is standing in front of a truck with "G.B. Alley" written on its side. The picture was taken in Brownsburg, probably in the 1920s. The Service Motor Company in Wabash, Indiana, built this truck, with "2 Ton" seen on its grill. The company manufactured trucks from 1910 to 1922. (Hendricks County Museum.)

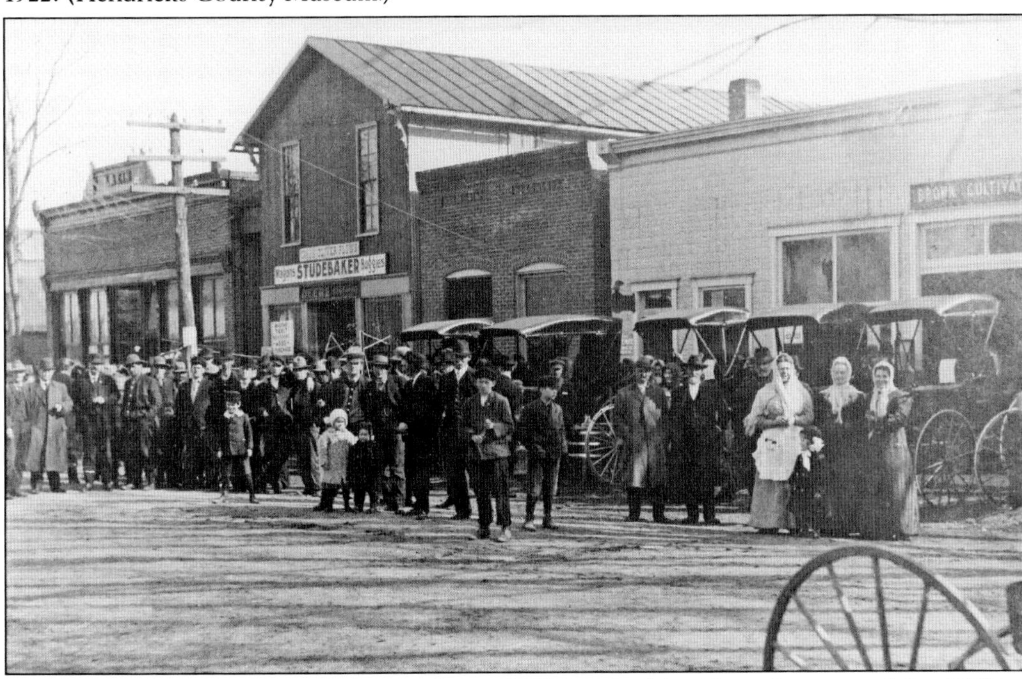

A large number of people turned out in front of W.N. Lakin's buildings for a special day. William N. Lakin worked in Danville before settling in Coatesville in 1869. He sold wagons and agricultural implements along with carriages and buggies. By 1885, he was very prosperous. (Guilford Township Collection–Plainfield Library.)

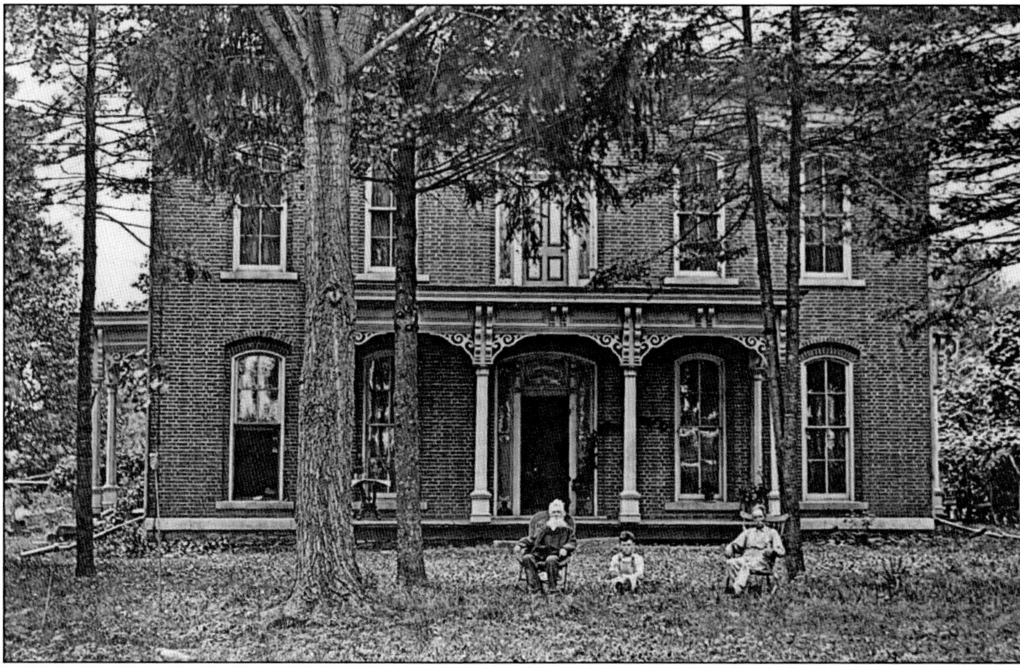

Located on US 40, west of Stilesville, is a beautifully restored brick home. Melville F. McHaffie built it in 1862. It is believed that Dan Patch, a famous racehorse, trained on Melville McHaffie's 1.5-mile racetrack on the grounds. In recent years, Walter and June Prosser bought and restored the property and named it "Rising Hall." (Clayton–Liberty Township Library.)

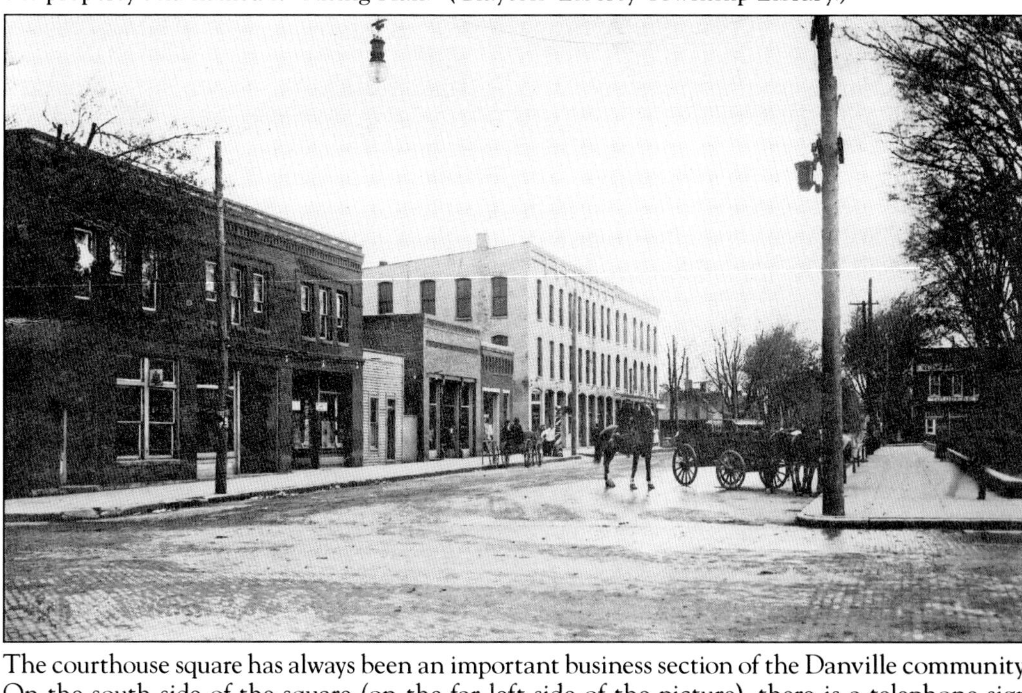

The courthouse square has always been an important business section of the Danville community. On the south side of the square (on the far left side of the picture), there is a telephone sign outside the store. A light hangs above the intersection, and horses and carriages travel on the bricked street. (Joseph Seiter.)

Two

Making a Living

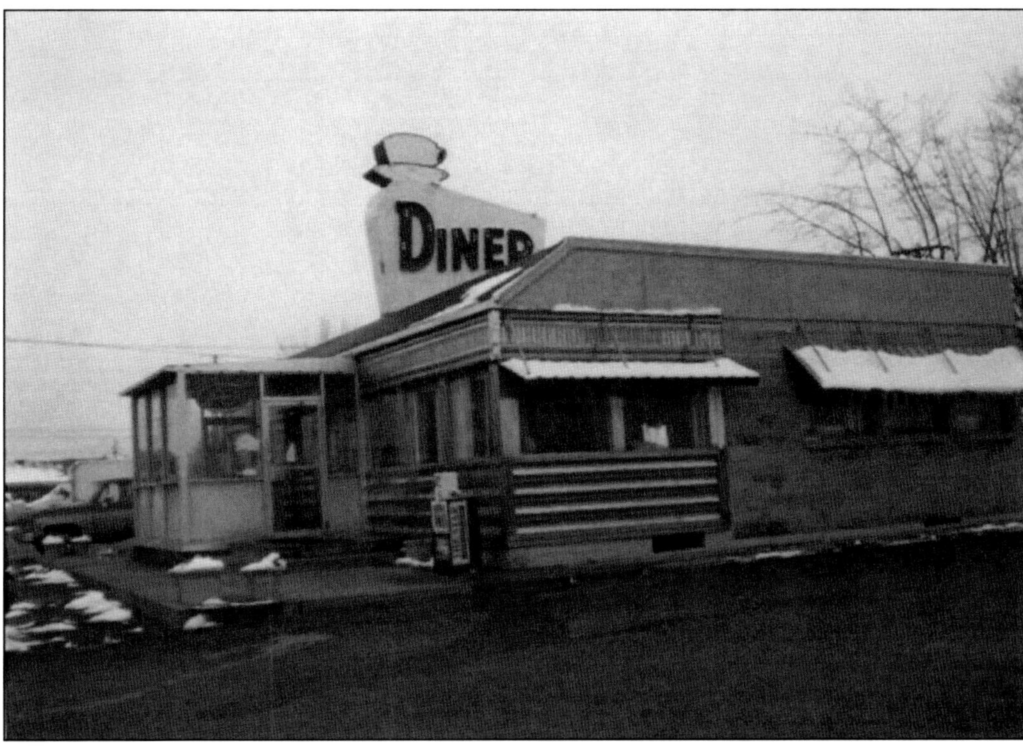

Early in Hendricks County history, most people worked close to home, either on the family farm or at a local business. As roads improved, making travel easier, citizens began to travel farther from home to earn their livings. In August 1954, the Oasis Diner opened for business at Six Points, on the east side of Plainfield. (Guilford Township Collection–Plainfield Library.)

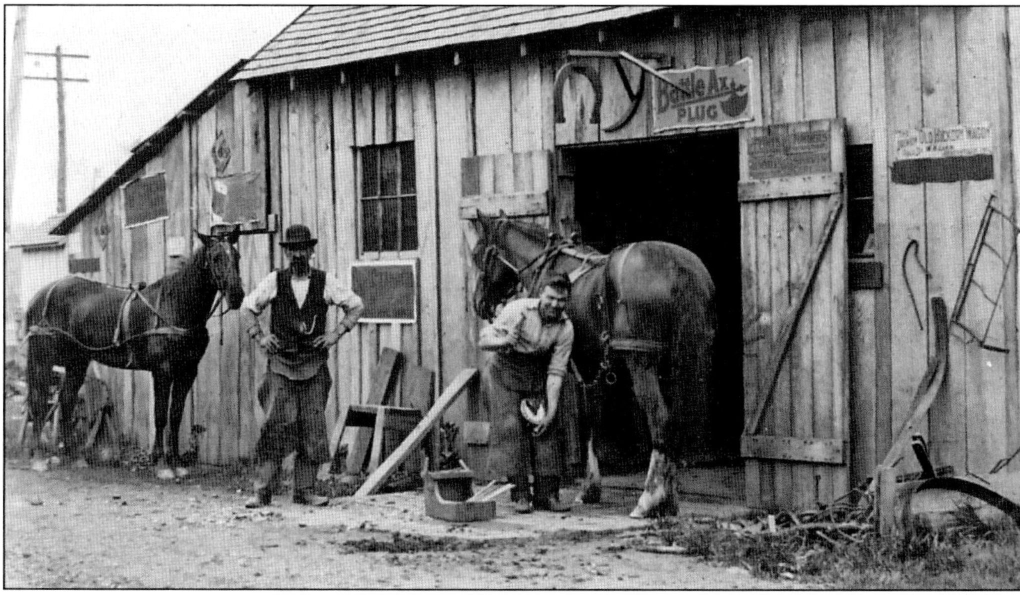

The blacksmith was vital to the early residents of the county. Charlie McCloud stands by as Lee Hollingsworth shoes a horse. Their shop was in Amo. The large horseshoe over the door advertises their trade. Another sign says, "The Premium Old Hickory Wagon, sold by W.N. Lakin, Coatesville, Ind." (Guilford Township Collection–Plainfield Library.)

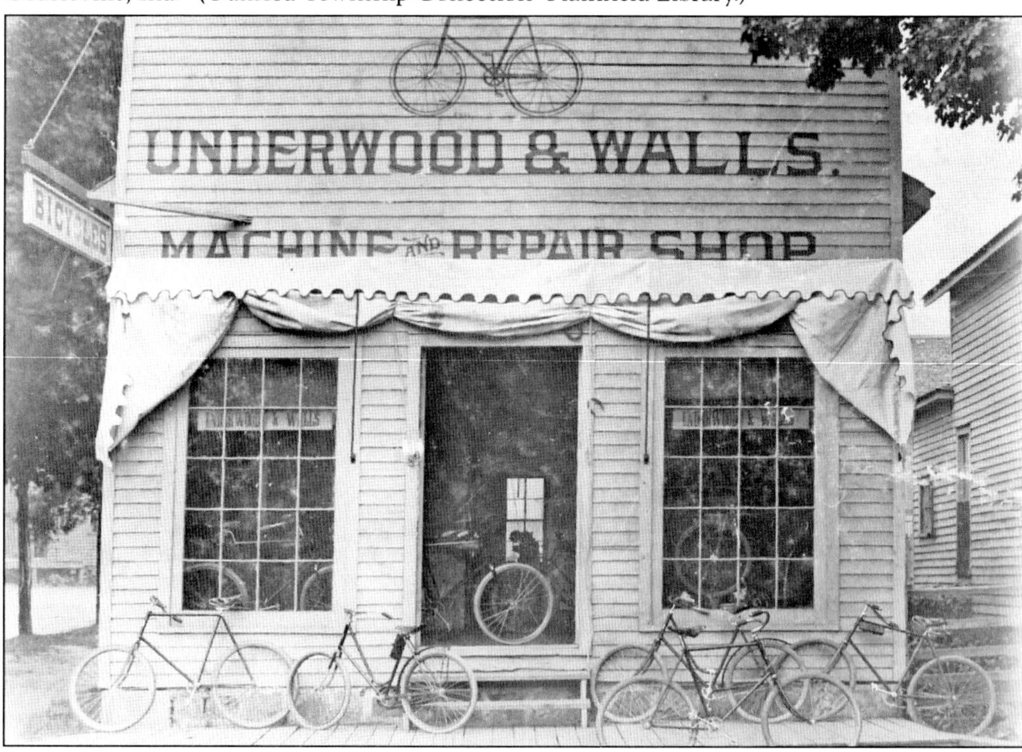

Bicycles became very popular in the 1880s, and a need for a bicycle shop arose. Selling and repairing bicycles, Underwood and Walls must have done a booming business at this shop at Amo. (Guilford Township Collection–Plainfield Library.)

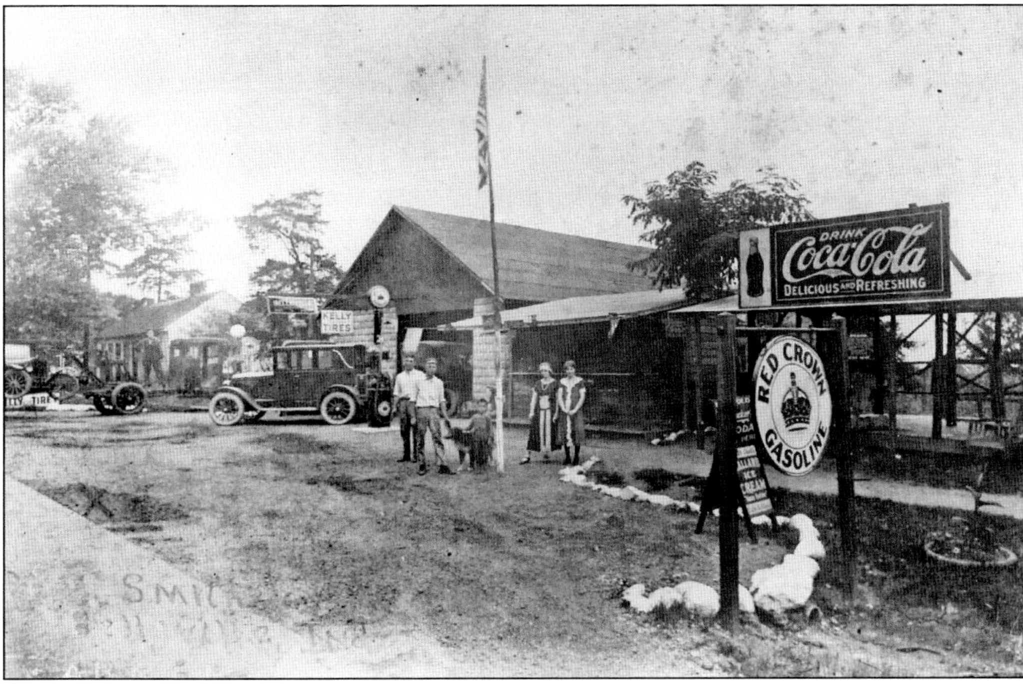

As the American flag flew above, H.J. Smith sold Red Crown Gasoline and Kelly tires and repaired automobiles in his Belleville Garage. One could also get Ballard Ice Cream and a Coca-Cola here. This building still stands on the north side of US 40. (Guilford Township Collection–Plainfield Library.)

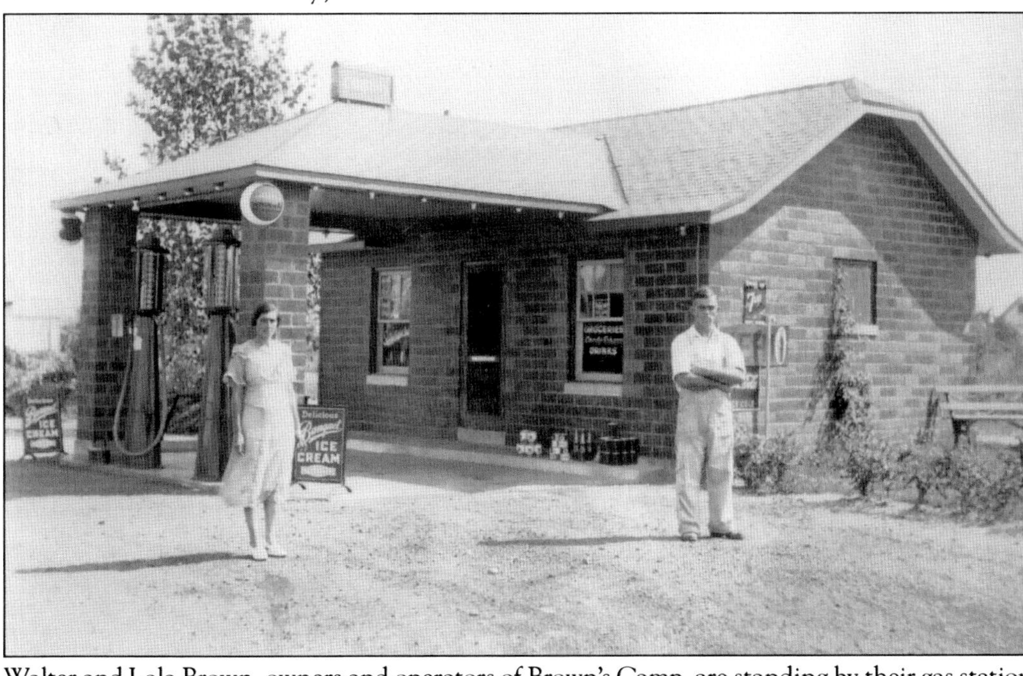

Walter and Lola Brown, owners and operators of Brown's Camp, are standing by their gas station in Washington Township. They also proudly sold Banquet Ice Cream. Some people referred to this as Brown's Cabins. (Sue Covey Wood.)

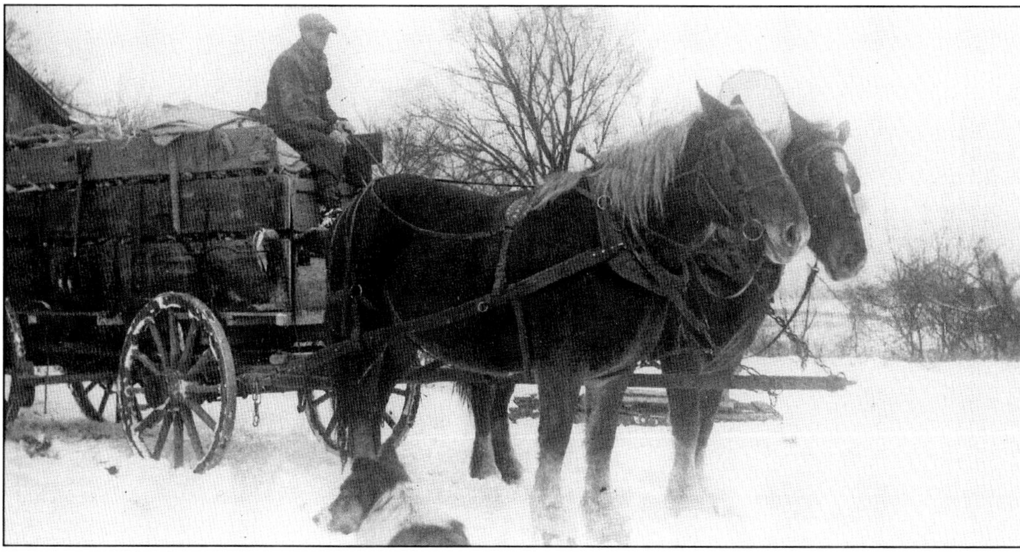

Farmers in the late 1930s and early 1940s were still using draft horses to do some of their work. In this picture, Roy Parker (1919–1984) is hauling corn to the Coatesville Elevator, where it will be ground into feed for his livestock. Considering the snow on the ground, it must have been a very cold ride. (Willa Dean Parker Yeager and Willis Parker.)

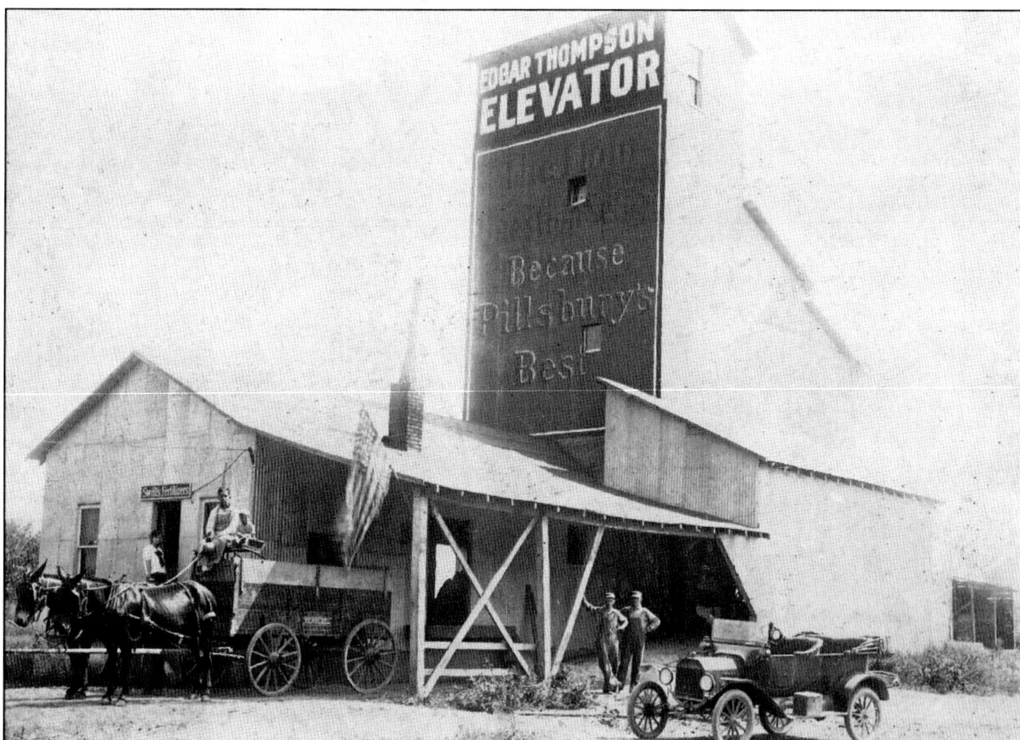

Grain elevators were important businesses for farmers. This elevator was located in Maplewood and was owned by Edgar Thompson. It was bought by Roy Fisher and later became the Wing Elevator. In this picture, Roy Fisher is the driver of the wagon, and Chester Martin stands farthest to the right of the elevator. (Judy Pingel.)

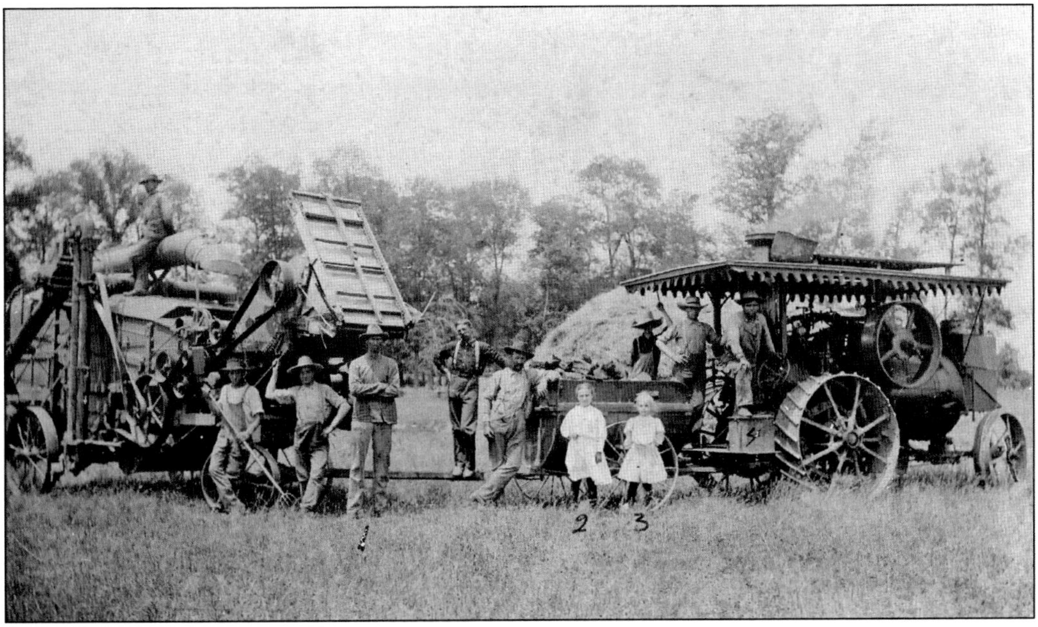

There was much excitement at the farm when the threshing ring arrived. Those identified here are Merritt A. Gregory (1), Lettie Hodge Sawyer (2), Christine Howson Wallace (3), and George Hodge (4). The picture was taken in 1907. (Hendricks County Museum.)

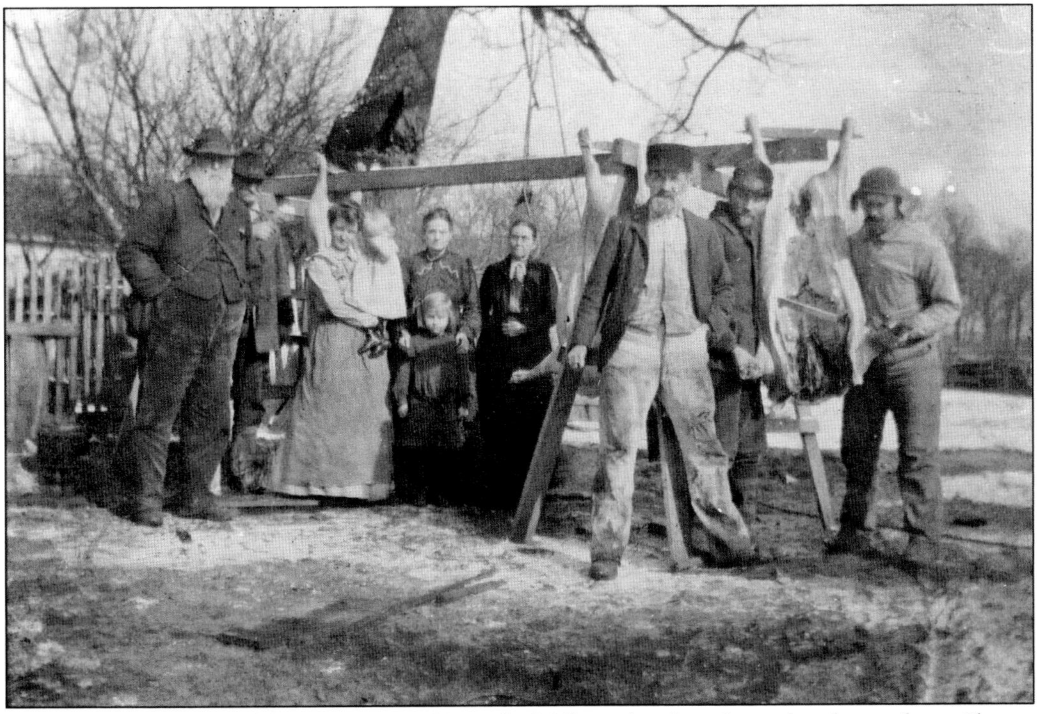

Many families butchered their own meat. Here, the Milhous family is shown butchering hogs. Shown are, from left to right, John Milhous, David Milhous, Ida Milhous, Laura Milhous, Wilma Milhous, Mary Ann Milhous, Lydia Copeland, David Copeland, Frank Milhous, and John T. Milhous. Laura and Wilma are Ida's daughters. (Guilford Township Collection–Plainfield Library.)

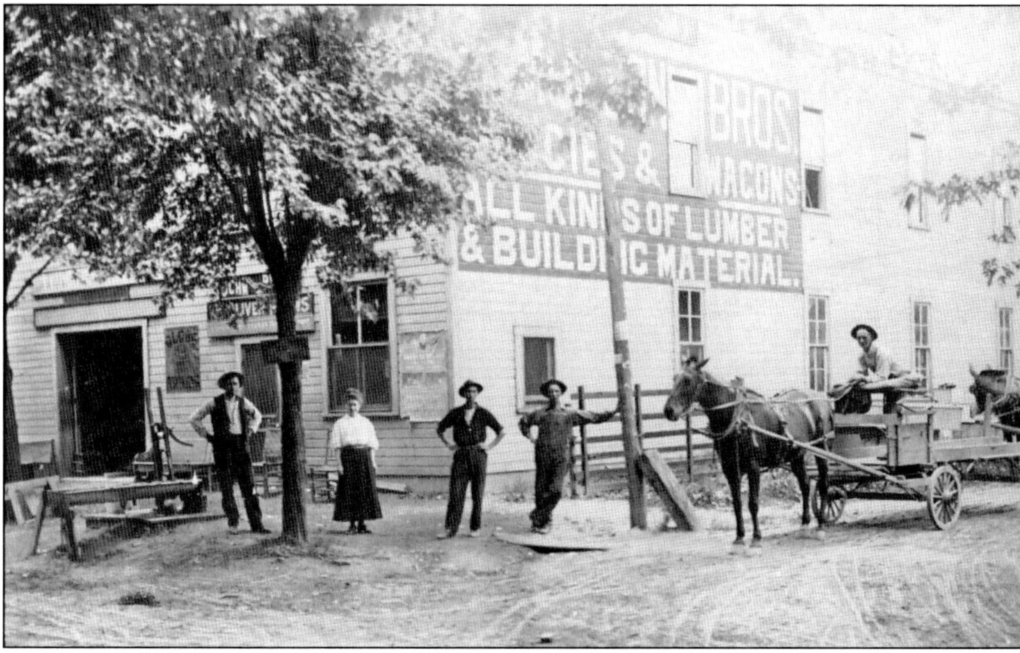

C. Art Edmondson's Vehicle and Implement Store stood south of the railroad in Clayton. It later became the Clayton Hardware and Lumber Company. Pictured are, from left to right, C. Art Edmondson, Claudia McCormack, Ed Busby, Ed Staley, and Sigel Bolen. This picture was taken about 1903. (Guilford Township Collection–Plainfield Library.)

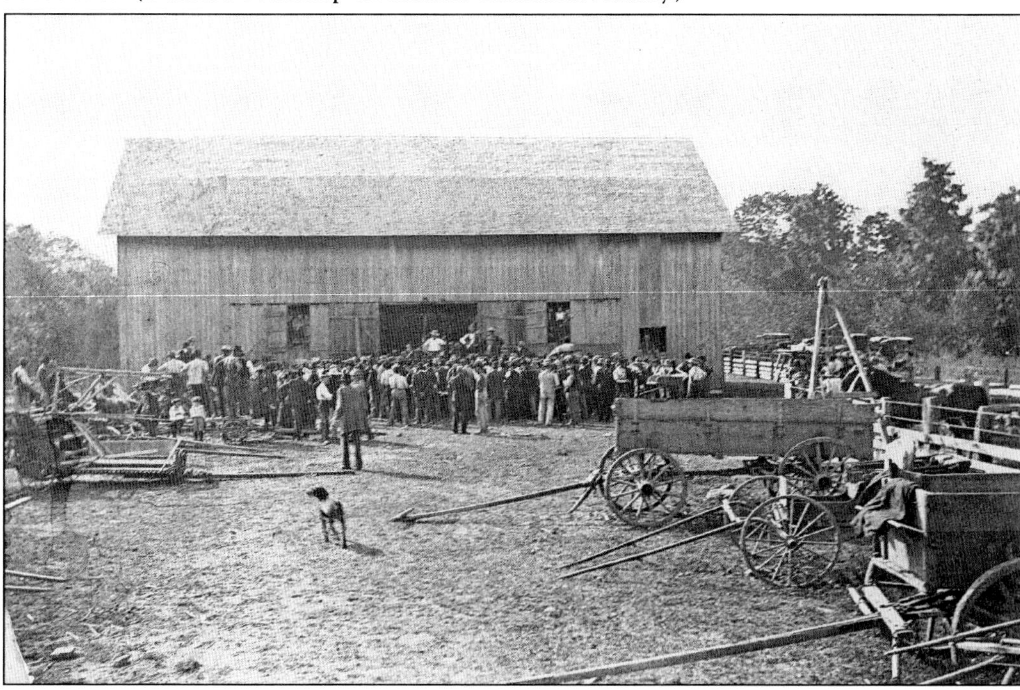

Men and women gathered from a wide area to attend this farm auction. Such auctions were often the sad result of the death of the owner or financial hardship. The cars in the background suggest that this was taken in the early 1900s. (Judy Pingel.)

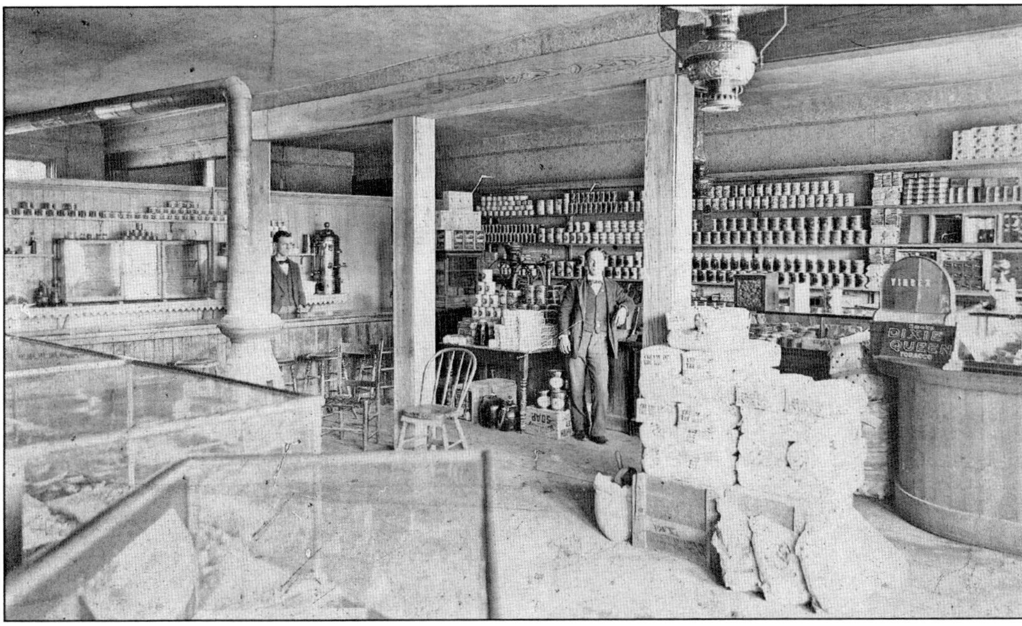

Claude Shane is shown in the McCoun Dry Goods Store on Main Street in Danville. It was located on the northwest corner of the square, currently the Mayberry Restaurant. James McCoun worked at the store for Shirley & Crabb. When Shirley & Crabb dissolved, James took over the operation. It was a popular business and gathering place for the community. Around 1920, James left the business, and Claude Shane took over. (Danville Public Library.)

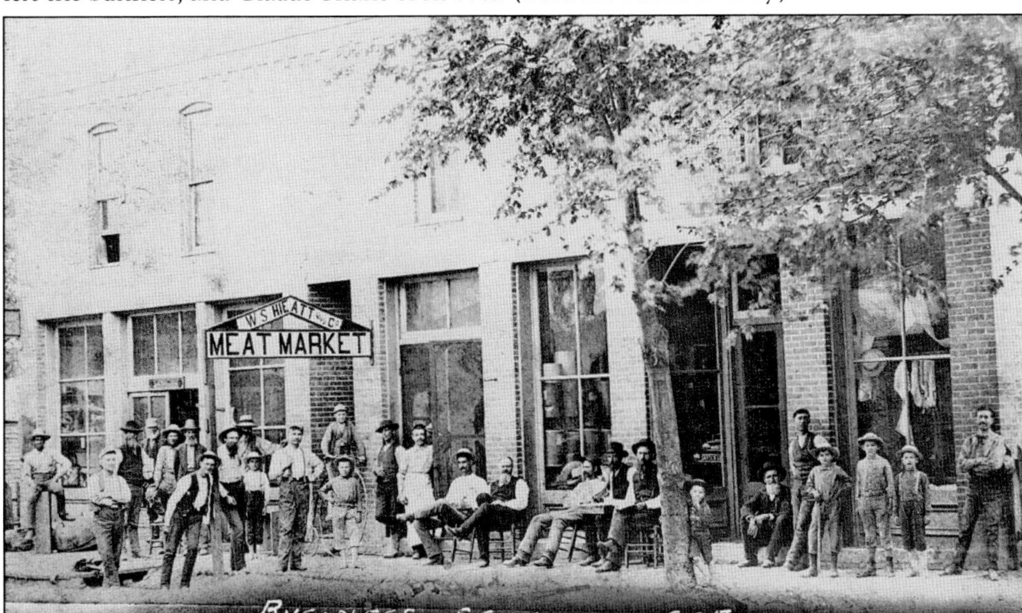

In this 1895 picture, men and boys are gathered in front of the W.S. Hiatt Meat Market at North Salem. They appear to be waiting for something—perhaps a parade. Hats must have been the attire for the occasion, since all but three people are wearing one. There is a young man astride a penny-farthing (high-wheeler) bicycle. This mode of transportation was popular in the late 1800s. (Bonnie Eggers.)

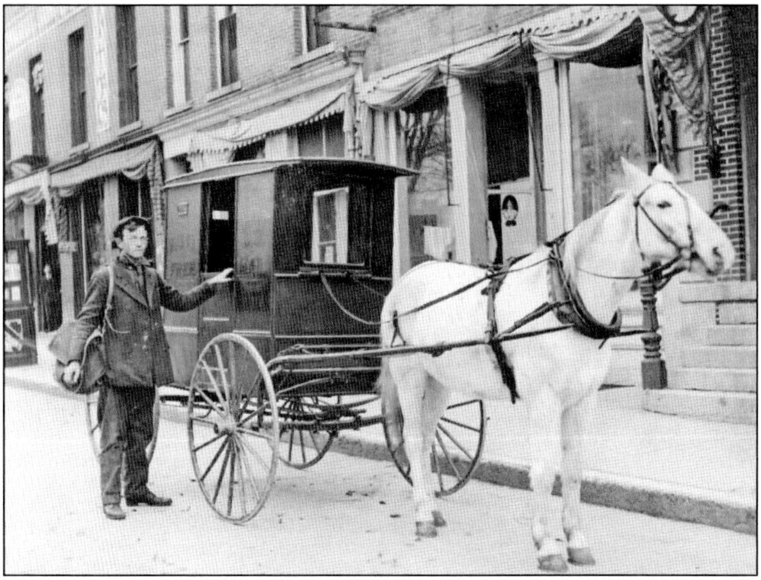

Through the years, mail was delivered in the county by various means. In 1908, Amos Harvey delivers mail on Main Street in Danville by horse and wagon. He is standing in front of the Thompson Drugstore, with his mail pouch over his shoulder. (Guilford Township Collection–Plainfield Library.)

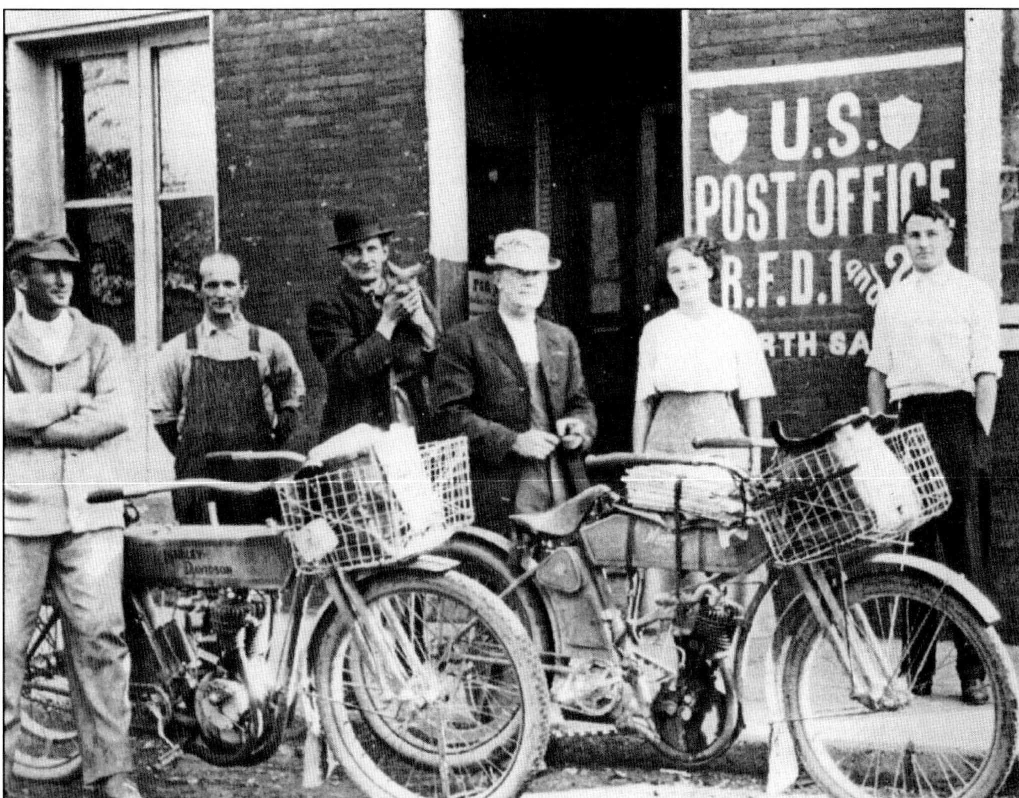

The North Salem Post Office opened on July 5, 1839, and continues in the same location today. The mail carriers used Harley Davidson motorcycles from 1912 to 1916. Pictured are, from left to right, Ed Hadley, mail carrier; Ed Elden; Postmaster Sherman Waters; John Adams, rural carrier; Vesta Gill, postal clerk; and Horace Waters, editor of the *North Salem Herald*. "R.F.D. 1 and 2" stands for Rural Free Delivery, routes 1 and 2. (Judy Pingel.)

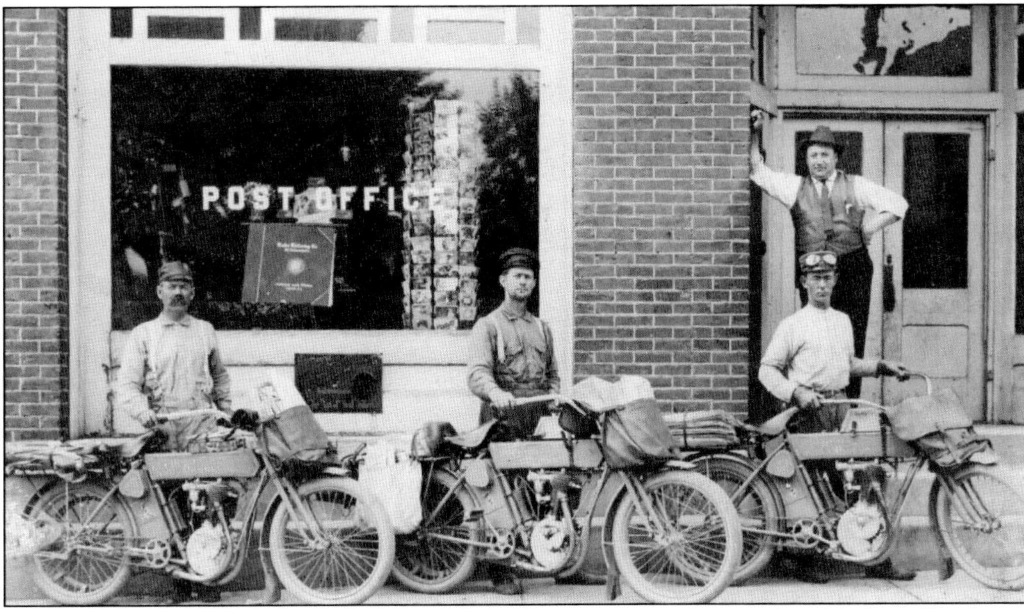

What a great way to have mail delivered—from left to right, James Wolford Noel, Harris Weesner, and Lee Weesner rode Harley Davidsons for the Clayton rural routes between 1912 and 1916. In the window are a lot of postcards for sale and an advertisement for Kahn Tailoring of Indianapolis. In 1915, the postmaster general decreed that motorcycles had to have weatherproof containers if they were used to deliver the mail. (Guilford Township Collection–Plainfield Library.)

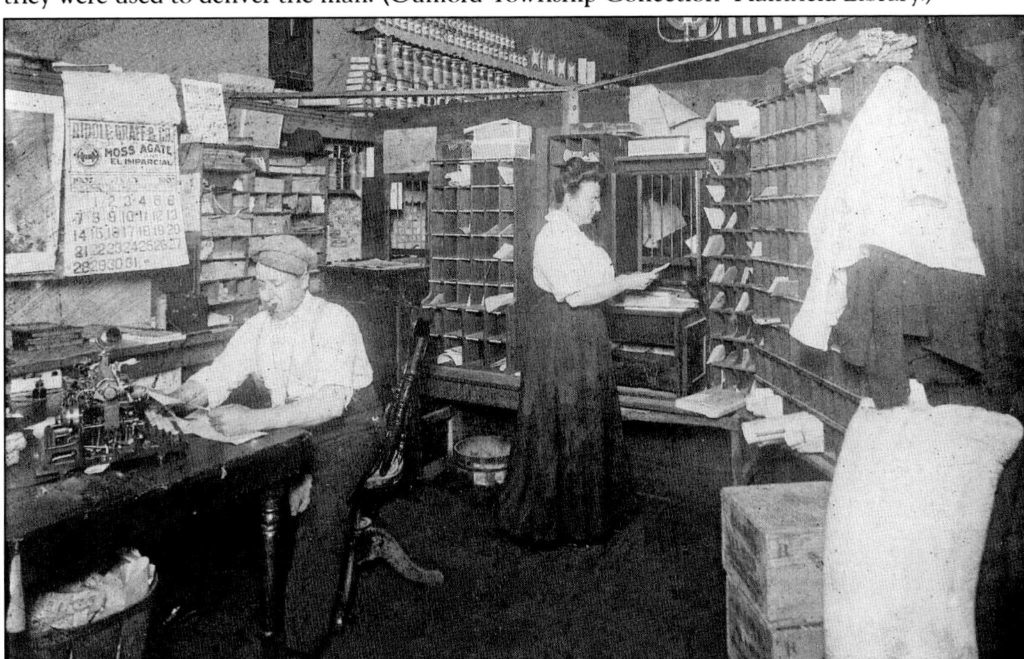

This is the inside of the Clayton Post Office, which was established in 1852. Looking closely at this picture of Oscar Harrison (1865–1912), one can see a calendar on the wall from July 1907. The advertisements are for Riddle Graff Co., Moss Agate, and El Imparcial Cigars. Oscar Harrison's sister Wilma (1873–1950) is seen sorting mail. (Guilford Township Collection–Plainfield Library.)

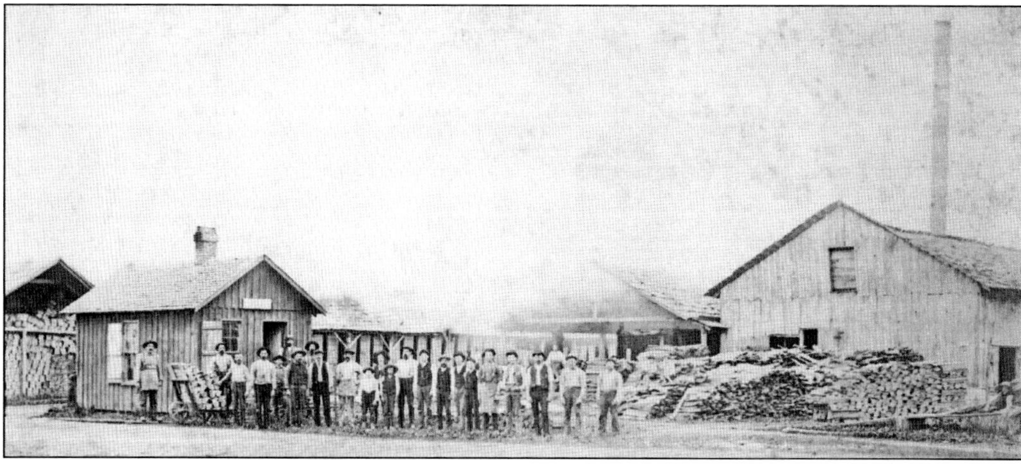

Daniel Feely, born in 1843 in New York, came to Pittsboro in the spring of 1873 and bought a stave factory from D.C. Cope. He had worked in other stave factories before coming to Indiana in 1864. He normally had about 20 people working for him in Pittsboro, but his business boomed and, at one time, he had over 100 workers making staves for barrels, which were shipped across the United States. (Phyllis Parsons.)

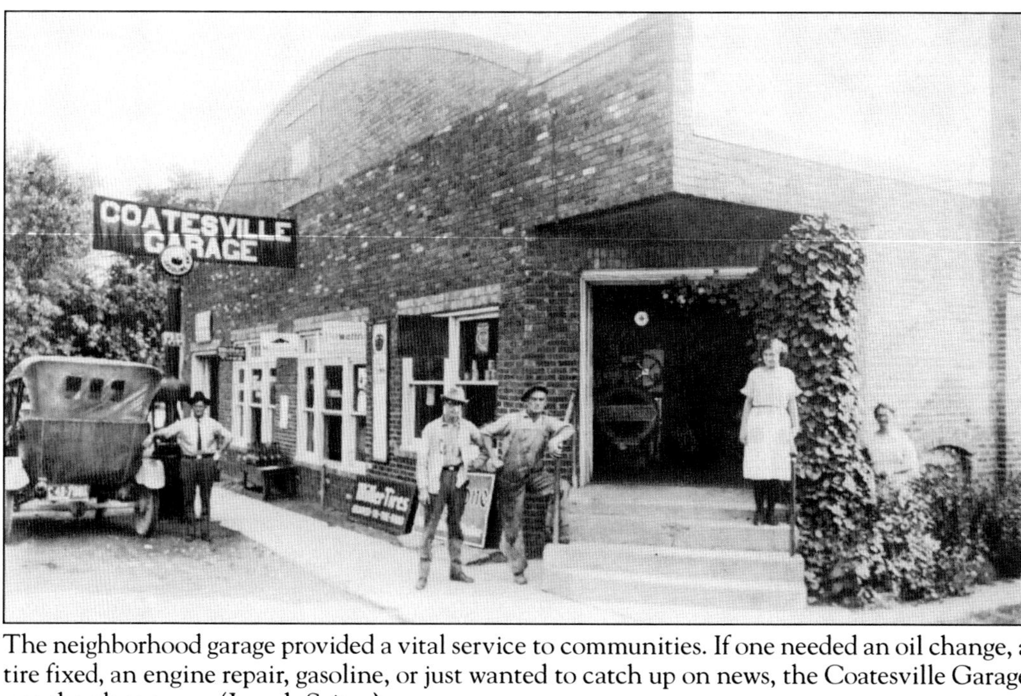

The neighborhood garage provided a vital service to communities. If one needed an oil change, a tire fixed, an engine repair, gasoline, or just wanted to catch up on news, the Coatesville Garage was the place to go. (Joseph Seiter.)

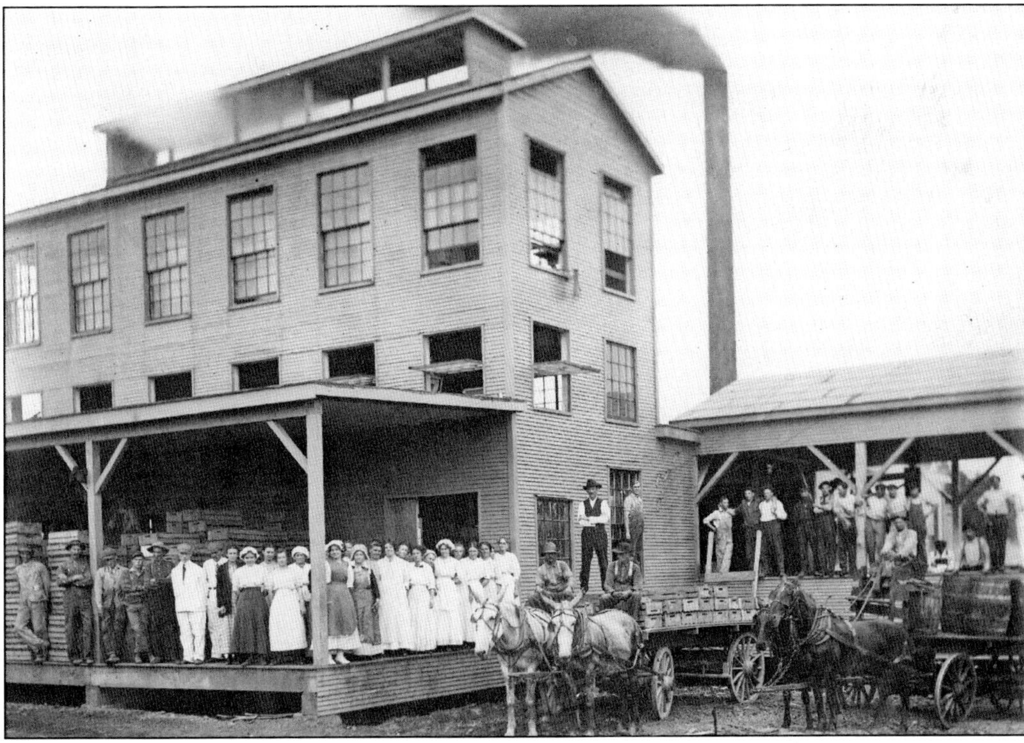

Hendricks County had at least two canning factories. The Van Camp Packing Company opened a factory on North Vine Street in Plainfield in 1913 and was there several years. Mules and horses were used to bring the wagons full of produce into the factory. In the late 1800s, the Princeton Canning Company was located on the west side of Green Street in Brownsburg and was owned by Charles F. Ruschaupt. Upon his death in 1932, the Princeton Canning Company was purchased by Scott Waddell and sons and became the Brownsburg Canning Factory. Loren Hufford was the last owner. After several years, the plant closed, and the building was burned as fire department training in 1956. (Above, Guilford Township Collection–Plainfield Library; below, Brownsburg Public Library.)

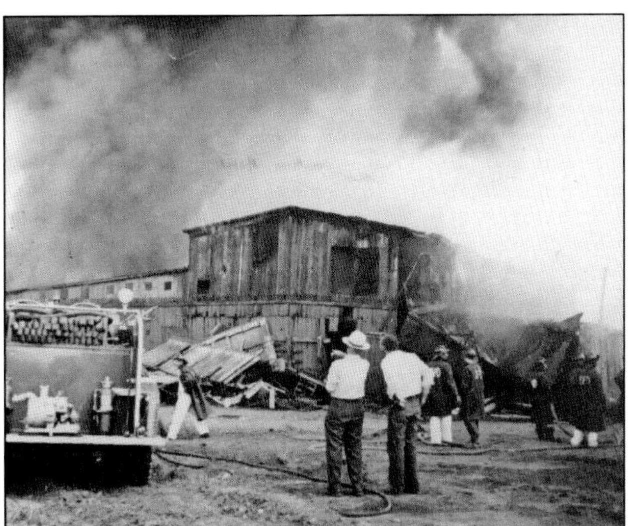

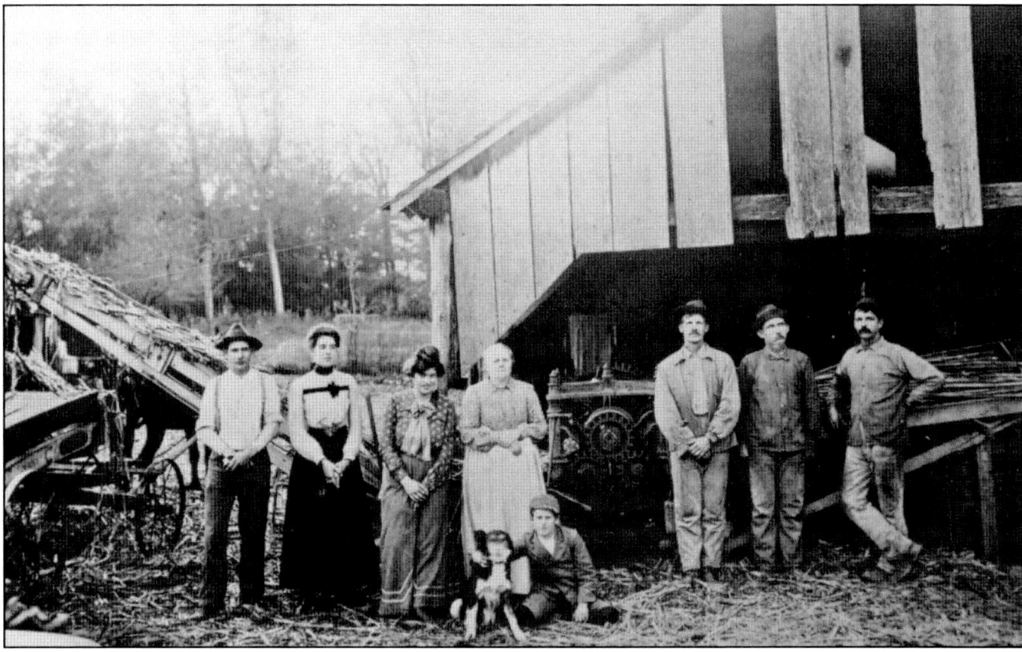

Some still remember the Nicholson Sorghum Mill. What a treat to ride in a wagon full of sorghum cane to the mill to be made into molasses. Many dishes would have been a lot less tasty without it. The employees in this picture, taken about 1904 or 1905, are, from left to right, Luther Caldwell, Edith Nicholson, Ruth Nicholson, Delia Nicholson, Charles Nicholson, Gus Bartholomew, Reuben Overman, and Cyrus Nicholson. The Nicholson Sorghum Mill was owned and operated by Charles B. and his wife, Delia, with the help of their daughters, Florence, Ruth, and Edith, and their son, Cyrus. Cyrus later ran the mill under the name of Nicholson and Sons. The mill closed in 1955. The picture below shows a label that Nicholson and Sons used on their containers. (Both, Hendricks County Museum.)

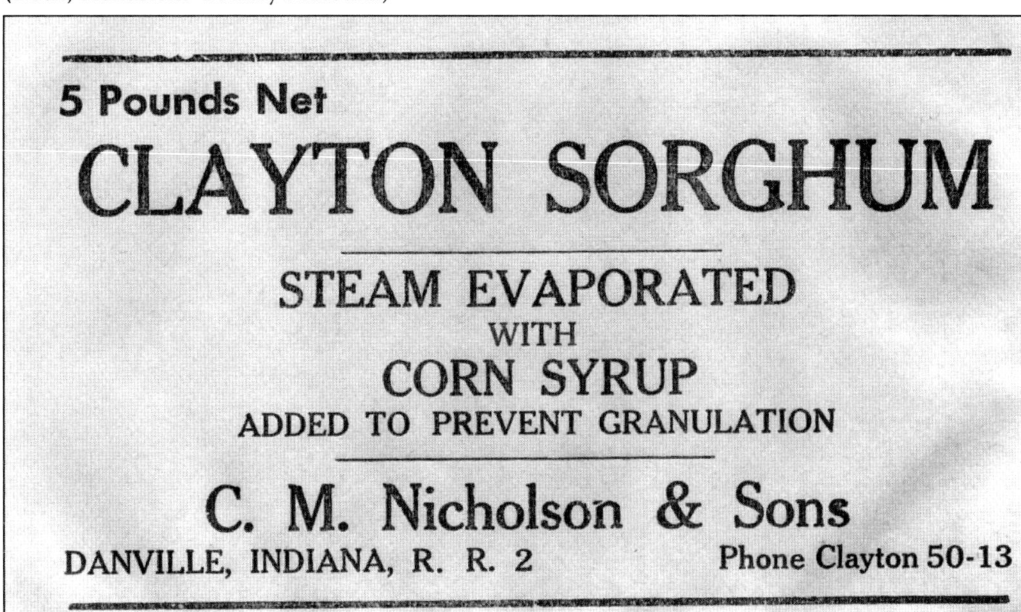

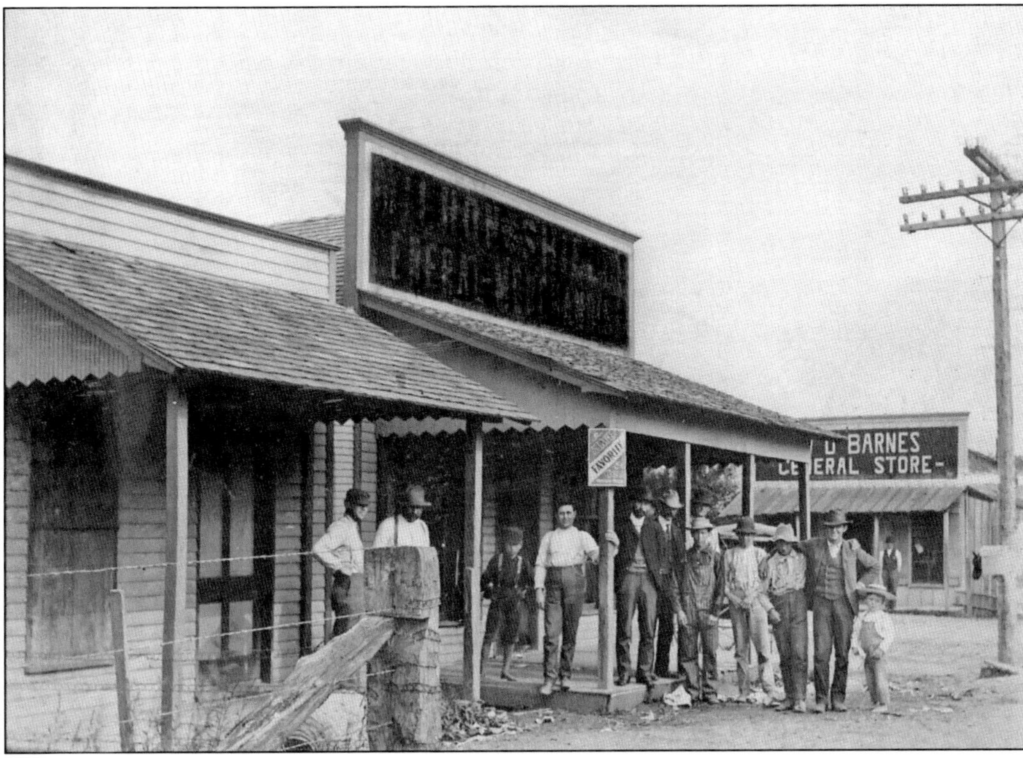

The Milhon and Shields General Merchandise Store was in the middle of Hazelwood. Ethor Milhon and Charlie Shields owned it. This store was replaced in 1914 by a new building. In the background is the Barnes General Store. (Phyllis Parsons.)

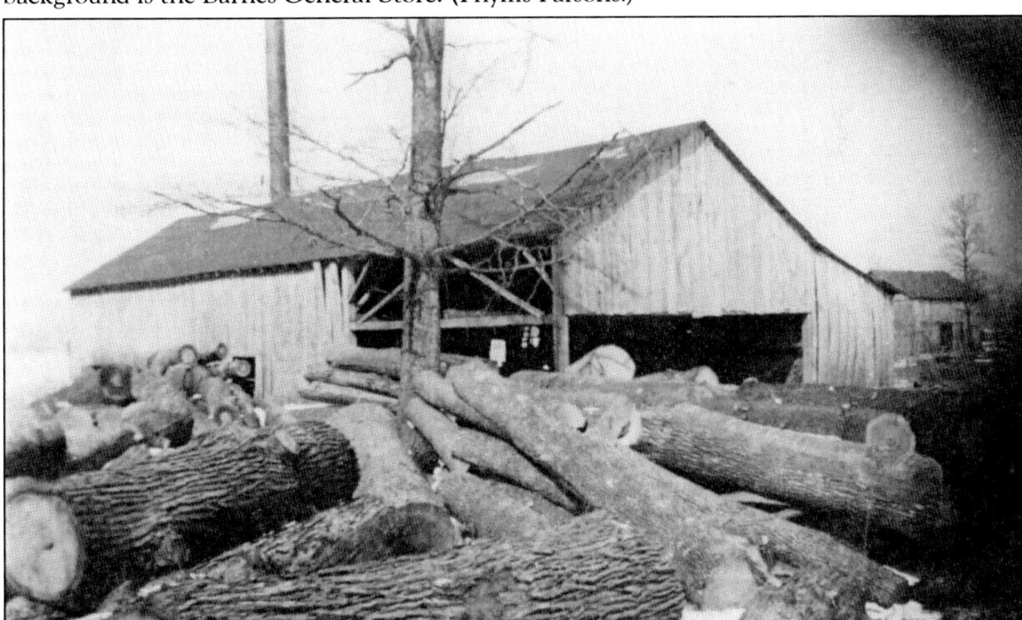
Sawmills were important businesses in many small communities. This one was located at Hazelwood, which was formerly known as Buzzards Roost. (Phyllis Parsons.)

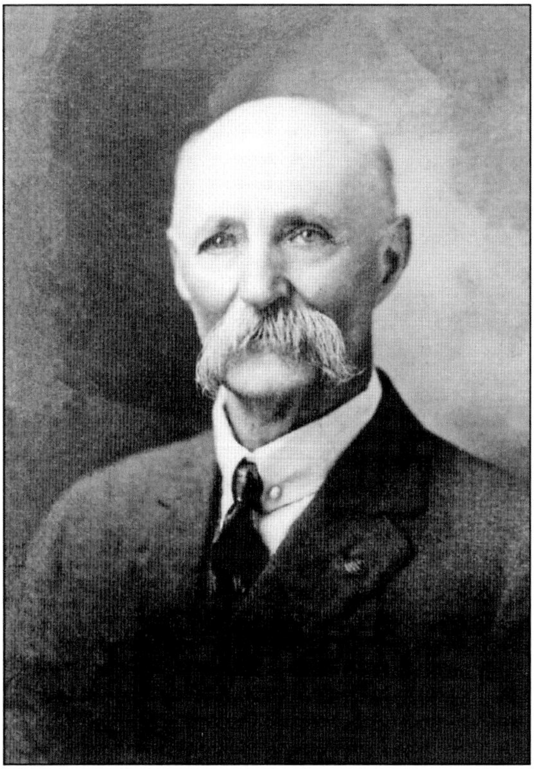

Adrian A. Parsons (1846–1929) represents the hardworking, patriotic, inventive men of his day. After being badly wounded in the Civil War, he served as county recorder. His experimenting with crops led him to soybeans that could be used in Indiana fields, and this pioneer farmer has enriched many. With his determined efforts on that small plot in Washington Township, Adrian showed how the soybean could be a useful and profitable crop. (Virginia Parsons Vapor Collection.)

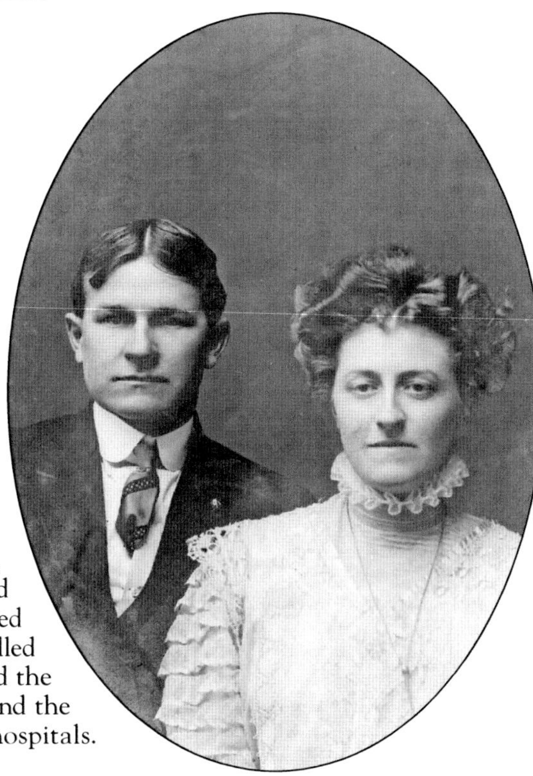

Dr. Frederick Wright grew up in North Salem, working on the family farm, until he left for medical school. He married Mamie Adams, a nurse, and they lived in the Hazelwood and Stilesville areas. As a country doctor, he delivered over 2,000 babies. When he passed away, he willed money to the Hazelwood Baptist Church and the Stilesville Christian and Baptist Churches and the Morgan County and Hendricks County hospitals. (Hendricks County Museum.)

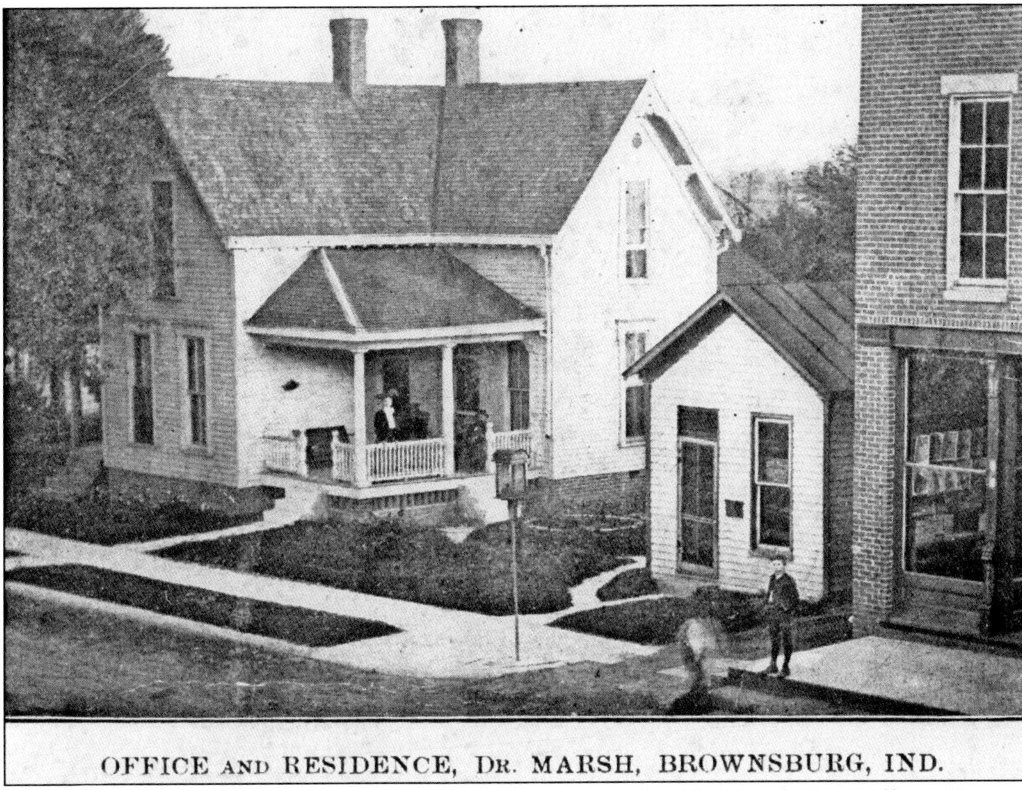

Dr. John L. Marsh, at the age of 18, trained as a medical student with Dr. William Trees at Warrington, Indiana. He received his medical degree from the Ohio Medical School in 1874. Upon graduation, he settled in Warrington (Hancock County) and then moved his practice to Greenfield in 1877. Dr. Marsh then took his medical practice to Brownsburg in the fall of 1881. He married Laura E. Trees, and they had three daughters, Florence, Mabel, and Kate. His office was located at 25 East Main Street. Kate and Mabel are seen below enjoying a ride around Brownsburg. (Both, Hendricks County Museum.)

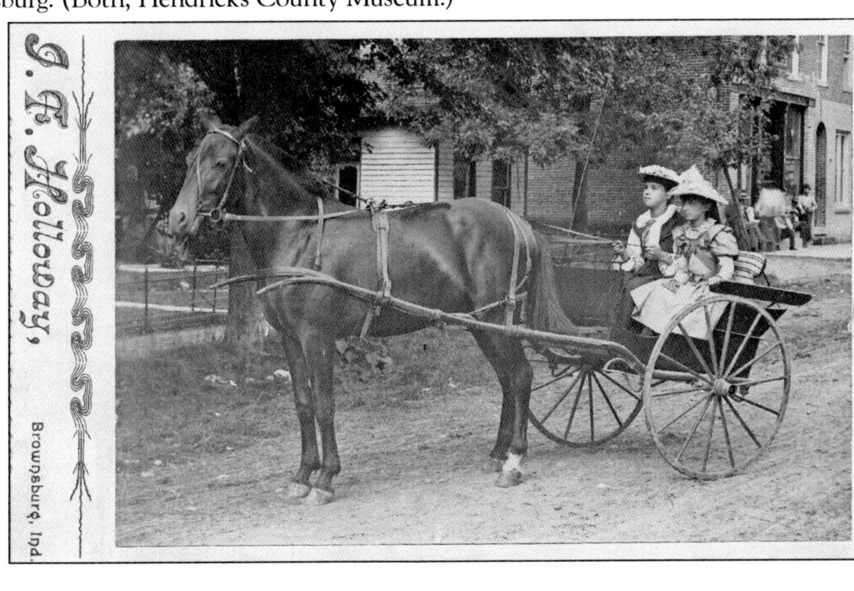

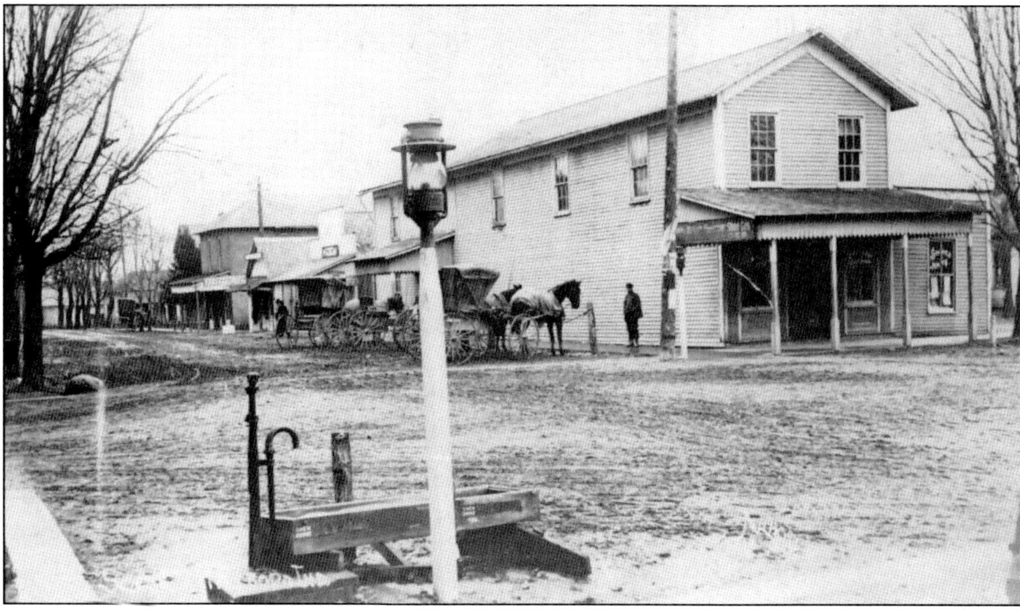

This 1899 picture shows the Weaver Store in Pittsboro. There, ladies could buy ribbons, buttons, dressmaking needs, and china for their homes. The second floor had clothing for boys and men, the west annex had shoes, and hardware supplies were at the east end. The Weaver family owned the store between 1872 and 1906 and then sold to Elwood Parker. He operated the business until 1923, when a fire destroyed it. (Hendricks County Museum.)

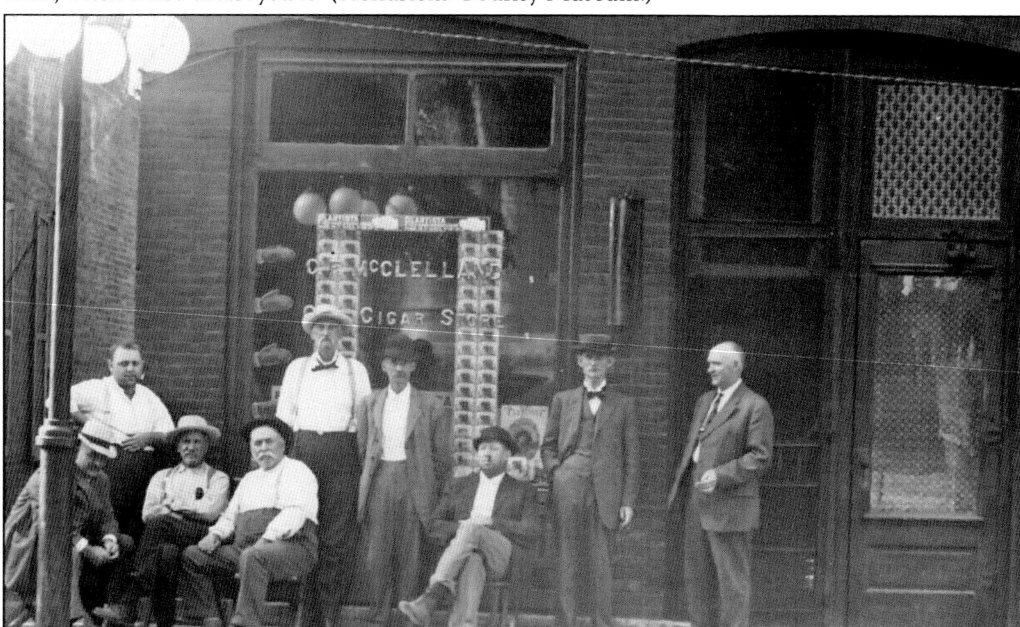

Men sit and talk over the business of the day in front of the Charles F. McClelland Cigar and Tobacco Shop in Danville. McClelland operated his store in the 1920s and 1930s. He also had a funeral business. From left to right are James Ham Wilson, Sam Ensminger, Alf Walters, William Tharp, Loyd Holtsclaw, Thad Adams, C.F. McClelland, Bob Hamilton, and Snow Wibbel. (Hendricks County Museum.)

The telephone company in North Salem was organized in 1899. The early phone exchanges were located in private homes. Vivian Gibson is the operator in this picture. The calendar indicates that it was February 1915. The operator usually sat on a high swivel chair and controlled the switchboard. At times, as many as eight families were on the same party line. (Jamie Neal.)

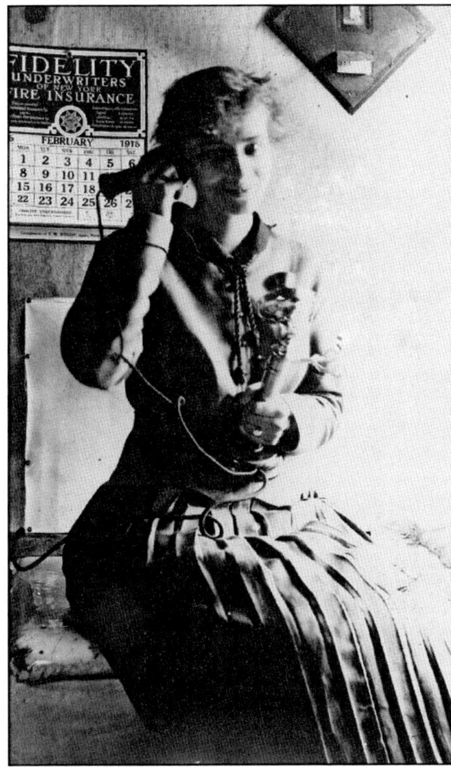

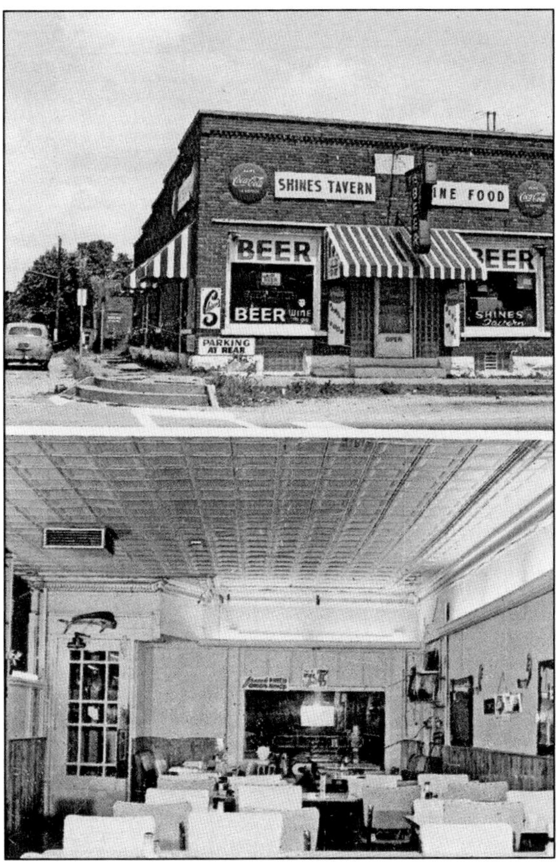

This postcard shows both the outside and inside of Shines Tavern in Stilesville. Many enjoyed a good meal and beverage there. The building is no longer standing. (Joseph Seiter.)

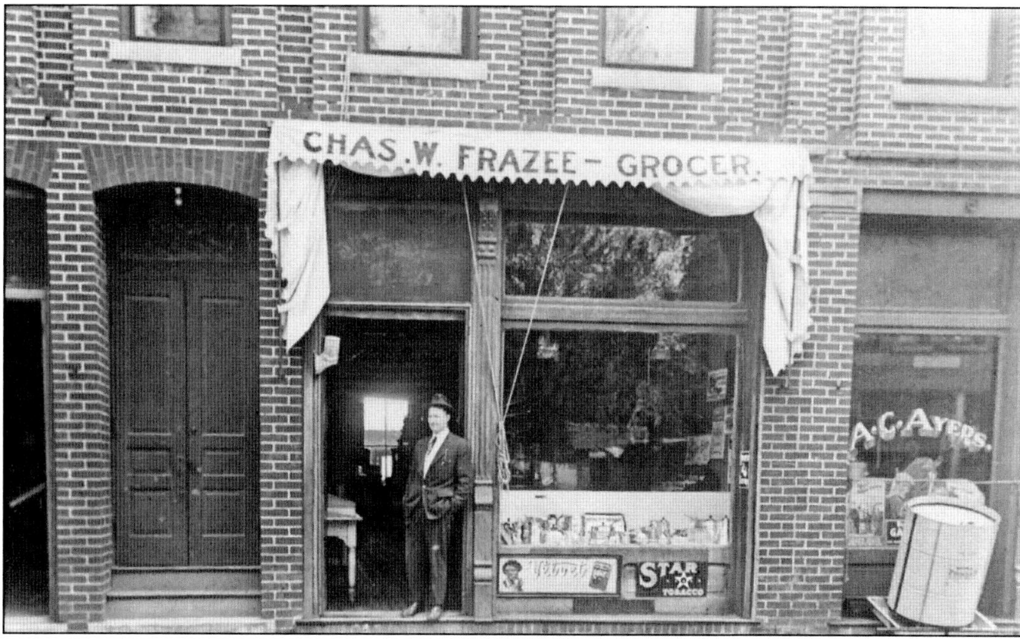

Grocery stores were not only places for families to shop but were also centers of community news. The Frazee Grocery Store was located in Brownsburg. Charles Frazee is listed as being in business on the 1920 and 1930 federal censuses. In the picture below, Leo Zerr and his brother Frank operated their grocery store on the south side of West Main Street in Pittsboro. (Above, Guilford Township Collection–Plainfield Library; below, Hendricks County Museum.)

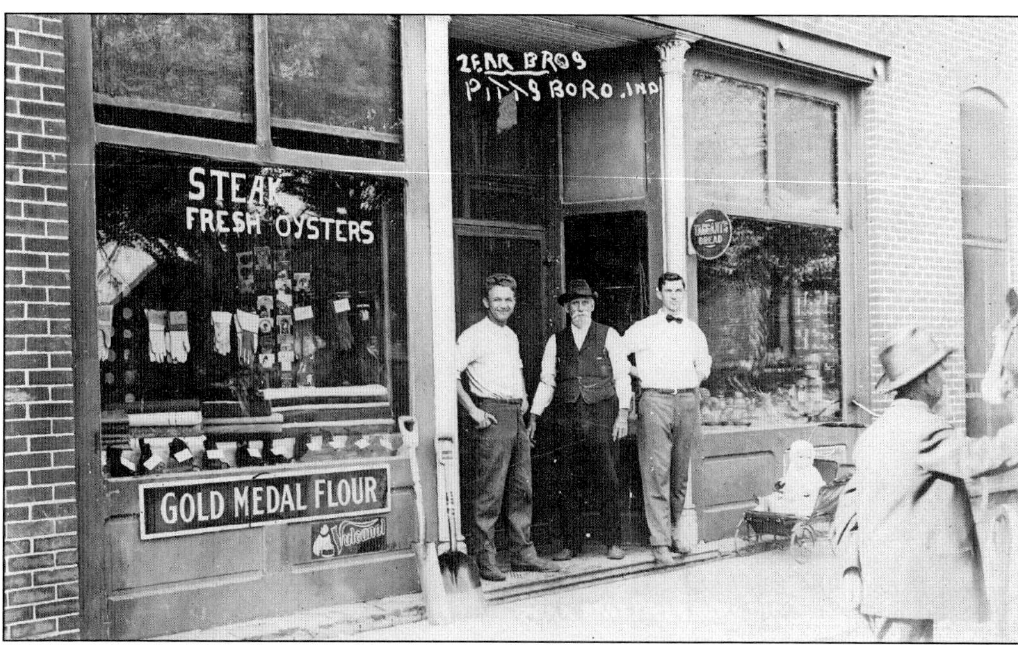

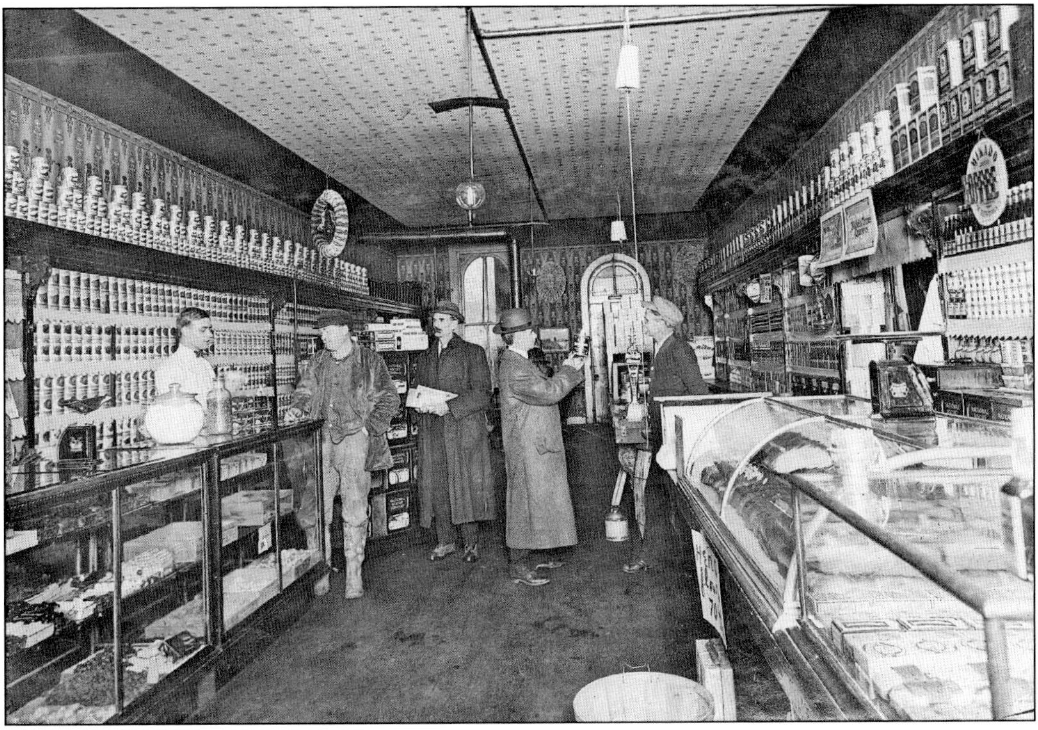

The Gibson Grocery Store in North Salem was located in the Odd Fellows Building, which later became the Red Dog Saloon, famous for its steaks cooked over apple wood. Hernando C. Gibson owned the grocery in 1920. The picture below shows a label for Gibson's Delight Baking Powder, which was featured at the Gibson Store. A handwritten note on the back of this label reads, "Place marshmallows upon thin wafers, put in oven to melt. While the wafers are hot, drop nuts over the top of the wafer and enjoy the treat." (Both, Jamie Neal.)

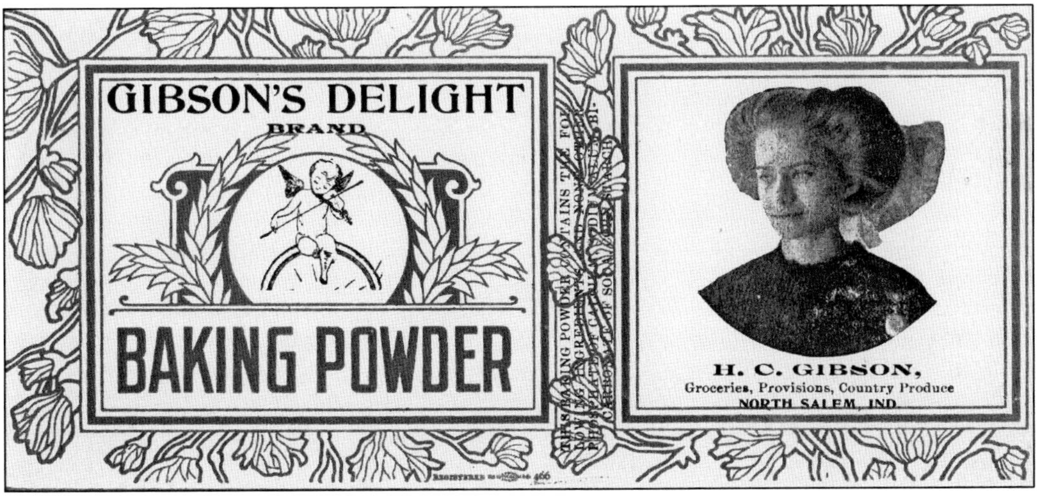

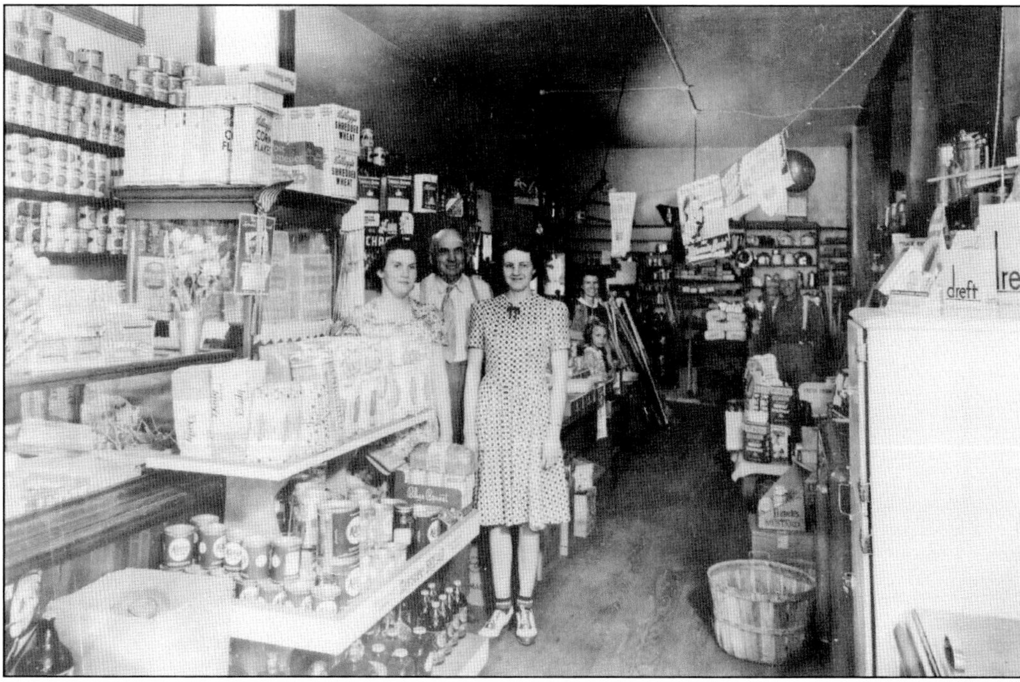

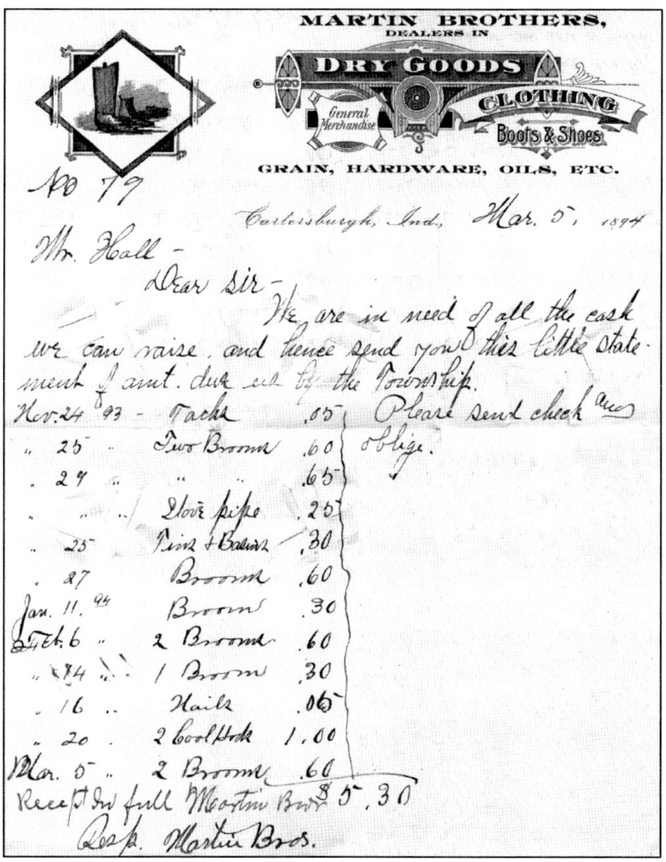

MARTIN BROTHERS,
DEALERS IN
DRY GOODS
General Merchandise
CLOTHING
Boots & Shoes
GRAIN, HARDWARE, OILS, ETC.

No 79

Cartersburgh, Ind., Mar. 5, 1894

Mr. Hall -

Dear Sir -

We are in need of all the cash we can raise, and hence send you this little statement of amt. due us by the Township.

Nov. 24 '93 - Tacks .05 Please send check and oblige.
" 25 " Two Broom .60
" 27 " " .65
" " " Stove pipe .25
" 25 Pins & Babies .30
" 27 Broom .60
Jan. 11, '94 Broom .30
Feb. 6 " 2 Broom .60
" 14 " 1 Broom .30
" 16 " Nails .05
" 20 " 2 Coal Hods 1.00
Mar. 5 " 2 Broom .60
Rec'd In full Martin Bros $5.30
Resp. Martin Bros.

Martin Brothers Store was located in Cartersburg for many years. Pictured are, from left to right, Marie Snodgrass Hargrave, Grant Martin, and Helen Snodgrass Stephenson. In the background is Leona Tomlinson, with daughter Imogene standing in front of her. Otto Low is off to the right side. Grant Martin, longtime postmaster, had the post office in his store. Note the variety of items stocked here. (Kim Snodgrass.)

The bill that Martin Brothers sent out in 1894 had the town's name spelled "Cartersburgh." It was sent to John Hall, trustee of Liberty Township. Hall was responsible for all the township schools and needed a new broom for each school. (Guilford Township Collection–Plainfield Library.)

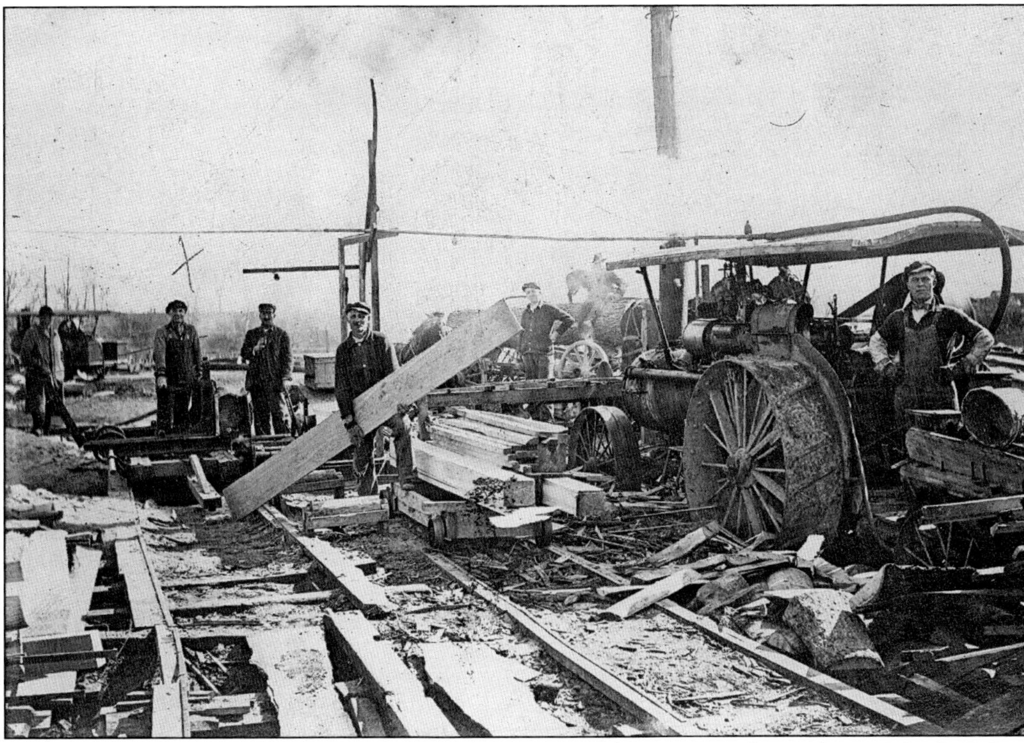

There were numerous sawmills in Hendricks County. This one was located near North Salem. The gentleman with the X over his head is Charlie Crispin. (Jamie Neal.)

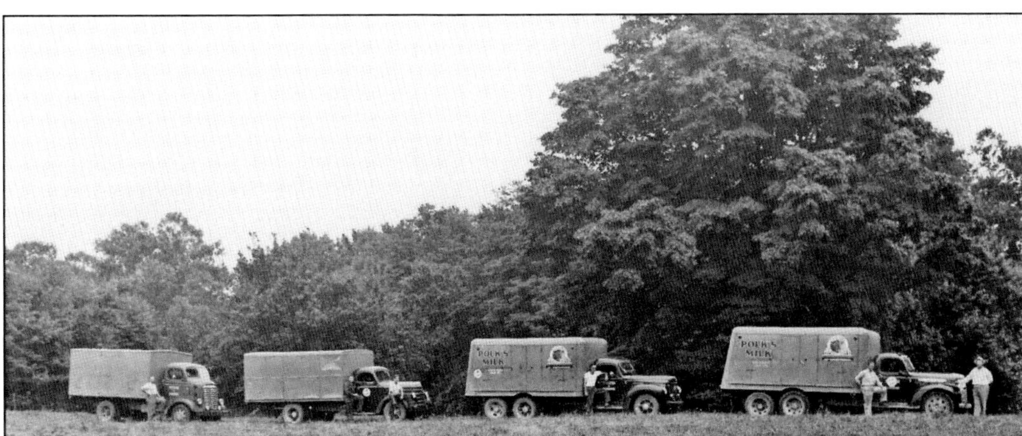

Carroll Harrison, general manager of Polk's Sanitary Milk Company, also ran a fleet of trucks that hauled raw milk in cans from the farmers to Polk's in Indianapolis. Harrison's brother Jay broke and trained the horses that were used by Polk's to pull the wagons that delivered the bottled milk in Indianapolis. Note the famous Polk cow decals on the trucks. (John O. Parsons Jr.)

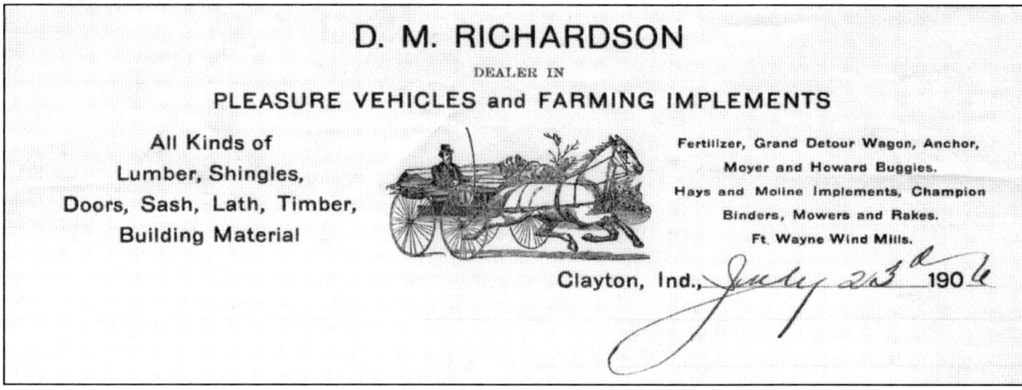

Letterheads could be used to tell customers many things about a business. D.M. Richardson, who was located in Clayton in 1906, was selling pleasure vehicles and farming implements, and he used a fine illustration of a horse and buggy to get one's attention. (Phyllis Parsons.)

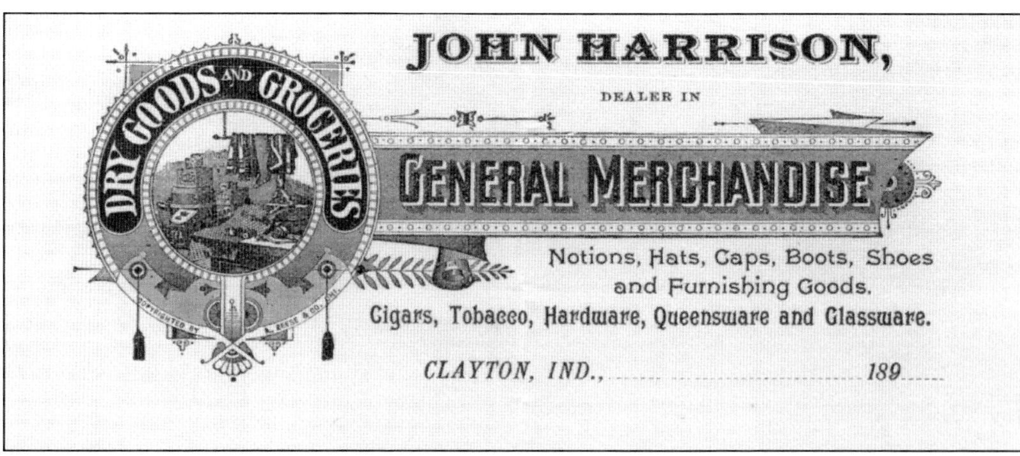

John Harrison had a general merchandise store in Clayton in 1897. His beautiful letterhead advertises his wares, which included notions, hats, caps, boots, shoes, furnishing goods, cigars, tobacco, hardware, Queensware, and glassware. He also sold dry goods and groceries. (Phyllis Parsons.)

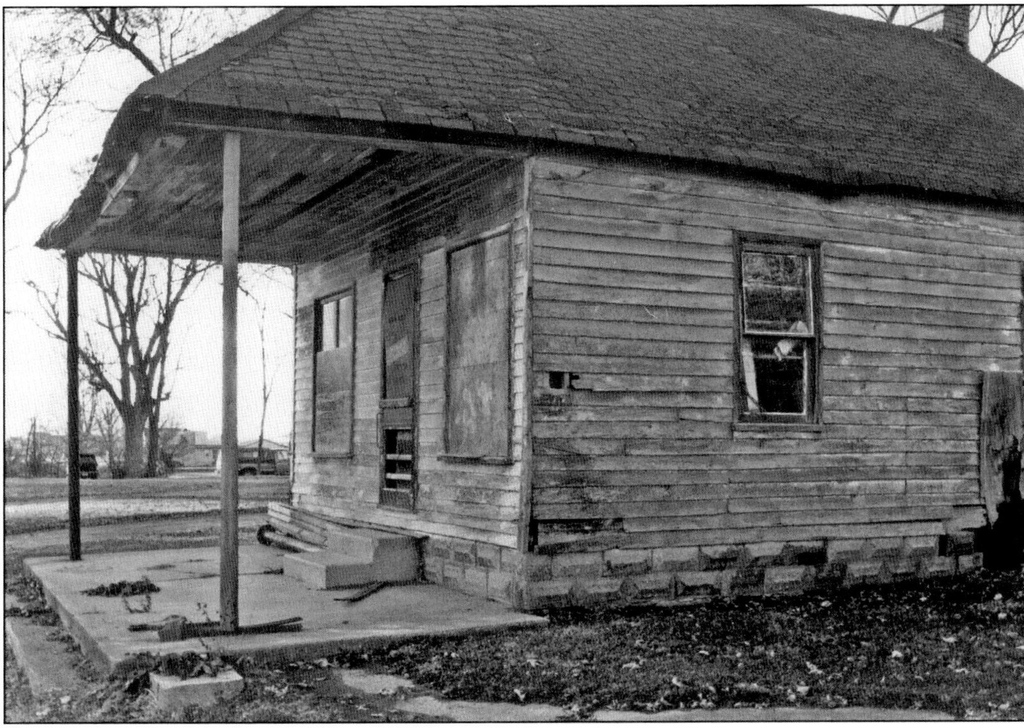

William Buchanan owned this New Winchester store. The building was moved 70 feet north when US 36 was widened in 1933. Later, the store was owned and operated by Hobert Steele. (Permission from John Bower, from Silent Workplace by Studio Publisher.)

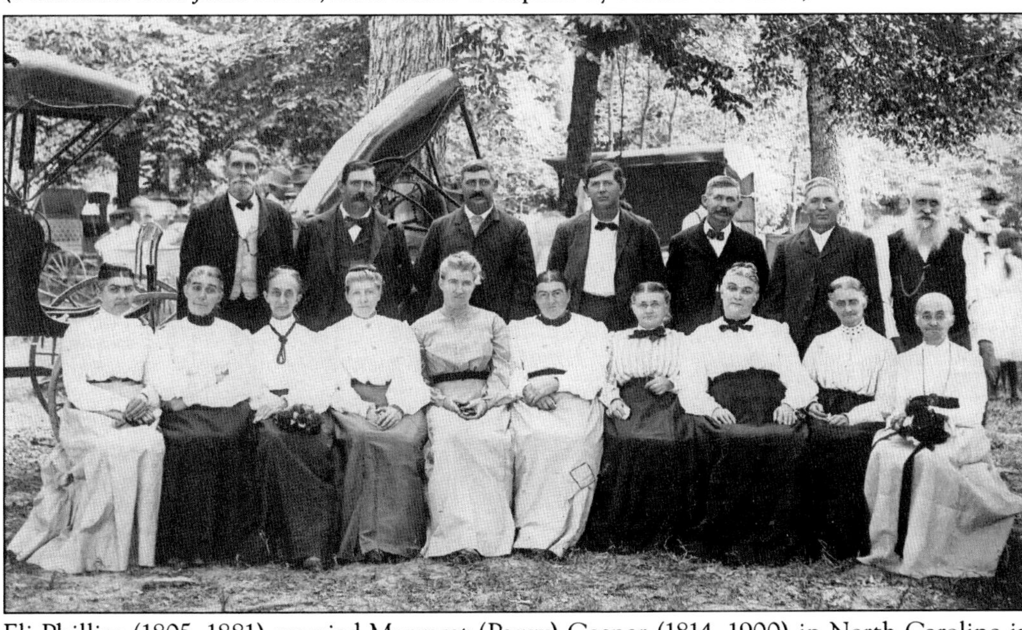

Eli Phillips (1805–1881) married Margaret (Peggy) Cosner (1814–1900) in North Carolina in September 1832. They moved to Clay Township, Hendricks County, and had a large family. The picture is labeled as the Phillips family but no names are listed. Eli and Peggy are buried in the Spring Friends cemetery and so are several of their children. (Hendricks County Museum.)

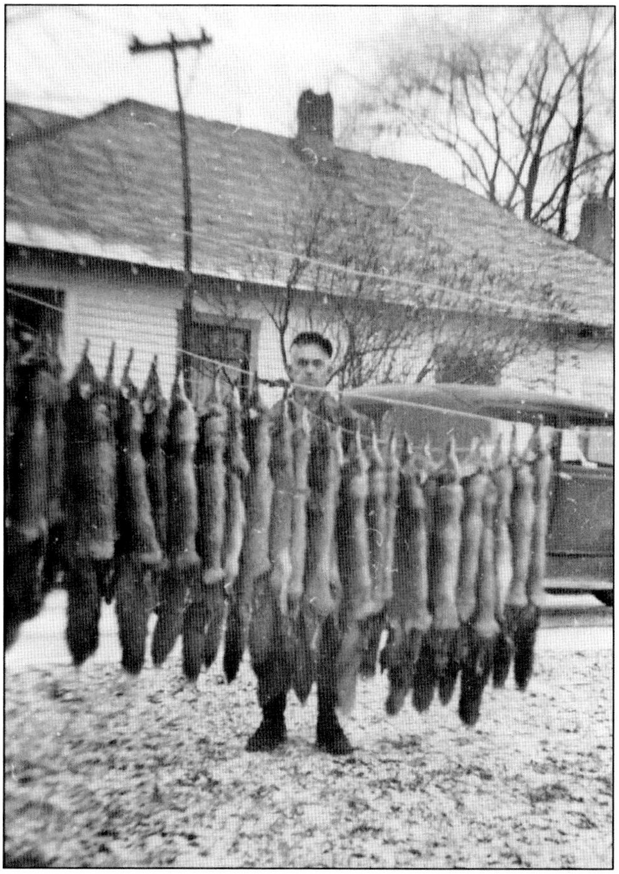

Some men made extra money by trapping animals and selling their pelts. In the winter of 1946–1947, Walter Brown trapped 26 foxes and displayed their skins, as seen here. He trapped them in Washington Township. (Sue Covey Wood.)

A plane flies over Brown's Camp in Washington Township. Brown's Camp had a column in the newspaper in the 1950s to report its community news. (Sue Covey Wood.)

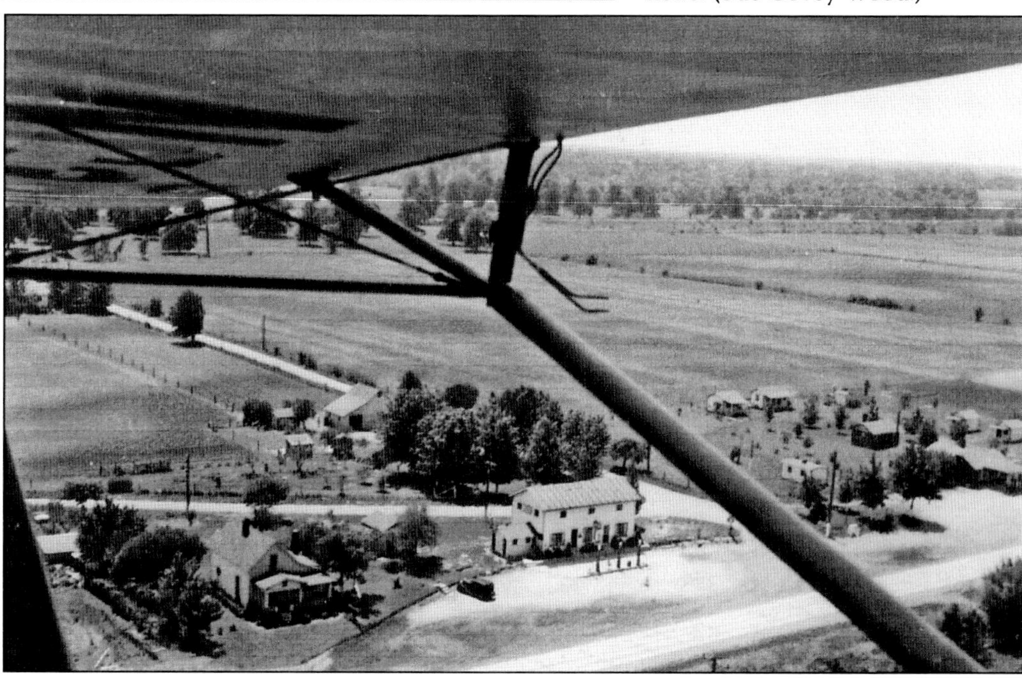

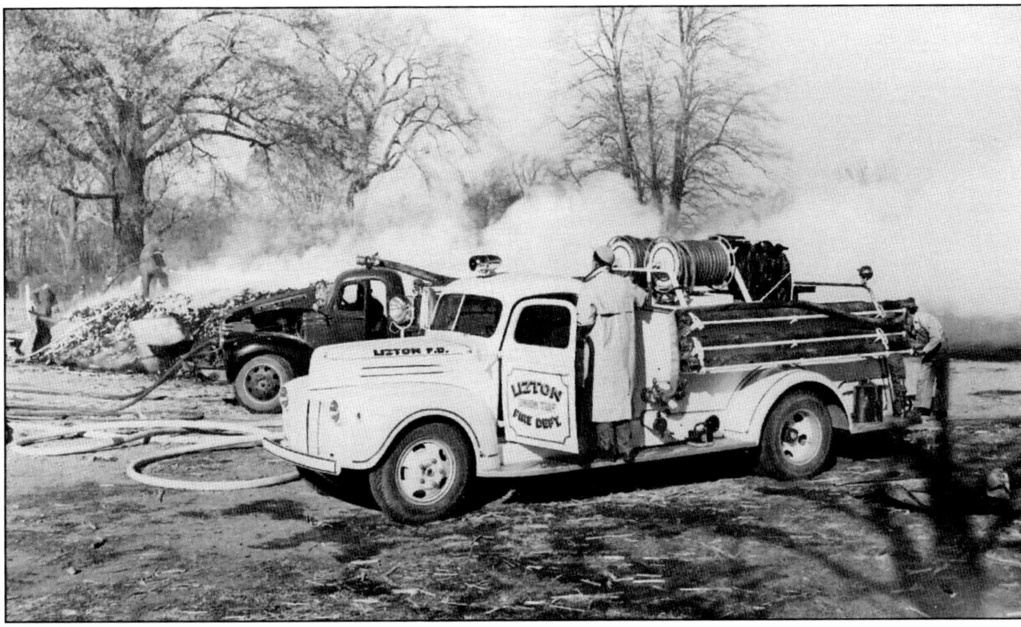

The fire department was very important to the communities. The town of Lizton has been fortunate to have a volunteer fire department through the years. The Lizton fire station is located on the corner of SR 39 and US 136. In the picture below, Bill Berzenye of the Danville Fire Department holds a clipboard as he talks with a coworker. As of 2012, Danville has two fire stations and a mix of both paid and volunteer firefighters. (Both, Hendricks County Museum.)

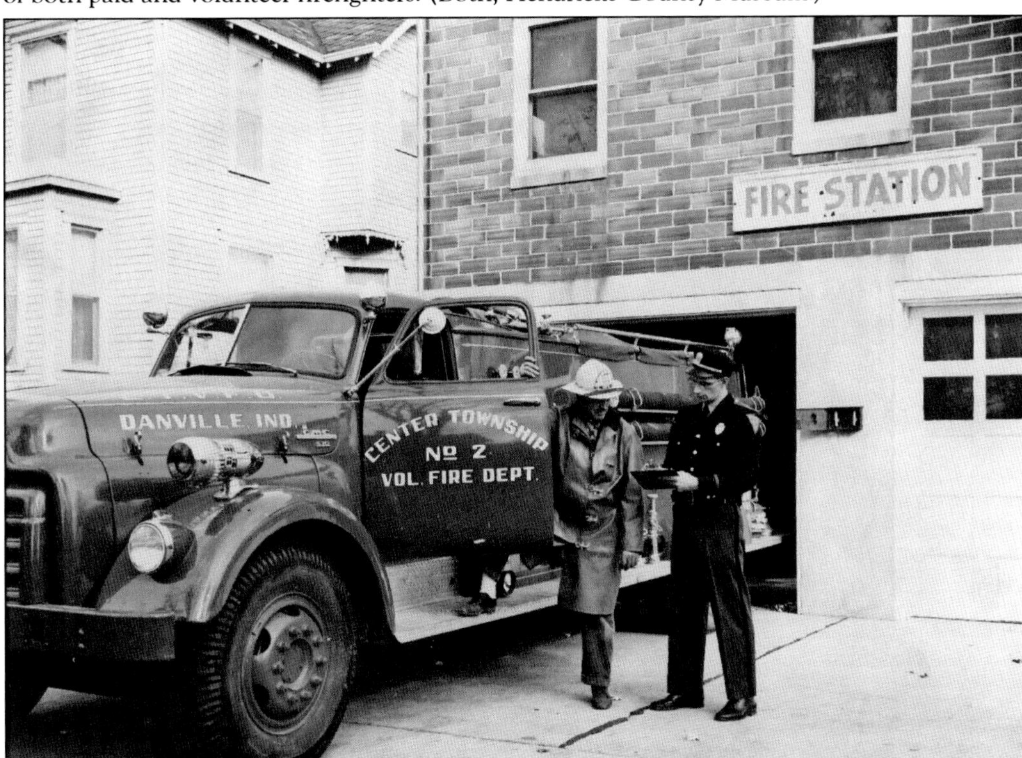

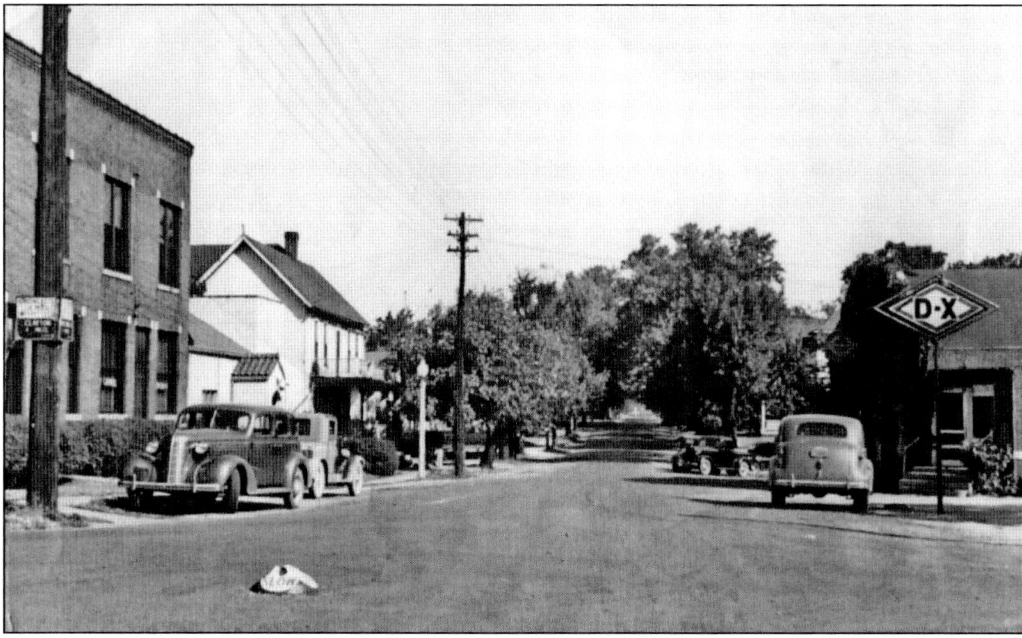

The above picture of Coatesville was taken at the intersection of Main and Milton Streets, looking north. There is a rock in the middle of the intersection that is advising drivers to "slow down." The sign on the post on the left points to Clayton (eight miles) and Greencastle (eleven miles). Most of these buildings were destroyed by the 1948 Good Friday tornado. The picture below shows Danville Motors. Chester Martin delivered DX gas to station owners. (Above, Coatesville–Clay Township Library; below, Judy Pingel.)

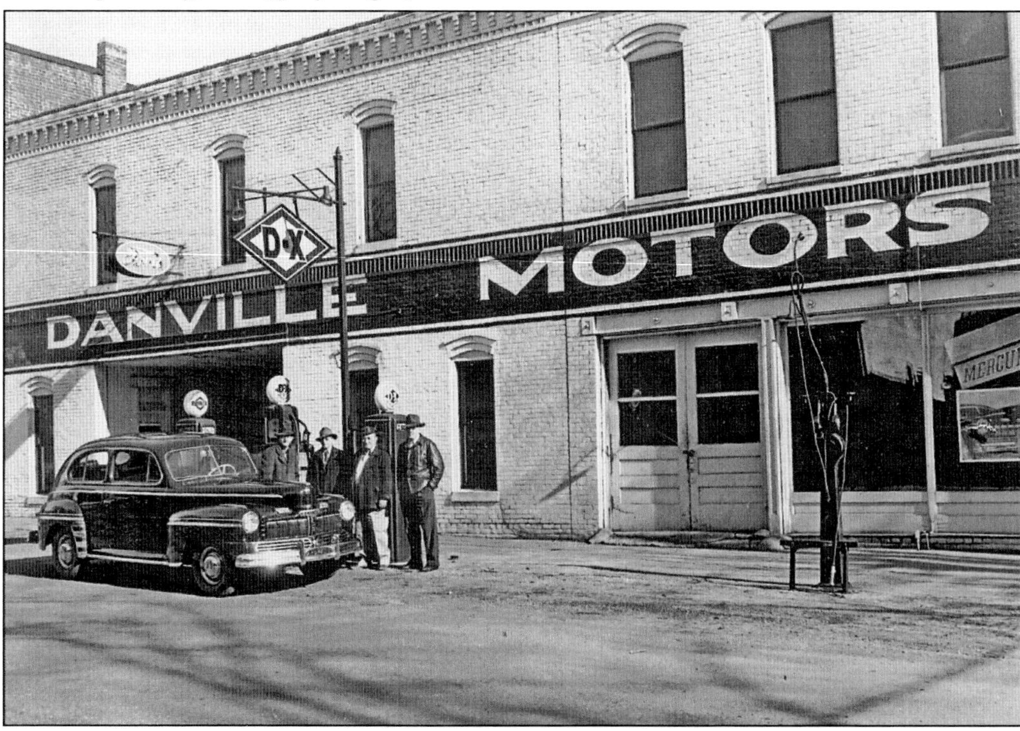

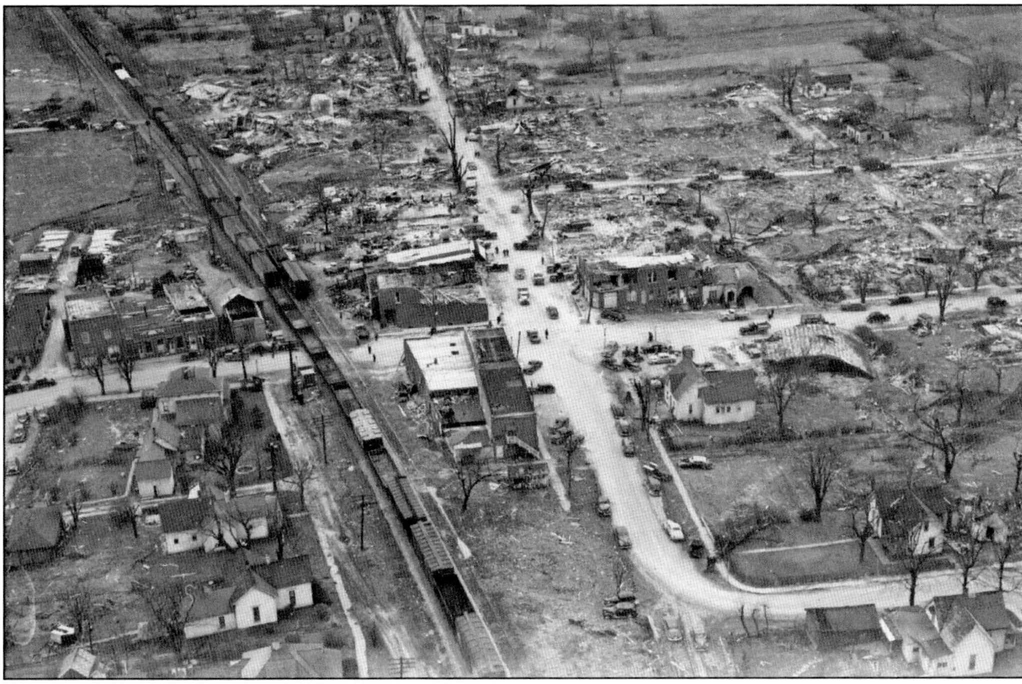

On Good Friday 1948, a tornado went through Hendricks County. In the town of Coatesville, 14 people died. This is an aerial photograph showing the devastation in Coatesville. Buildings and trees are destroyed and people are arriving to help rebuild this community. (Hendricks County Museum.)

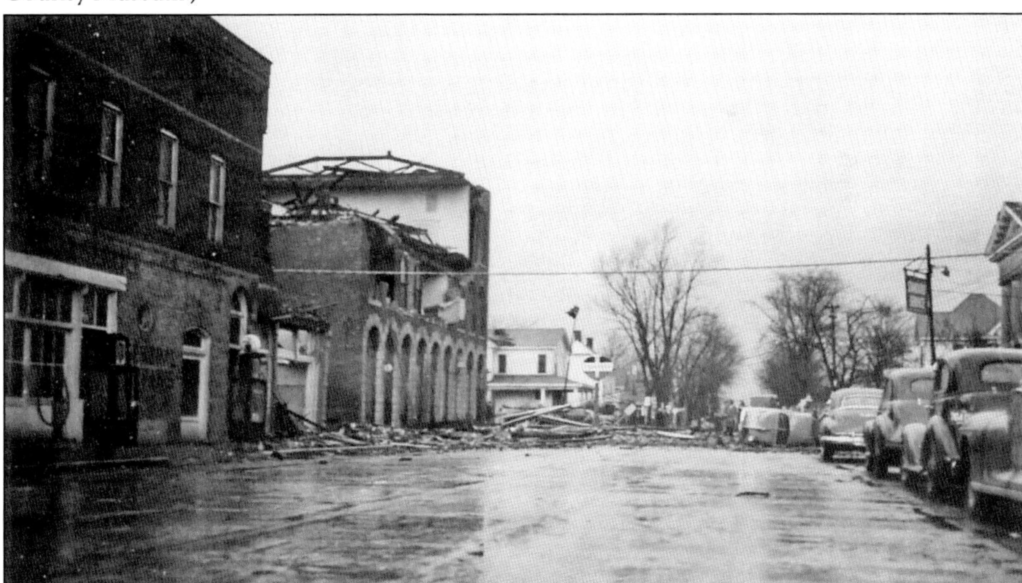

After leaving Coatesville, the tornado went through Hadley and Danville and then traveled northeast through the county. Lives were lost, buildings were torn apart, and trees were uprooted. In this picture, an overturned car blocks traffic on US 36 on the west side of Danville, near the Danville Christian Church. The damaged Christian church can be partially seen on the right. (Hendricks County Museum.)

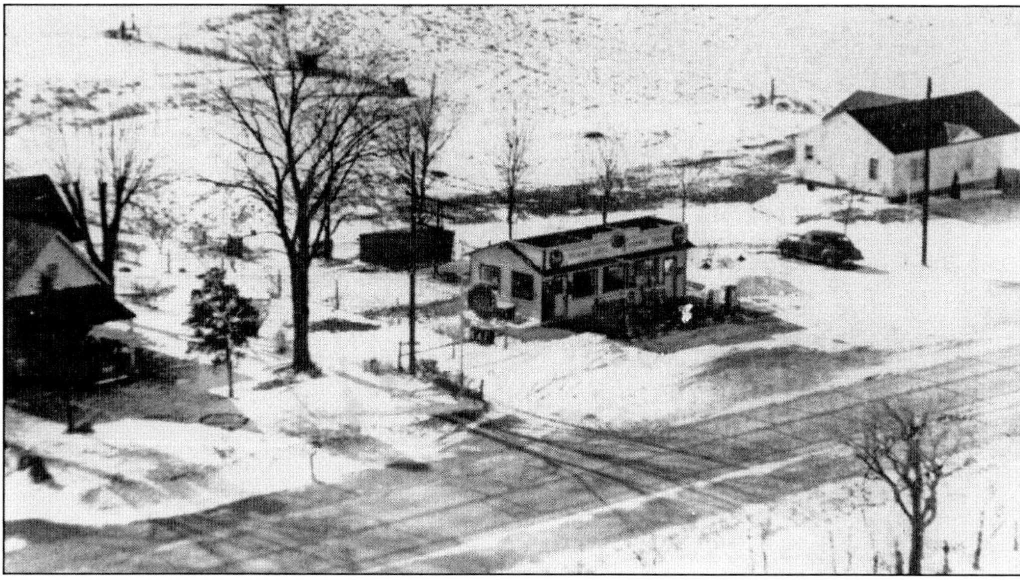

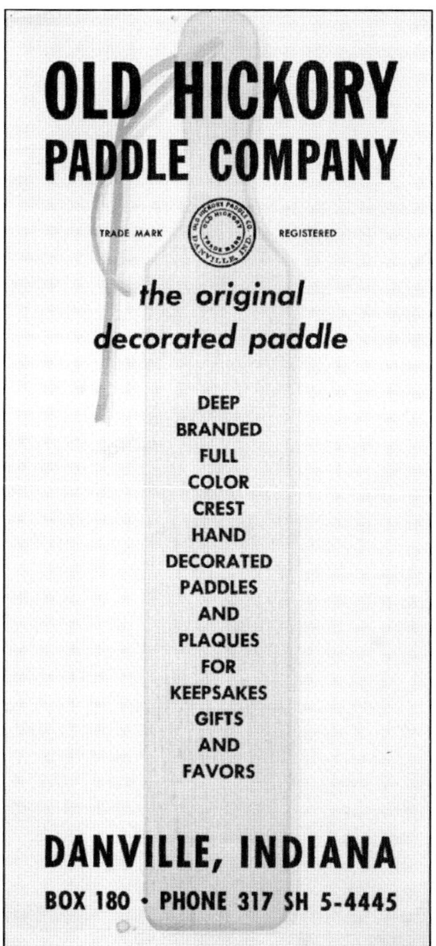

The Van Horn Grill and Gulf station was located on old US 36, two miles east of Danville. It was listed in the Danville phone directory from 1959 to 1963. This was before the era of "self-service," so customers enjoyed the personal service of an attendant who filled their gas tanks, washed their windows, and checked their oil. (Bonnie Eggers.)

John Rader ran the Old Paddle Shop in Danville. It was located at various addresses (462 East Broadway, Lawson Street, and finally on old US 36). The company produced hickory college paddles and mugs with fraternity and sorority insignias. It was in operation from the 1950s through the 1980s. (Hendricks County Museum.)

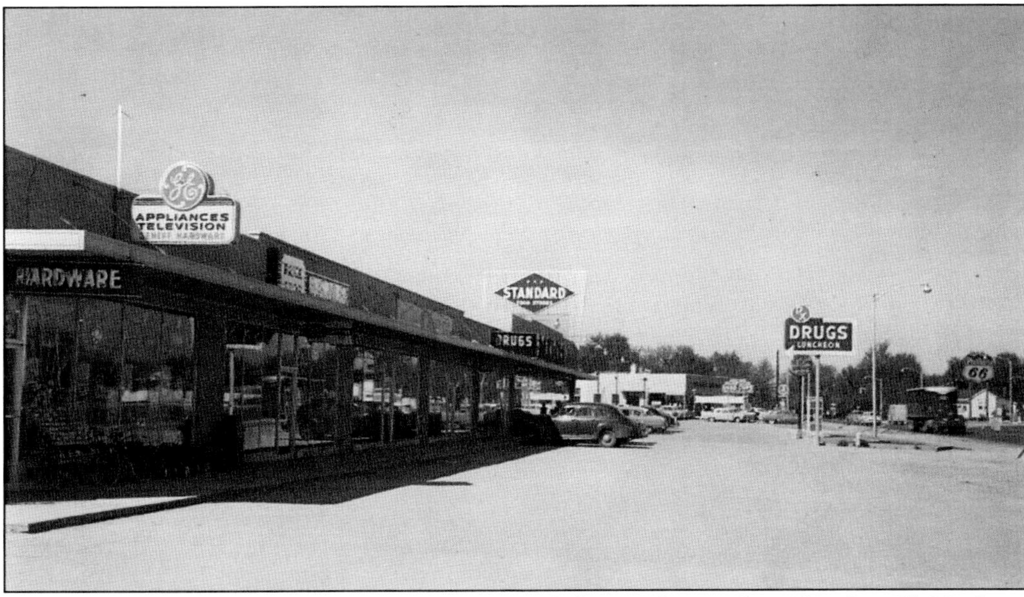

The Plainfield East Hill Shopping Center was a good place to shop in the 1950s. Seneff's Hardware Store was located here, along with a drugstore and the Standard Food Store. At the end of the shopping center, there was a car dealership that sold Chrysler products, and across the street was a Phillips 66 gas station. Telephone booths like that hardly exist today. (Bonnie Eggers.)

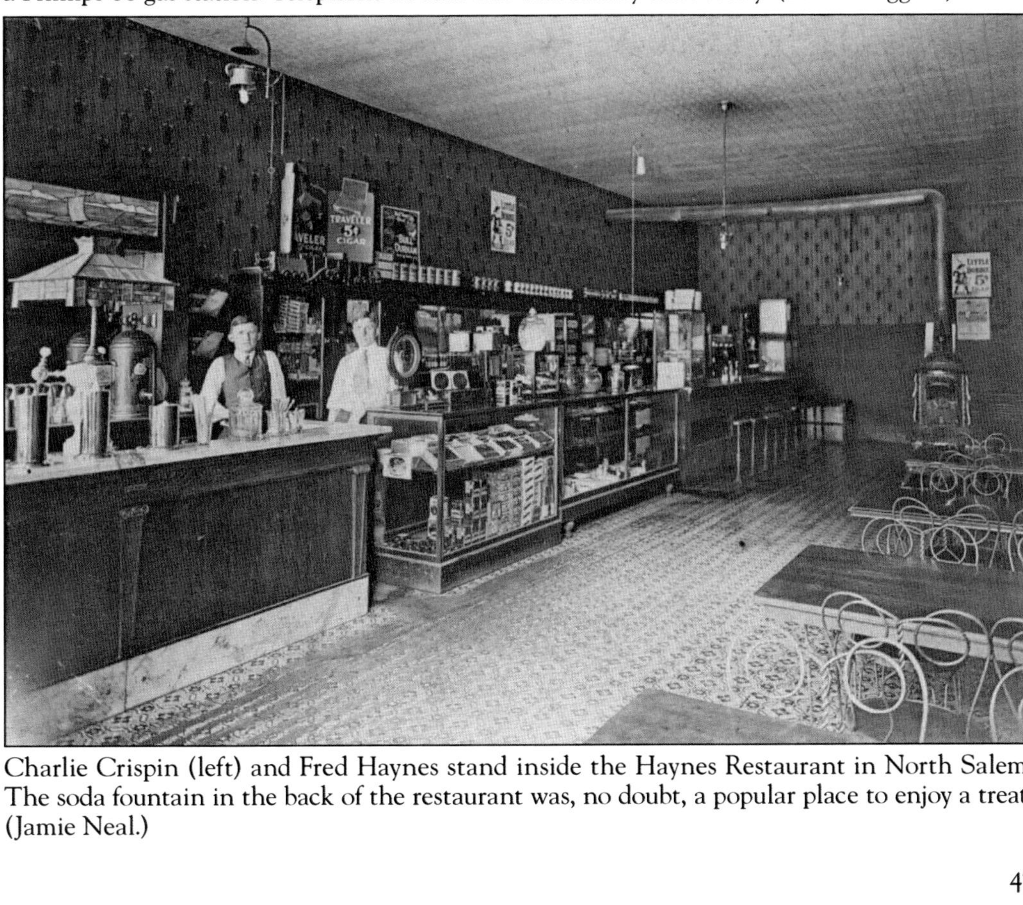

Charlie Crispin (left) and Fred Haynes stand inside the Haynes Restaurant in North Salem. The soda fountain in the back of the restaurant was, no doubt, a popular place to enjoy a treat. (Jamie Neal.)

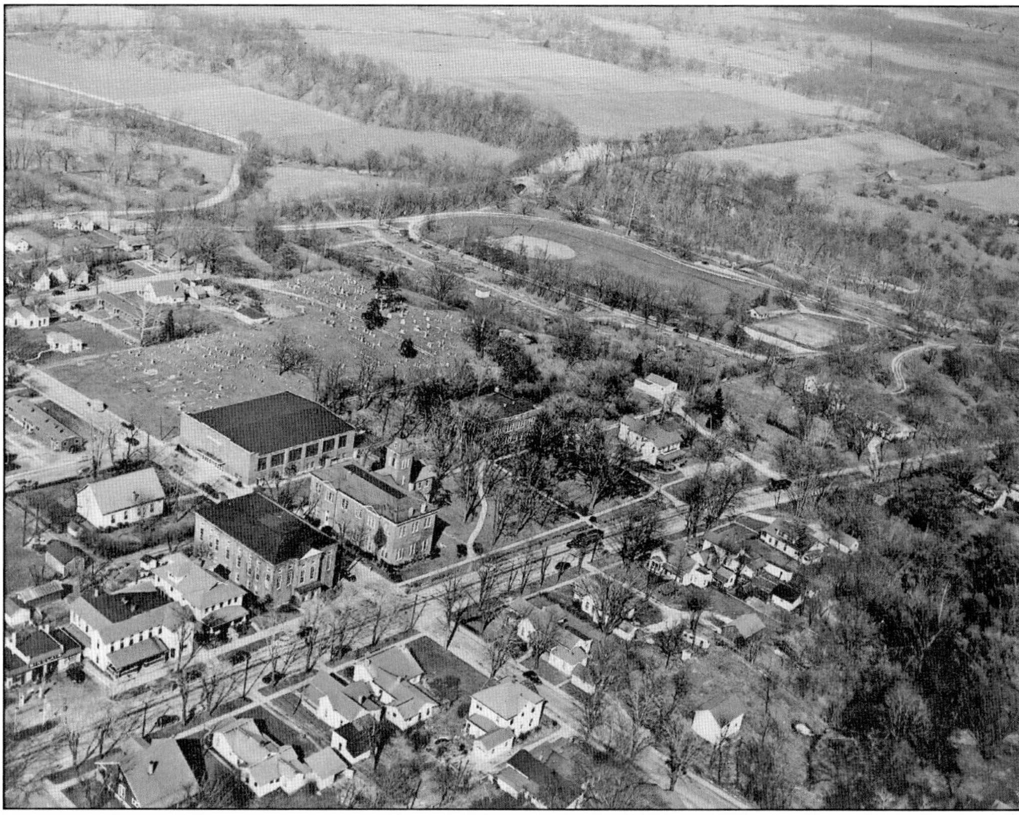

This overhead view of Danville shows Central Normal College buildings next to the Danville East Cemetery. Ellis Park is at the top. The small white building in the left center, across from the Central Normal College gym, is the Danville Regular Baptist Church, which was later purchased and demolished by the Danville School Corporation to make a parking lot. (Danville Public Library.)

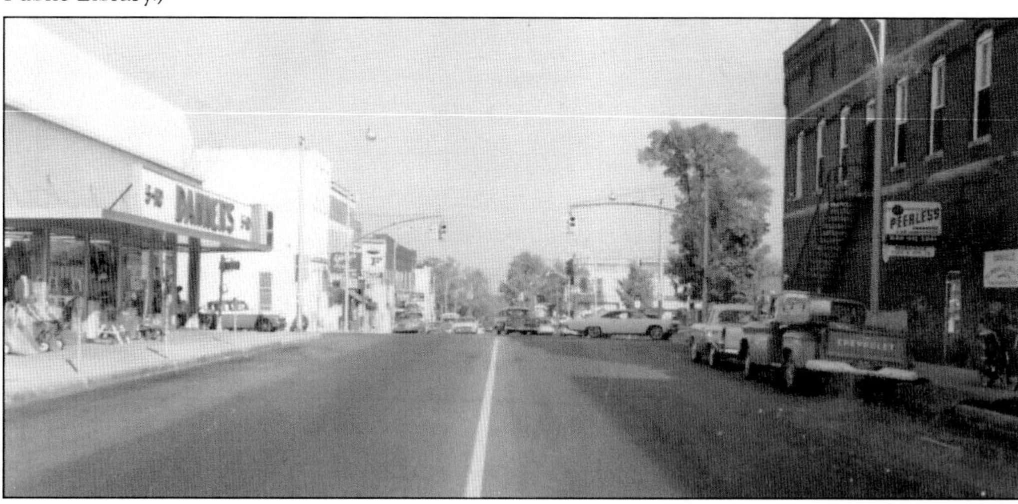

As drivers in their automobiles move about town, Danville appears to be bustling in the early 1950s. Danner's, which was located on the north side of Main Street, was a popular place to shop. (Phyllis Parsons.)

Hendricks County has had four courthouses. Men in this picture are installing telephone poles around the third courthouse. It was demolished in 1912 after the roof collapsed from too much snow. Fortunately, no one was in the building at the time. Sheriff John Ader had the key to the courthouse and kept it as a memento since it was no longer needed. A few years ago, his granddaughter Barbara McIntyre donated it to the Hendricks County Museum, and it is on display there. Signs on the post read "Baths" and "John's Gaming Parlor." The picture below shows the courthouse that currently serves Hendricks County, as it has been doing for 100 years now. (Both, Phyllis Parsons.)

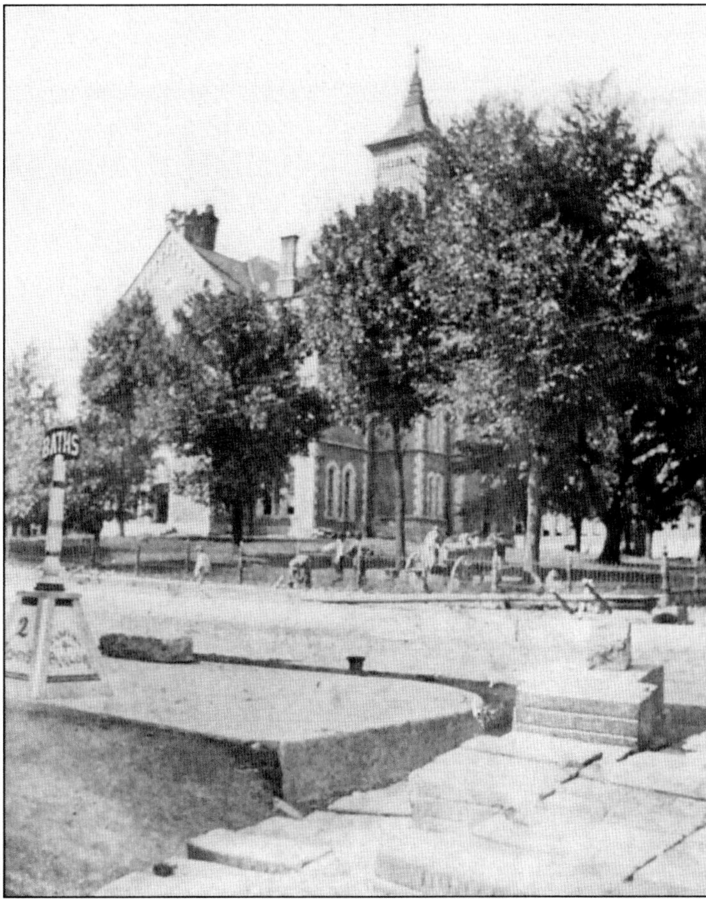

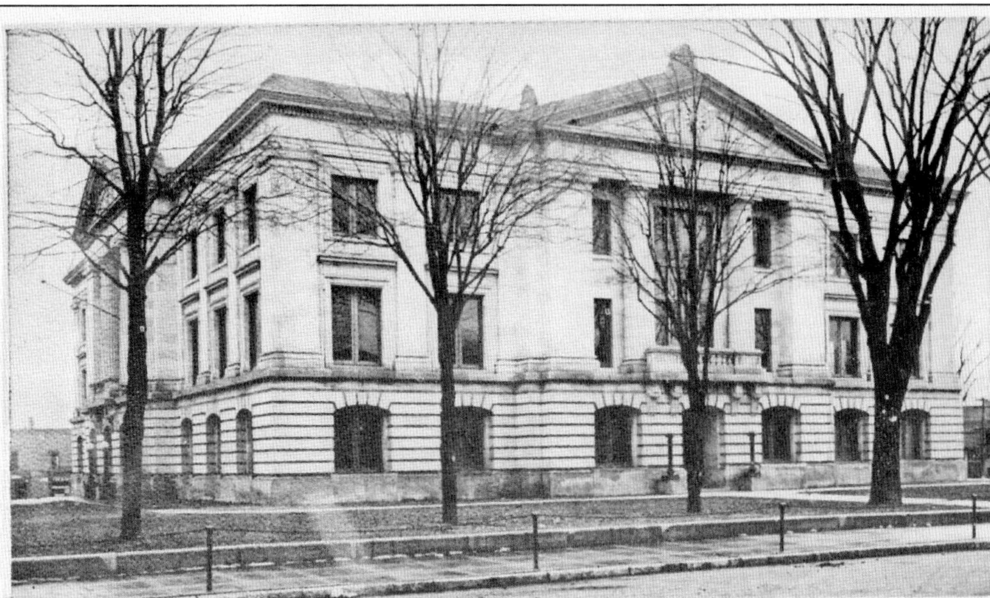

Court House, Hendrick County, Danville, Ind.

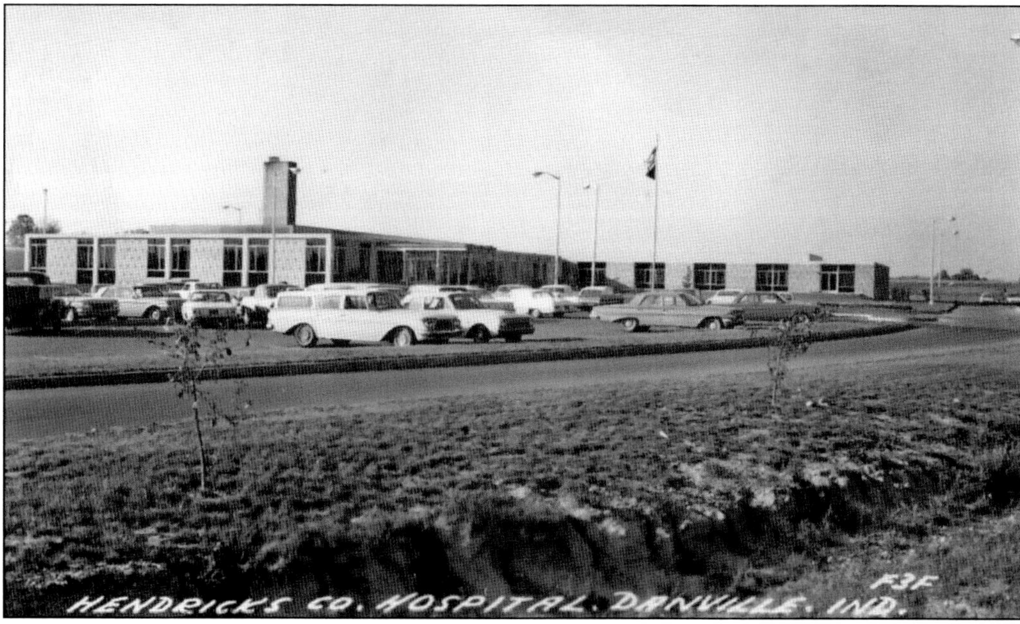

Hendricks County citizens were fortunate when a county hospital was built to serve the medical needs of the area. Ground breaking was in 1960, and the hospital opened its doors in Danville on May 21, 1962, with 70 beds. After many changes and expansion, it is now called Hendricks Regional Health. As the county has grown, other hospital facilities have been added, including IU Health and St. Francis Hospital. (Phyllis Parsons.)

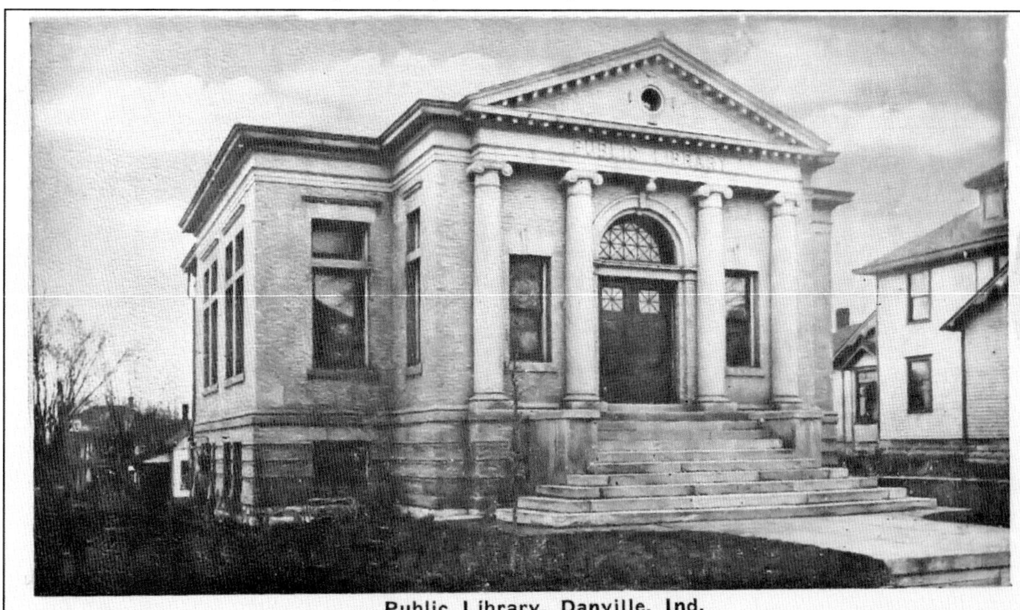

At one time, Hendricks County had four Carnegie public libraries. They were located at Brownsburg, Coatesville, Danville, and Plainfield. Brownsburg was the last one built in 1916. The Brownsburg and Clayton libraries have been replaced by newer structures. The former library in Plainfield is now an office for the Triangle Fraternity. Danville's Carnegie library is the only one still in use as a library. It has been expanded. (Phyllis Parsons.)

Three

GETTING FROM HERE TO THERE

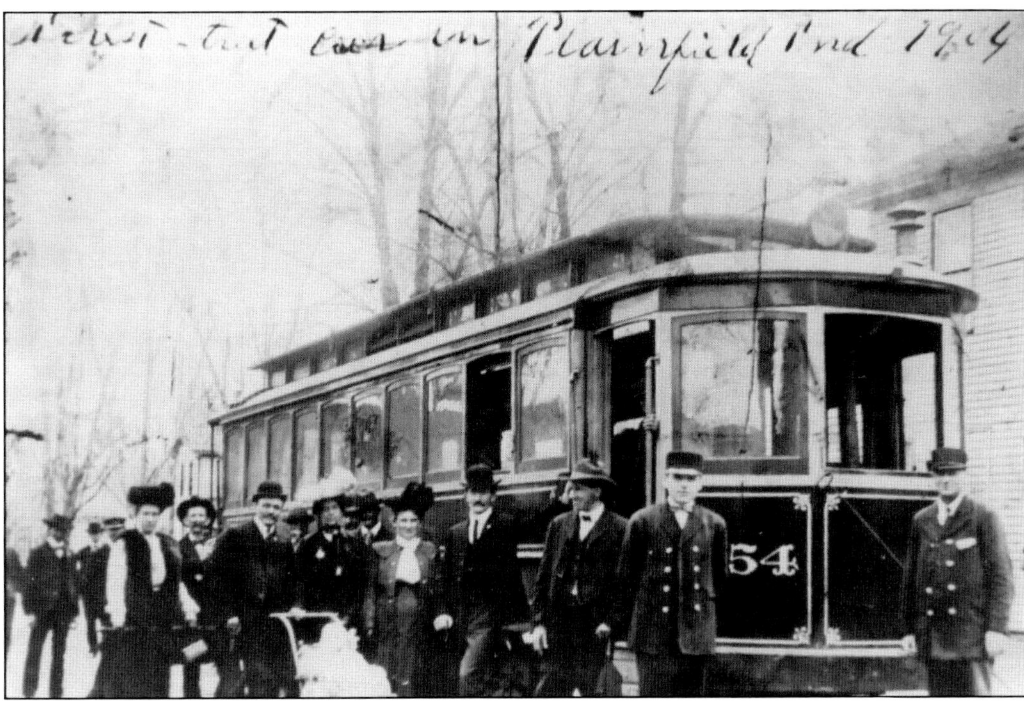

The earliest settlers either walked or rode horses into the area that became Hendricks County. As time passed, getting from here to there became easier with the advent of trains, automobiles, and buses. County travel improved with the introduction of hard surfaces. This picture shows an interurban car in Plainfield in 1904. (Guilford Township Collection–Plainfield Library.)

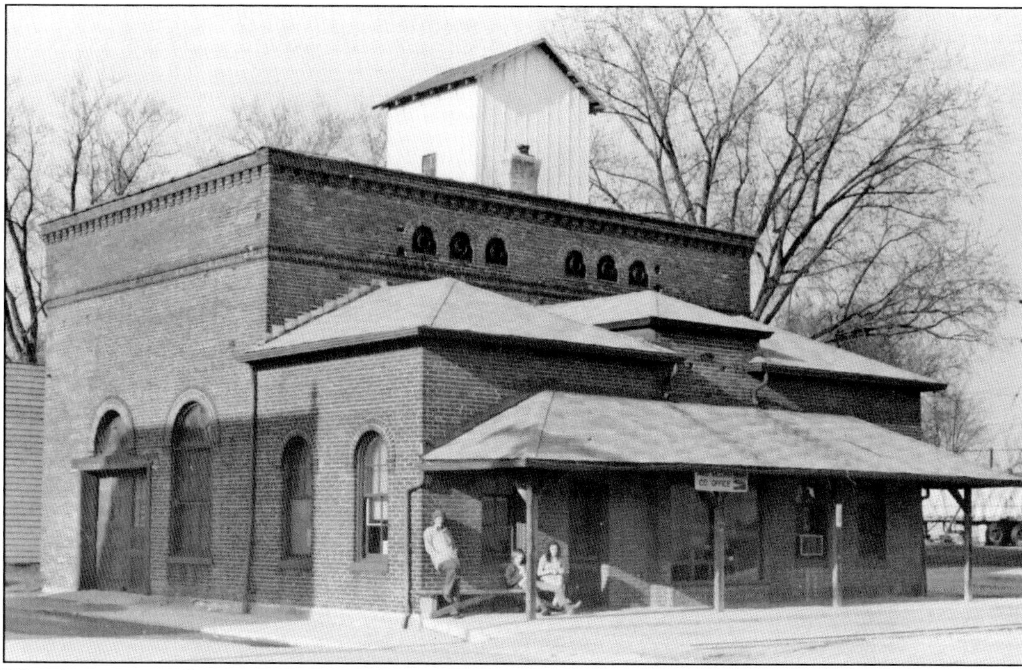

The Amo interurban station proved useful when it was built and still serves the community today as the Amo Interurban Reading Room. It is listed in the National Register of Historic Places. It was put into use in July 1907 and was operational until the early 1940s. At one time, 15 interurban cars came into the station daily from Indianapolis. (Hendricks County Museum.)

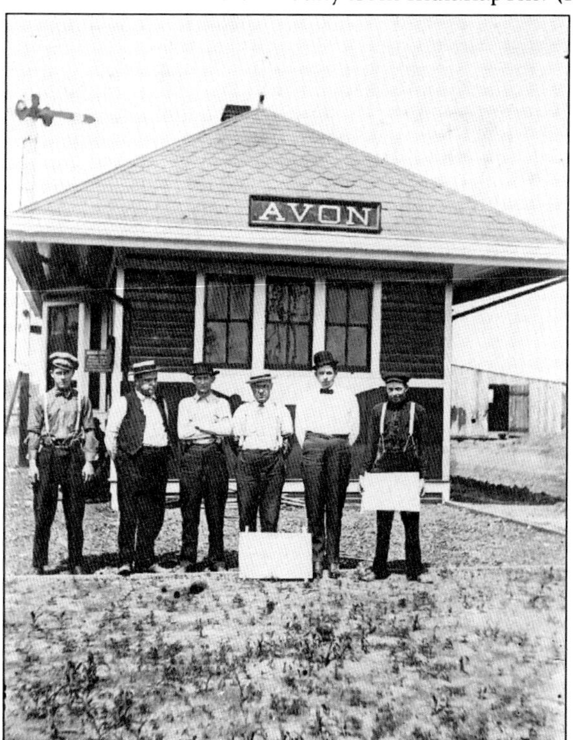

This is the Avon train station. It was located on Dan Jones Road where the grain elevator later stood. The men standing here are, from left to right, Eddie Barker, Jumbo Hurin, unidentified, Bill Barker, unidentified, and Bill Wear. Bill Barker was the stationmaster and telegraph operator. (Guilford Township Collection–Plainfield Library.)

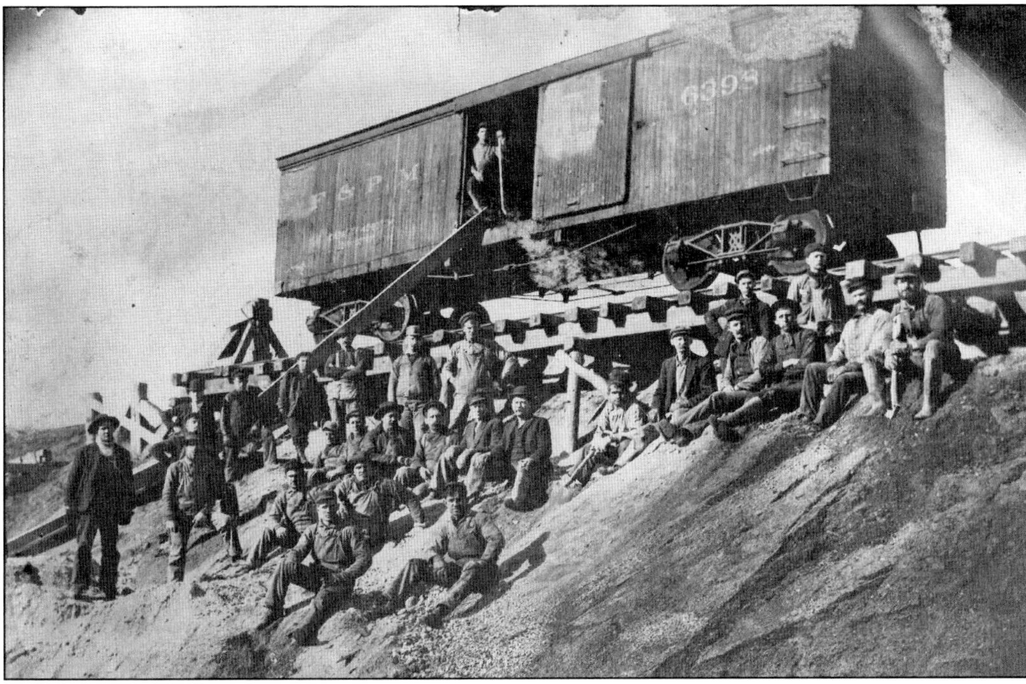

Building a railroad was no easy task. These men are working in the Washington Township area in 1910. As the tracks were being laid, a railcar would follow along, carrying needed supplies. (Huron Heritage Collection, Avon–Washington Township Library, Avon, Indiana.)

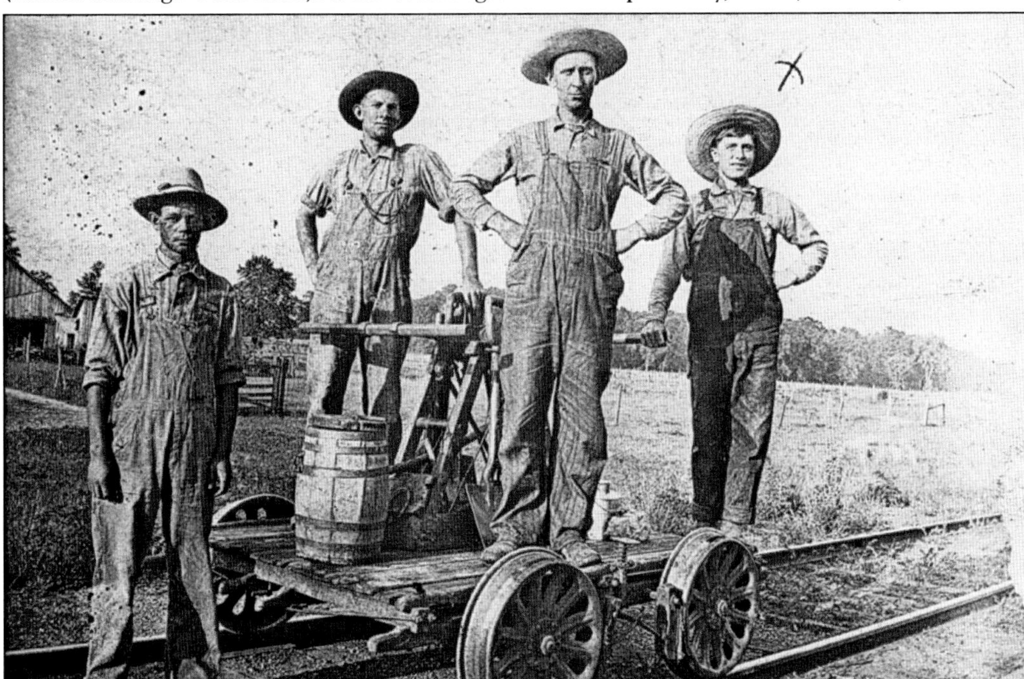

Railroads needed constant maintenance to assure safe travel. These railroad workers are from the North Salem area. Charlie Crispin is the man with the X over his head. (Jamie Neal.)

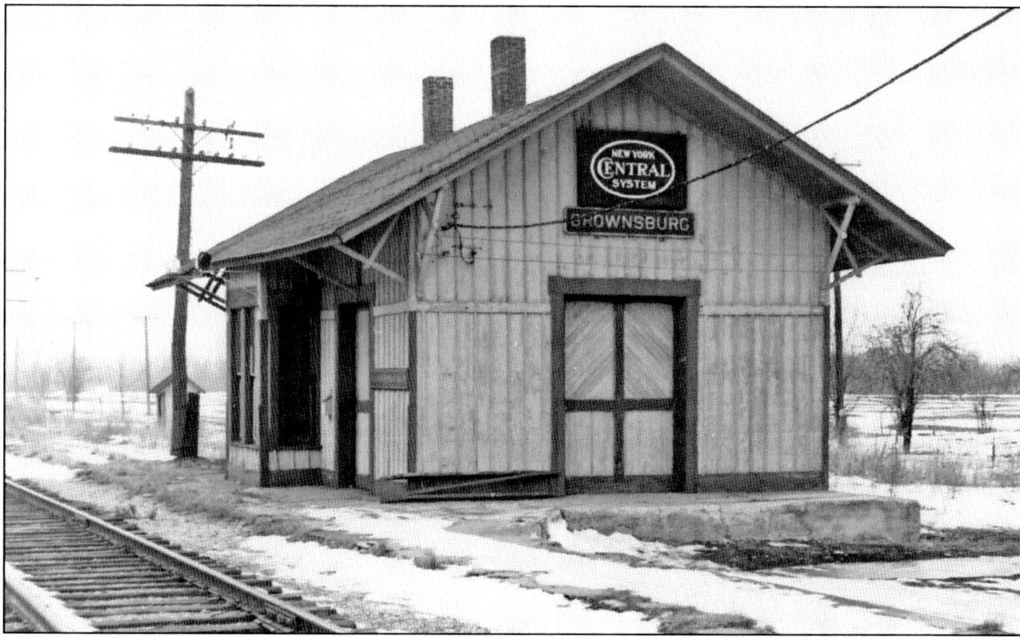

In the early 1900s, the railroads were of great importance in transporting goods and passengers both inside and outside the county. A ride from Brownsburg to Indianapolis took as long as an hour, due to several stops along the way. This is the New York Central depot at Brownsburg. It had a telegraph office, and a water tower stood outside the station until it was taken down in 1951. (Brownsburg Public Library.)

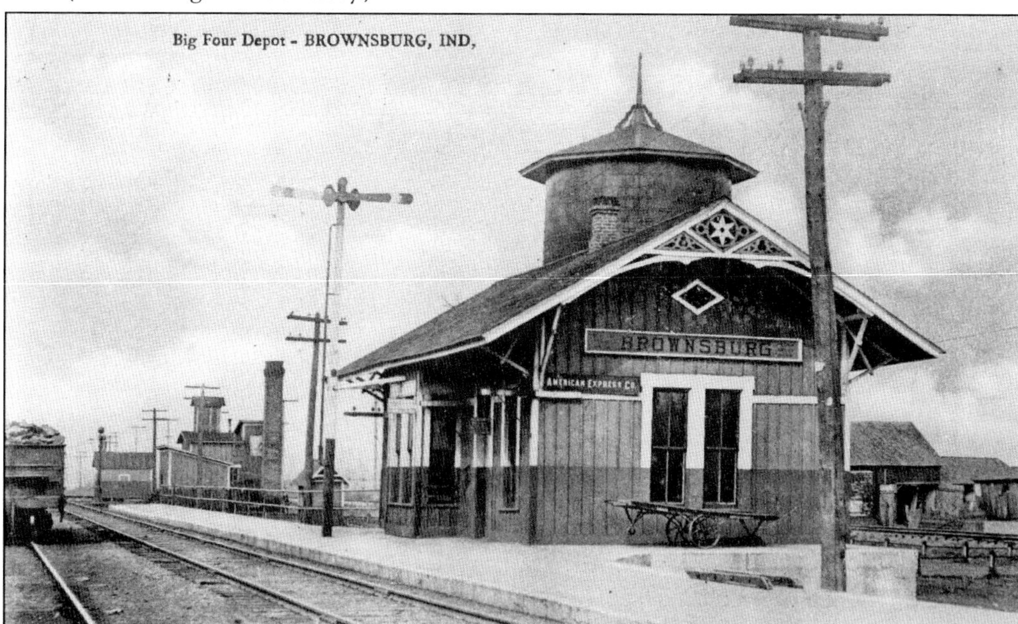

The ornate Big Four depot in Brownsburg was built in 1911. It sat west of Green Street, near the entrance to Arbuckle Park. In 1964, the town considered turning the unused building into a museum. However, the costs involved made the plan prohibitive, so the building was demolished. (Brownsburg Public Library.)

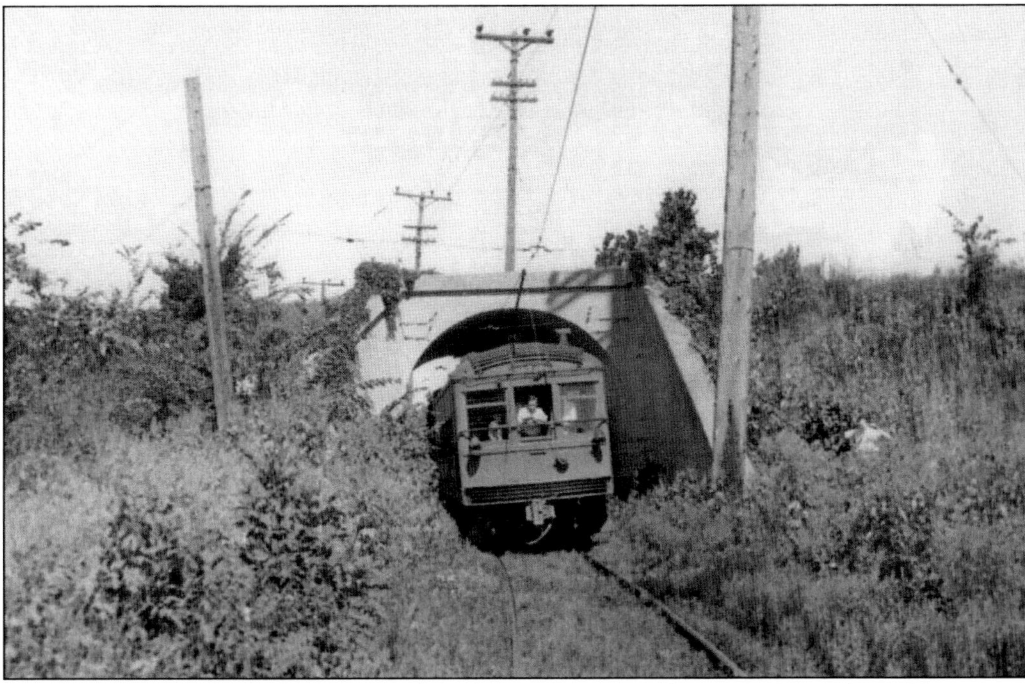

The interurban was nearing its end when this picture was taken near Cartersburg. Trains were running infrequently, and brush was growing along the rails. The electric lines that run the train can be seen as the car leaves the tunnel. (Hendricks County Museum.)

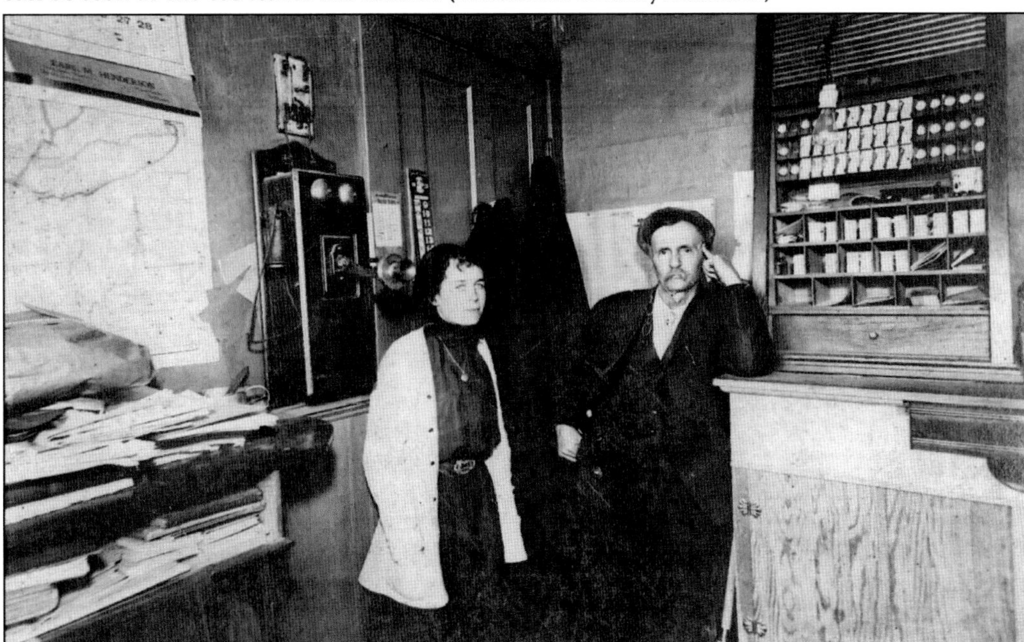

Inside the Terre Haute, Indianapolis & Eastern (THI&E) interurban station at Brownsburg are agent O.E. Parsons and his daughter Leota Parsons Hughes. Oliver worked here for many years. According to the calendar on the wall, this picture was taken between February 9 and 15, 1913. (Virginia Parsons Vapor Collection.)

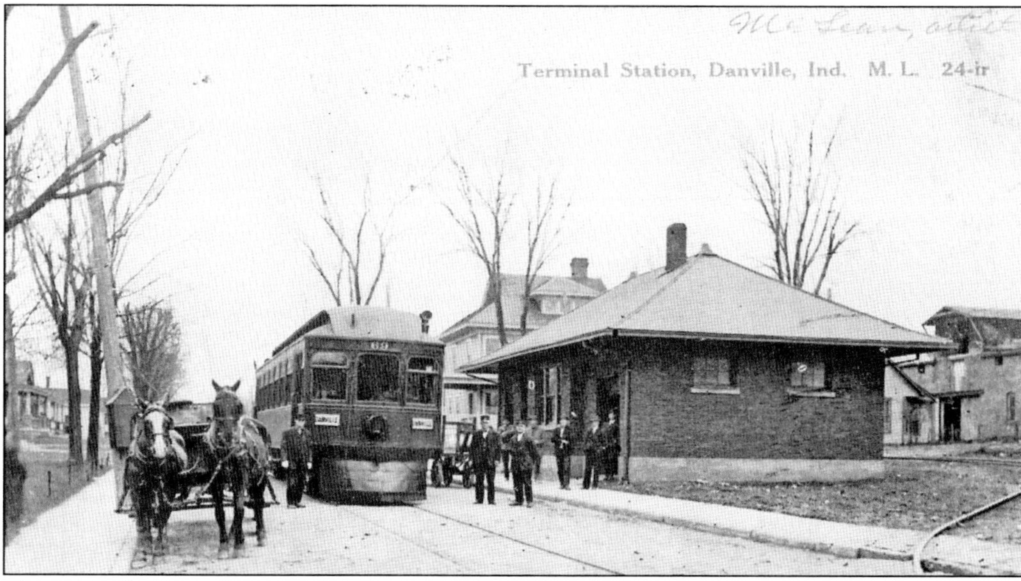

The Danville interurban station was located on the corner of Marion and Indiana Streets. Electric trains ran in Danville from 1906 to 1930, coming from Indianapolis and crossing over an elevated bridge in Ellis Park. The bridge was torn down in May 1961. Today, the former station building is a part of Hackleman's Auto. (Hendricks County Museum.)

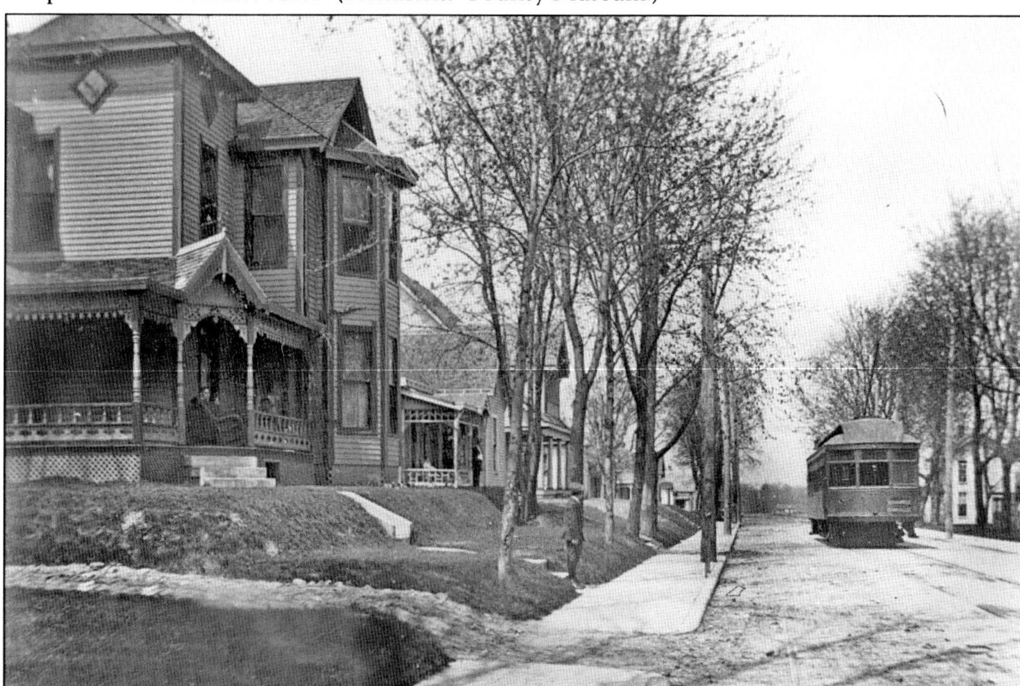

The electric interurban train system, with its hub in Indianapolis, had three lines that ran through Hendricks County from 1902 to 1940. One line passed through Brownsburg, Pittsboro, and Lizton on its way to Crawfordsville. Another line went through Plainfield and then on to Terre Haute. A third line traveled from Indianapolis, through Avon, and ended at Danville. These trains were powered from overhead electric wires. (Danville Public Library.)

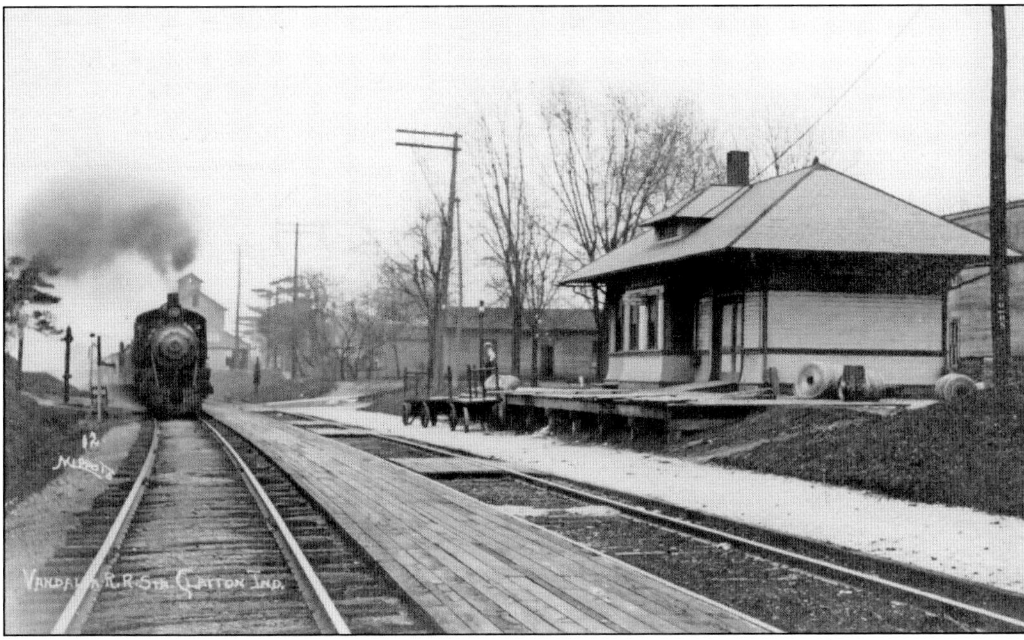

Many towns had the advantage of having both a train station and an interurban station. Here is the Clayton train station. The mill in the background was later destroyed by fire. For many years, it was known as Blanton's Mill. (Guilford Township Collection–Plainfield Library.)

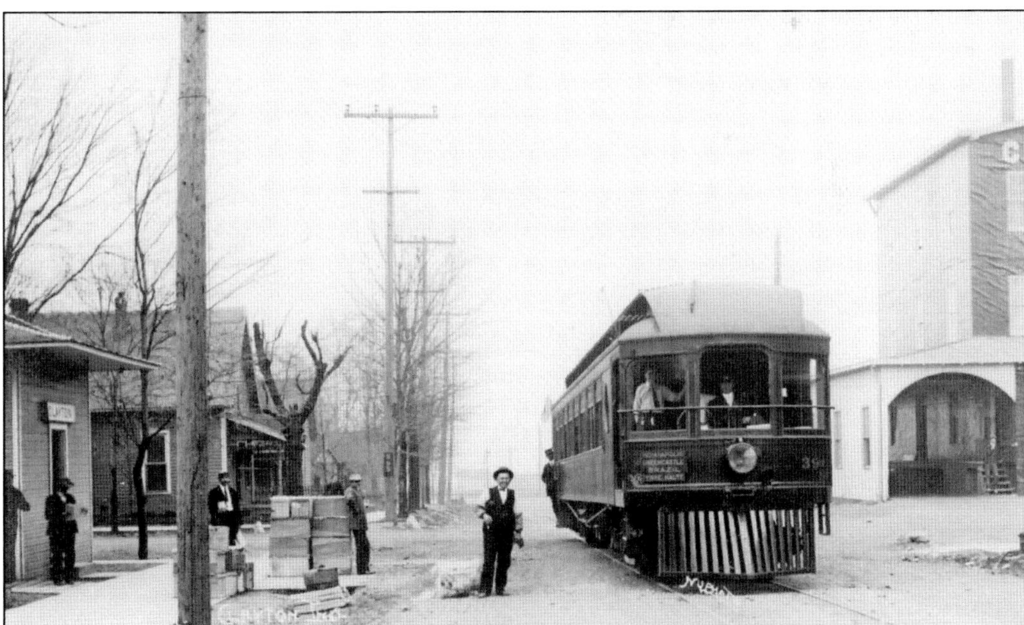

The former Clayton interurban station is still located today on the north side of SR 39. As can be seen, this was handy when the interurban train was running, as it came right down SR 39. The car has the following city names on the front: Indianapolis, Greencastle, Brazil, and Terre Haute. The mill can also be seen. (Guilford Township Collection–Plainfield Library.)

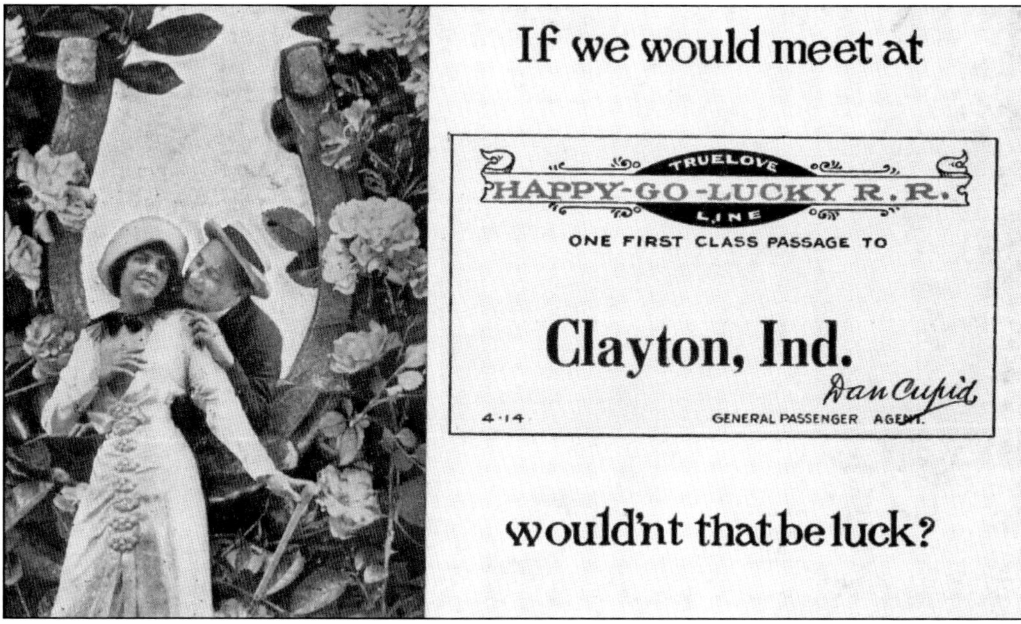

"If we could meet at Clayton, Ind., wouldn't that be luck?" One really needs to visit a town that advertises, "Truelove Line on the Happy-Go-Lucky R.R. One first class Passage to Clayton, Ind. General Passenger; Agent: Dan Cupid." (Phyllis Parsons.)

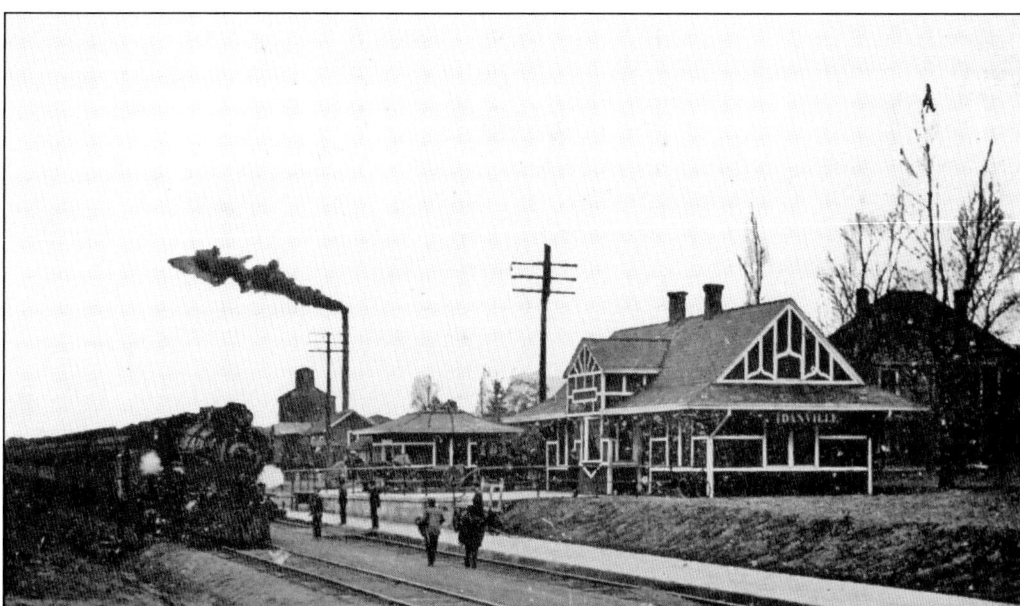

The Danville train depot was located in the southern part of town, near Lincoln Street. The trains delivered lumber and other needed products. Passengers, including students of Central Normal College, also used it. (Guilford Township Collection–Plainfield Library.)

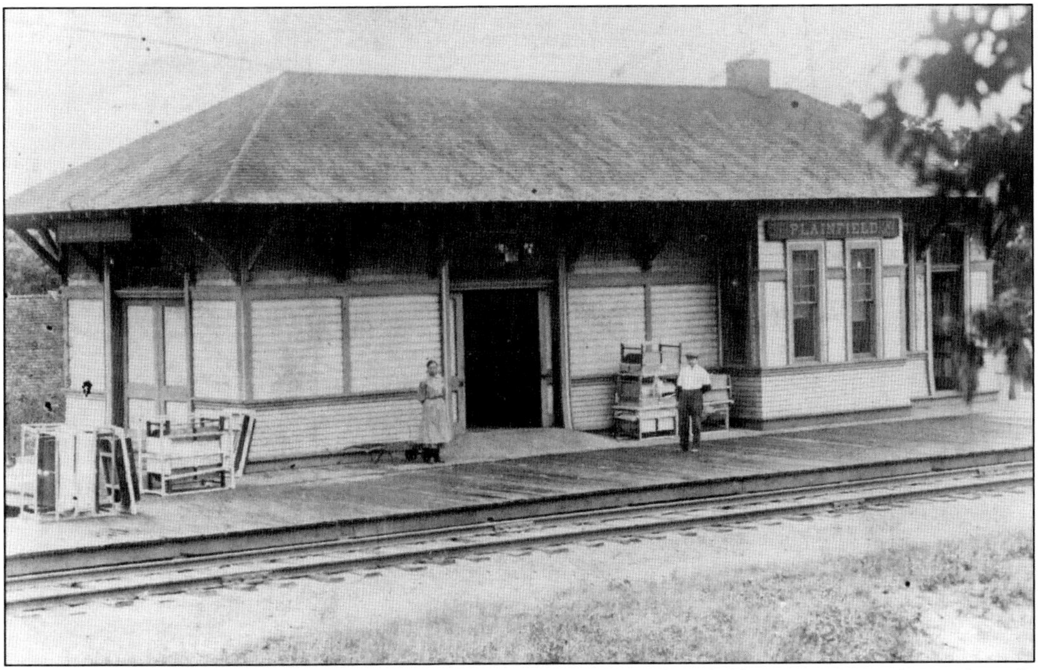

Many of the Vandalia stations looked similar. Here is the one in Plainfield in 1908. It was located north of town. The people are not identified. (Guilford Township Collection–Plainfield Library.)

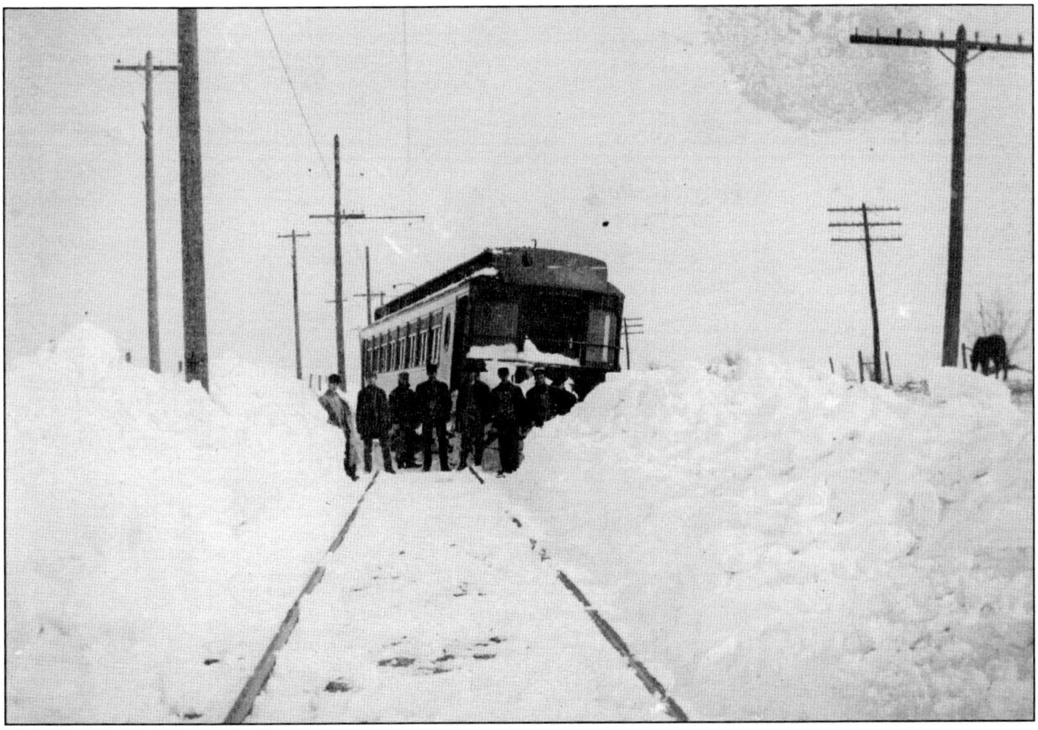

When a blizzard hit Hendricks County, life stood still for a time. The note on the back of this picture relates that this interurban car was stuck in the snow for three days and that it took 25 men to free it. The year and exact location are not known. (Hendricks County Museum.)

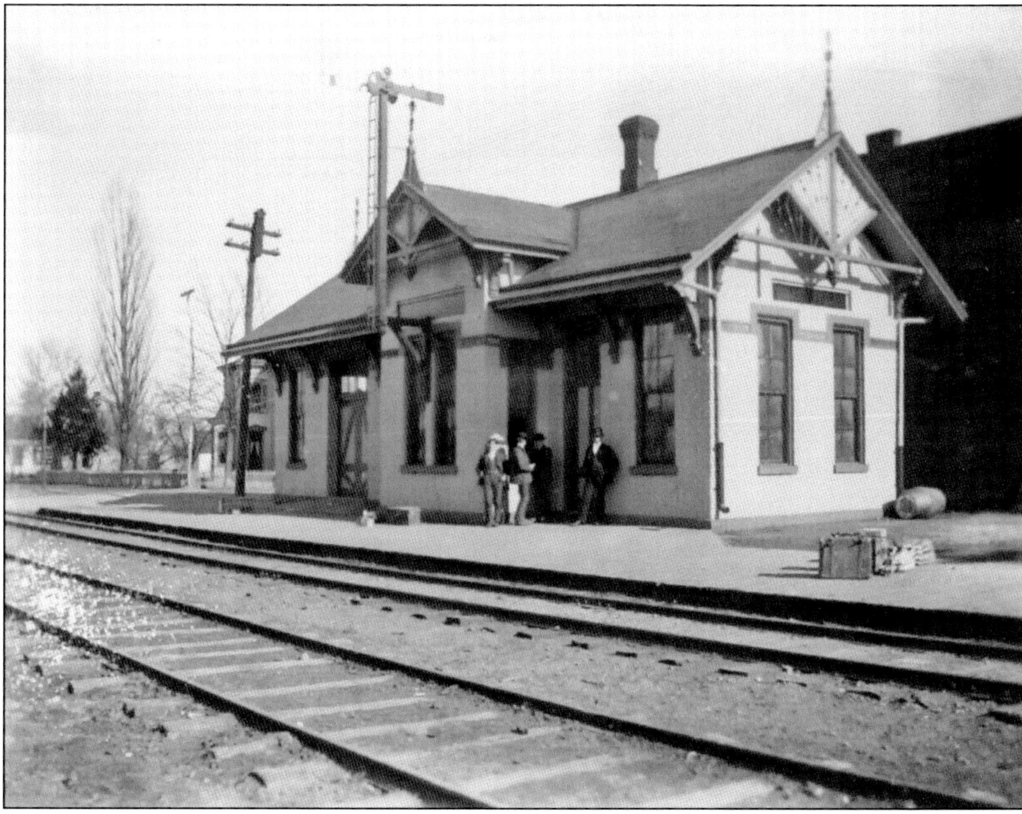

Coatesville was another community with both a regular train depot and an interurban station. This attractive building is the interurban station. (Guilford Township Collection–Plainfield Library.)

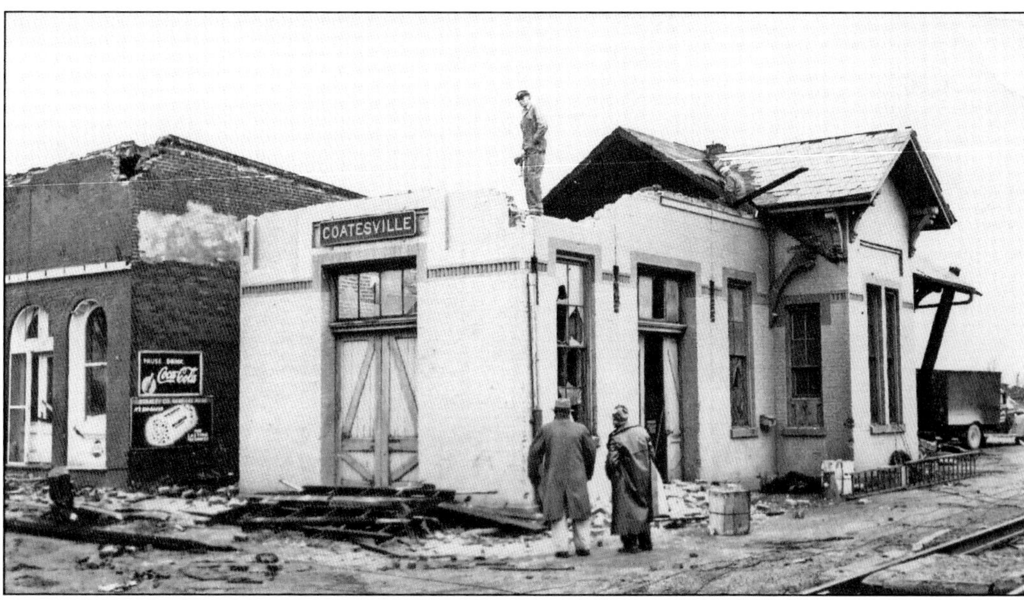

This is the interurban station in Coatesville after the 1948 Good Friday tornado. It shows the destruction that this storm caused. Those pictured are unidentified. (Hendricks County Museum.)

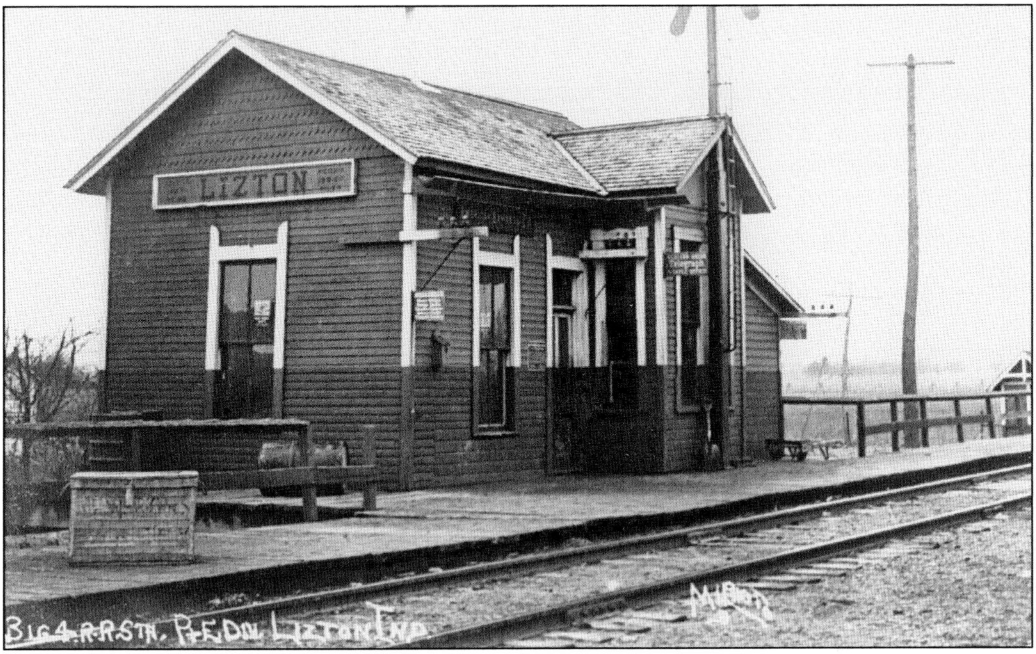

This is the Lizton depot, around 1905. The sign on the side of the building lets travelers know that it also had a telegraph operation. (Guilford Township Collection–Plainfield Library.)

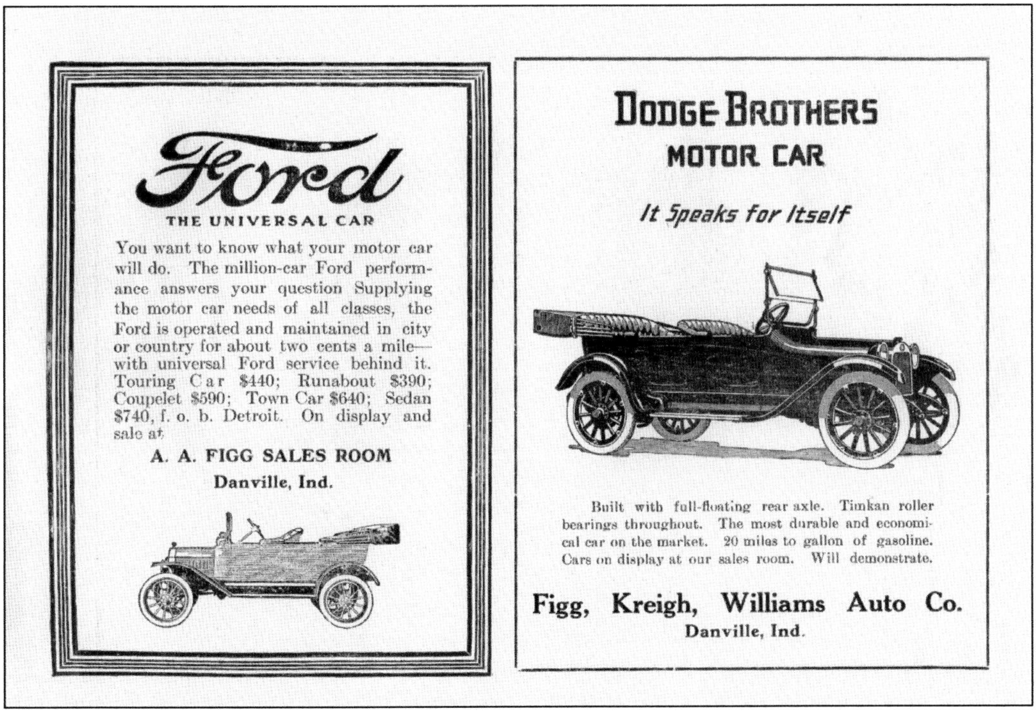

Many businesses chose high school yearbooks, or annuals as some called them, to advertise their products. A.A. Figg, who once served as Hendricks County sheriff, sold Fords and Dodges at Danville. These two ads were side by side in the 1916 Amo annual, which was called *The Blue and White.* (Guilford Township Collection–Plainfield Library.)

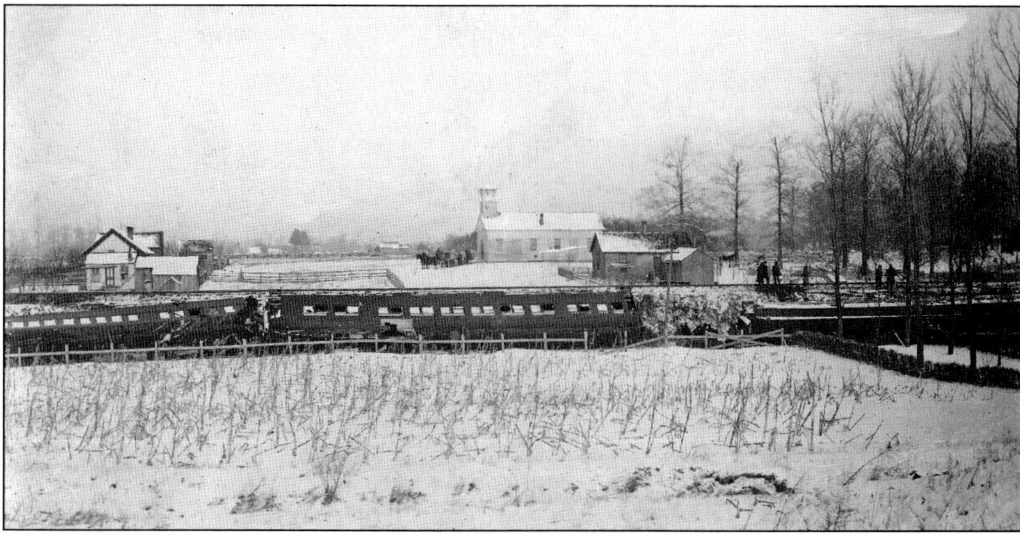

Two railroad tragedies occurred in Hendricks County. Coatesville and Maplewood each had a train wreck. The Vandalia wreck at Coatesville occurred on January 28, 1895. In the background, people are leaving the church to enter the carriage pulled by horses. It is believed to be the West Branch Friends Church. At least three people died in this terrible wreck, and many were injured. (Guilford Township Collection–Plainfield Library.)

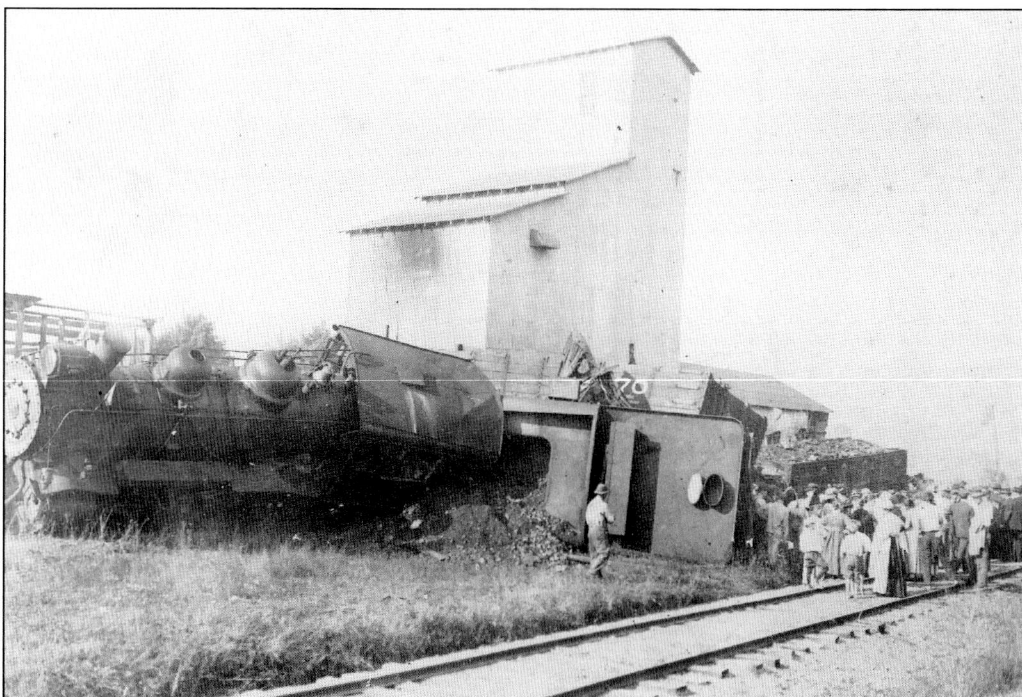

In October 1916, engineer O.J. Owen, fireman G.R. Carpenter, and head brakeman W.S. Monce were killed as two engines crashed in Maplewood. The eastbound freight on the Cincinnati, Indianapolis & Western (CI&W) ran through an open switch and crashed into the engine of a westbound freight. The crew of the westbound train jumped clear. Cars were piled high, and the nearby elevator was badly damaged. (Hendricks County Museum.)

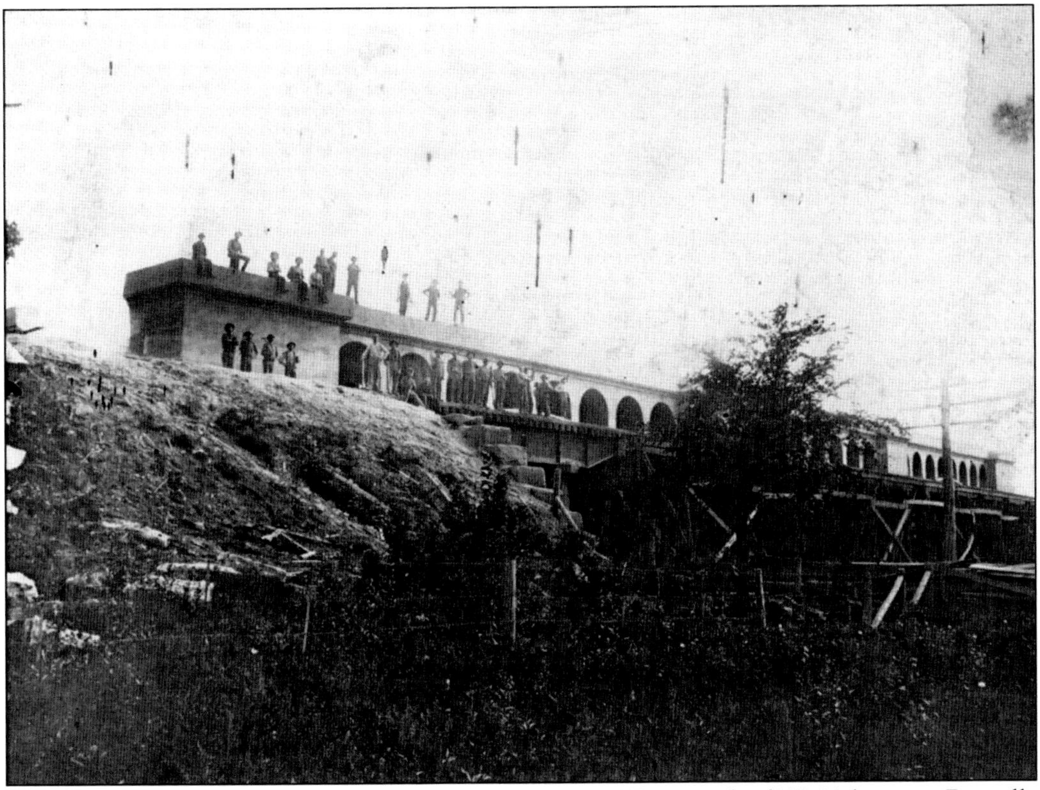

These workers are building the railroad trestle over CR 625 East, south of US 36, between Danville and Avon. (Huron Heritage Collection, Avon–Washington Township Library, Avon, Indiana.)

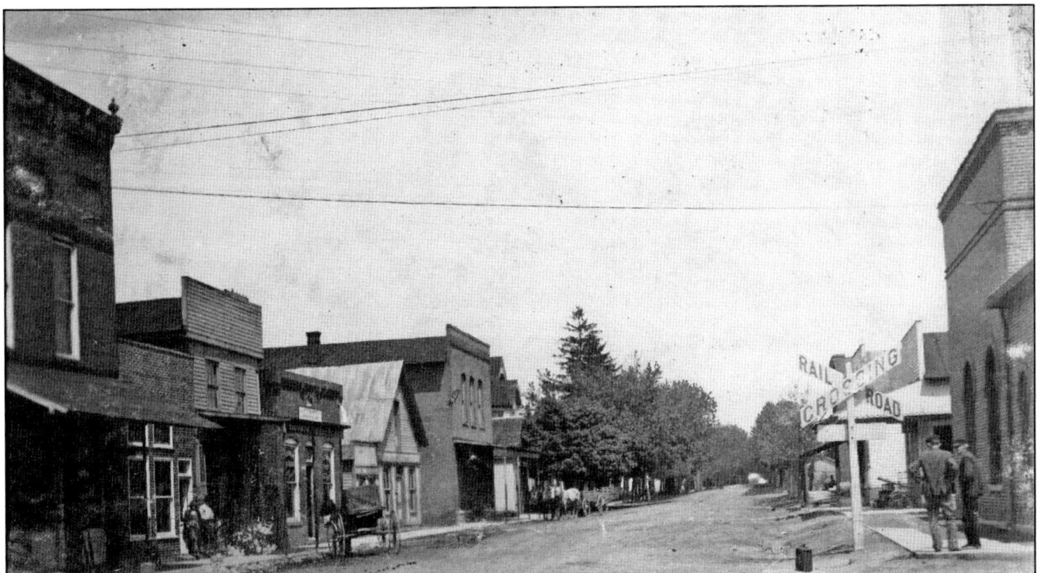

This picture looks north on Pearl Street across the Vandalia tracks in Amo. To the right is the interurban station, which is still standing and is used as a reading room today. (Joseph Seiter.)

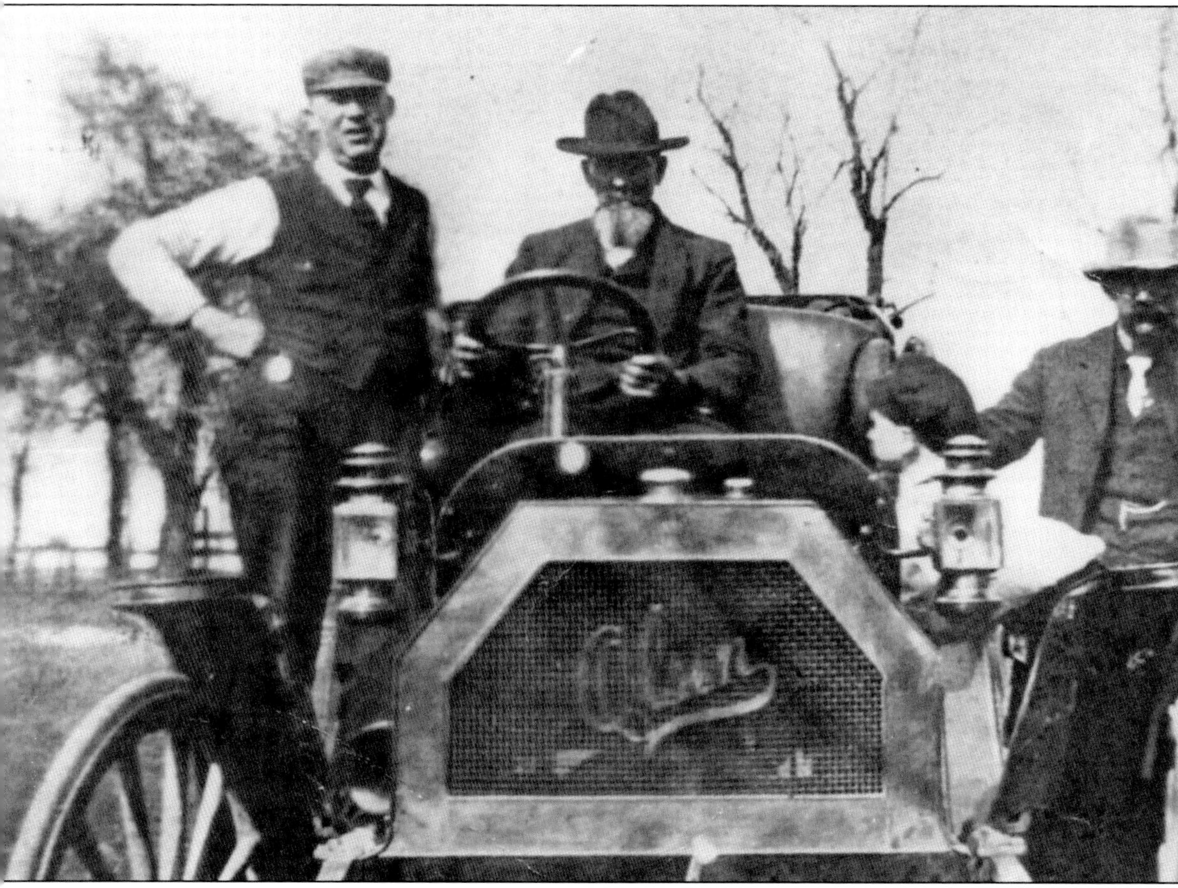

C.J. Olsen was very successful in the manufacture of school wagons, or hacks, but his automobile was not as well received. This picture shows one of the few he made. The Olsen is thought to be the only automobile manufactured in Hendricks County. C.J. Olsen was described as a gracious, kind, and honest gentleman. Behind the steering wheel is the owner of the car, James Hughes. (Hendricks County Museum.)

Four

Reading, 'Riting, 'Rithmetic, and Religion

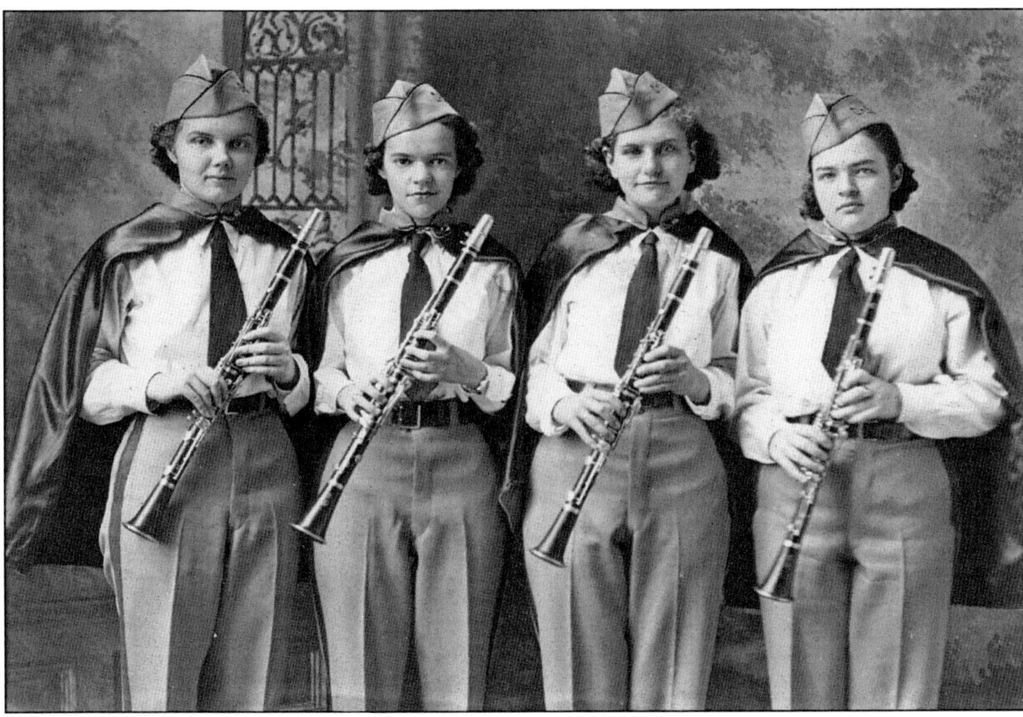

Academic, as well as religious, instruction was very important as families settled in Hendricks County. Schools and churches were community centers for revivals, picnics, reunions, association meetings, weddings, funerals, and so on. This photograph shows the Danville High School band quartet around 1936; members are, from left to right, Doris Jean Miller, Eva Tharp, Frances Cox, and Lee Collins. (Kerry Trout.)

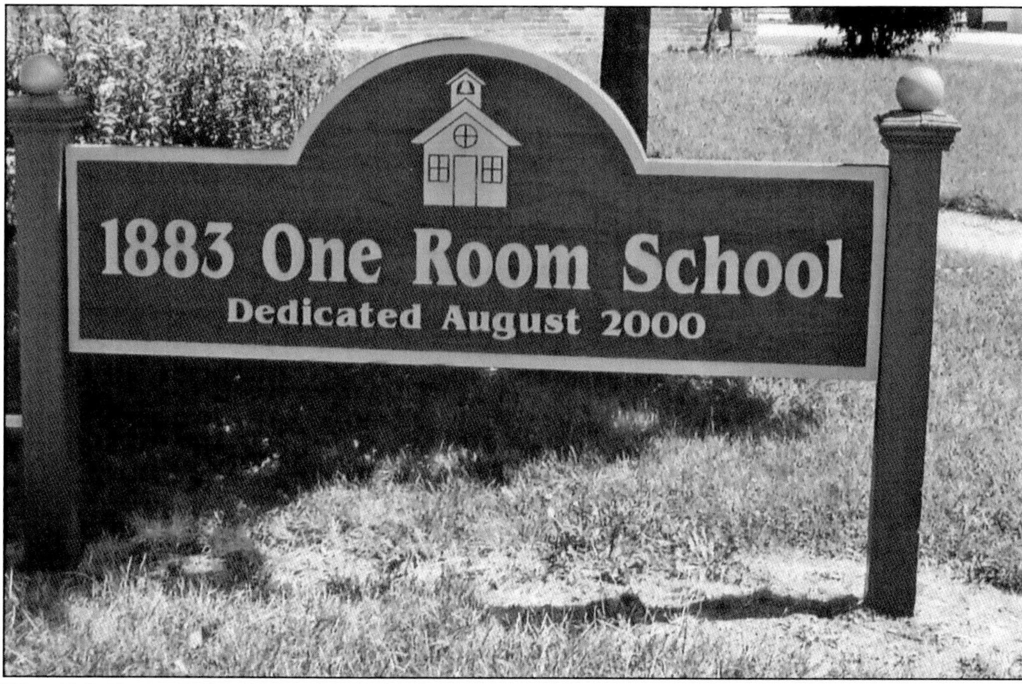

The Caledonia School No. 3 was built in 1883. After it ceased to be used as a school, it sat abandoned for many years on the Frank McClung property near Pittsboro. There was interest in having the building restored as a historical teaching tool for future generations, so it was moved to the North West Hendricks School property in Pittsboro. Hundreds of hours of work went into the restoration. Today, volunteers maintain and operate it as a model one-room schoolhouse. (Both, Hendricks County Museum.)

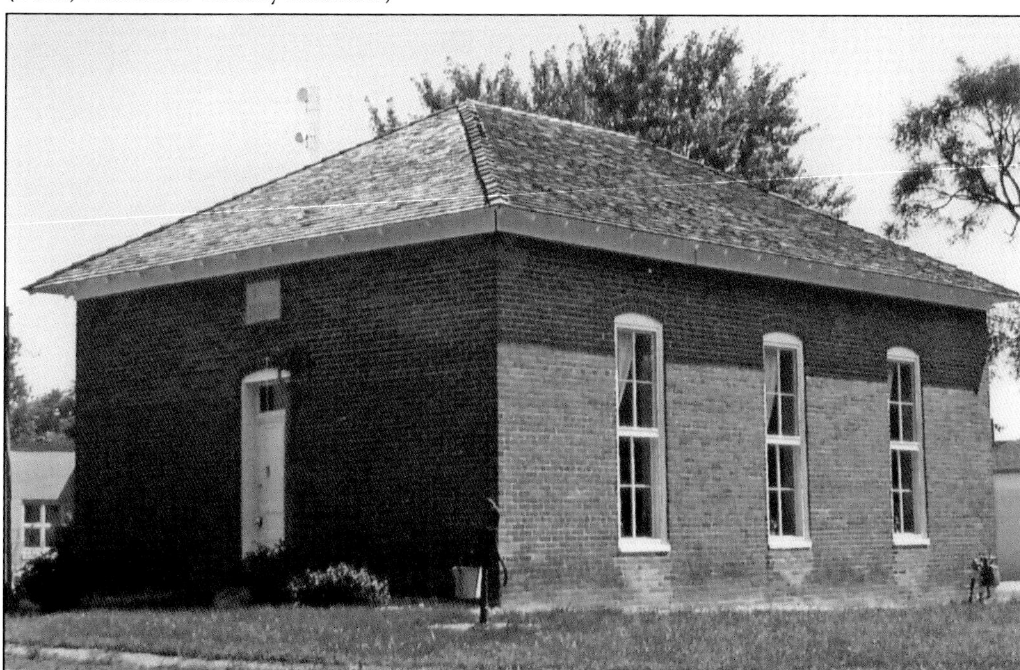

Room No. 2 of the North Salem School, of Eel River Township, announces a program during the 1897–1898 school year. J.D. Hostetter was the county superintendent, and E.M. Murphy was the trustee. Laura Bryant was the teacher for that room. (Hendricks County Museum.)

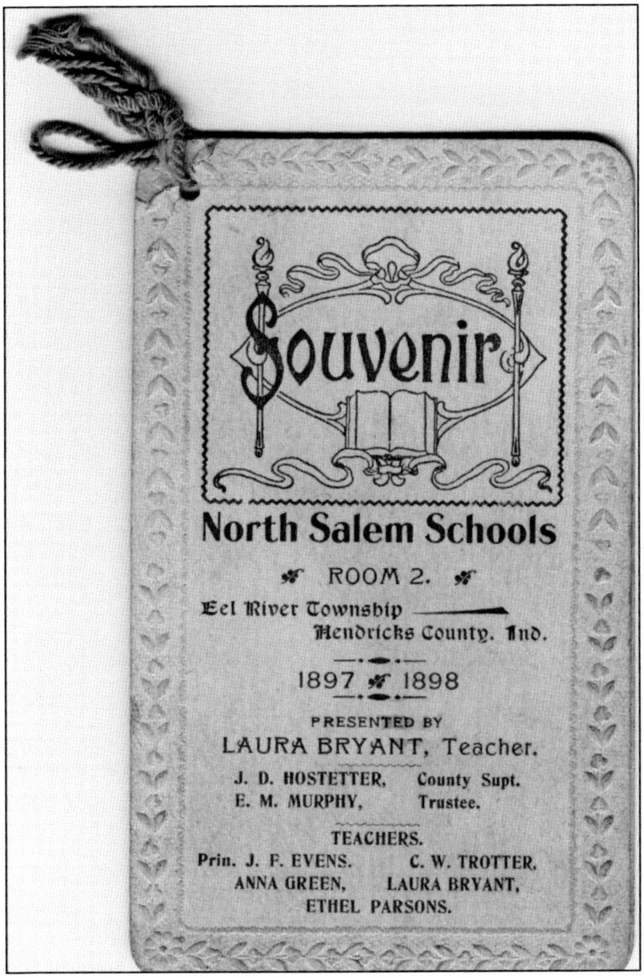
Souvenir

North Salem Schools

ROOM 2.

Eel River Township
Hendricks County. Ind.

1897 1898

PRESENTED BY
LAURA BRYANT, Teacher.

J. D. HOSTETTER, County Supt.
E. M. MURPHY, Trustee.

TEACHERS.
Prin. J. F. EVENS. C. W. TROTTER.
ANNA GREEN. LAURA BRYANT.
ETHEL PARSONS.

This 1902 Certificate of Promotion card belonged to Osie Kurtz. Osie had completed the third-grade course in the North Salem School and was ready to advance to the fourth grade. In 1910, she was living at home in Marion Township with her mother, Mary, who was a widow, along with a sister and three brothers. (Hendricks County Museum.)

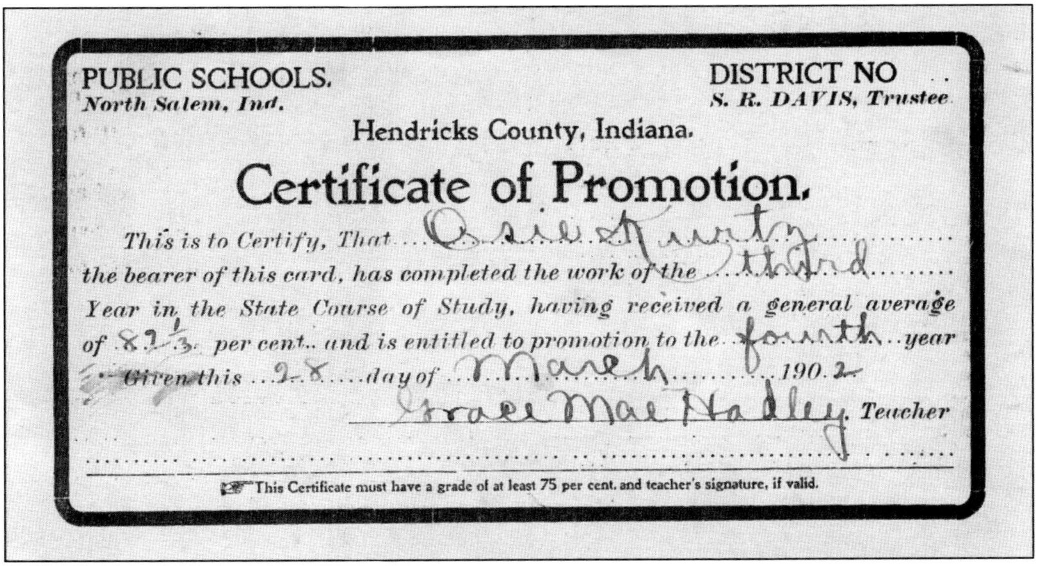
PUBLIC SCHOOLS.
North Salem, Ind.

DISTRICT NO ..
S. R. DAVIS, Trustee

Hendricks County, Indiana.

Certificate of Promotion.

This is to Certify, That Osie Kurtz
the bearer of this card, has completed the work of the third
Year in the State Course of Study, having received a general average of 82 1/3 *per cent., and is entitled to promotion to the* fourth *year*
Given this 28 *day of* March *190*2
Grace Mae Hadley *Teacher*

This Certificate must have a grade of at least 75 per cent. and teacher's signature, if valid.

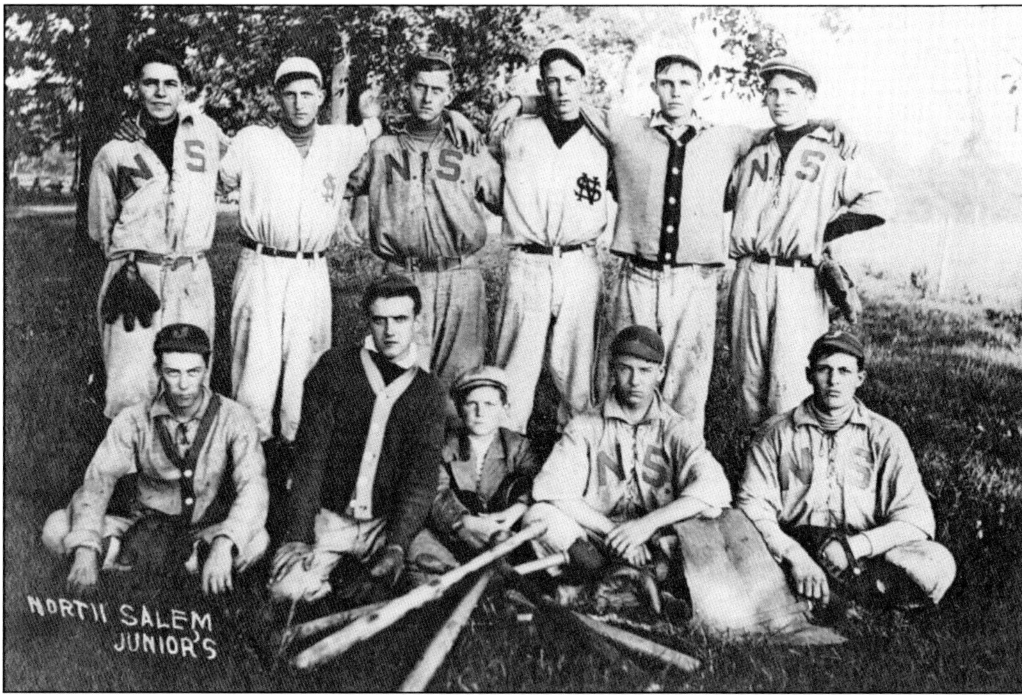

Most towns had a baseball team to represent them. This is the North Salem Junior's baseball team around 1908. Seated on the far left is Dora "Dode" Miller, and fourth from left in the back row is Ralph Kurtz. The others are not identified. (Kerry Trout.)

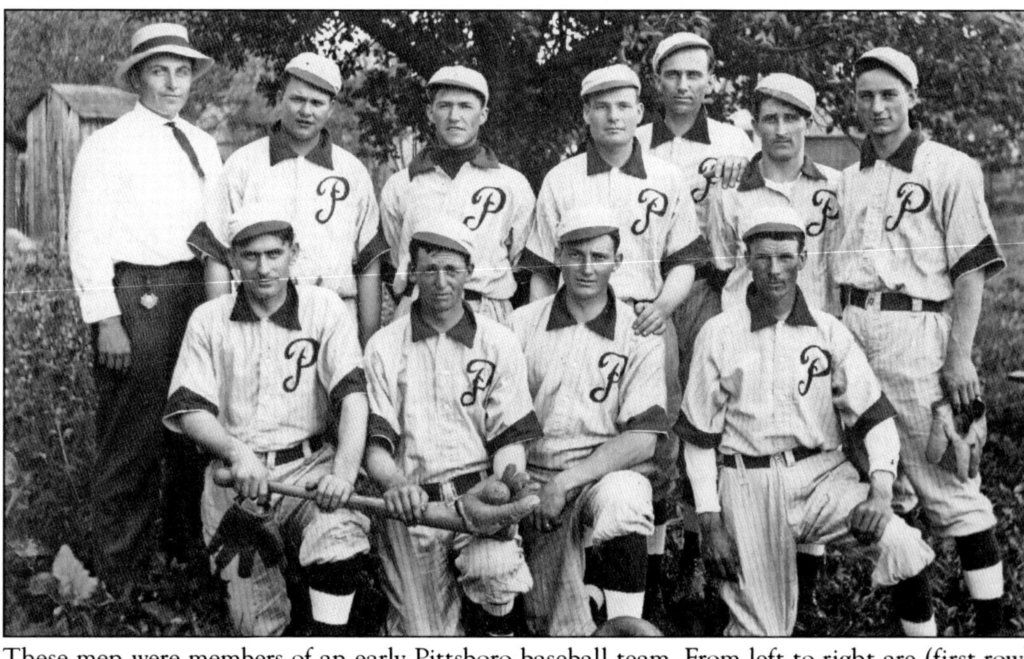

These men were members of an early Pittsboro baseball team. From left to right are (first row) Hollis Arnold, Check Gregg, Ralph Morgan, and Jess McIntire; (second row) manager Chester Peckinpaugh, Sam Hollingsworth, Bob Mitchell, John Holley, Bill Feeney, Ovid Layton, and Wib Starkey. (Hendricks County Museum.)

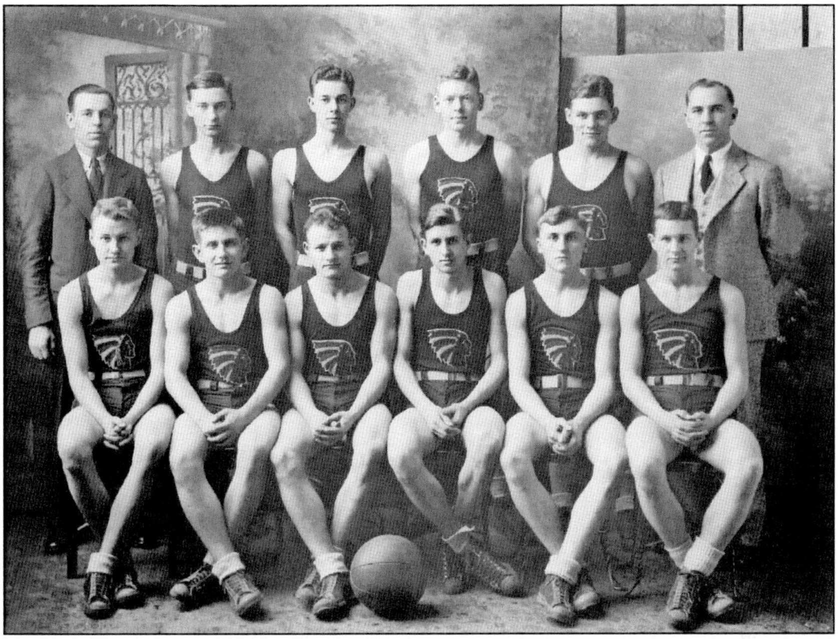

The Danville basketball team proudly displays the warrior emblem on their shirts. The players are, from left to right, (first row) M. Williams, ? Edwards, ? Wilson, H. Boll, ? Martin, and ? Reed; (second row) coach Amos Shelton, ? Hicks, J. Williams, ? Fleece, ? Kernodle, and principal Landis. Check out the short uniforms of the day. (Hendricks County Museum.)

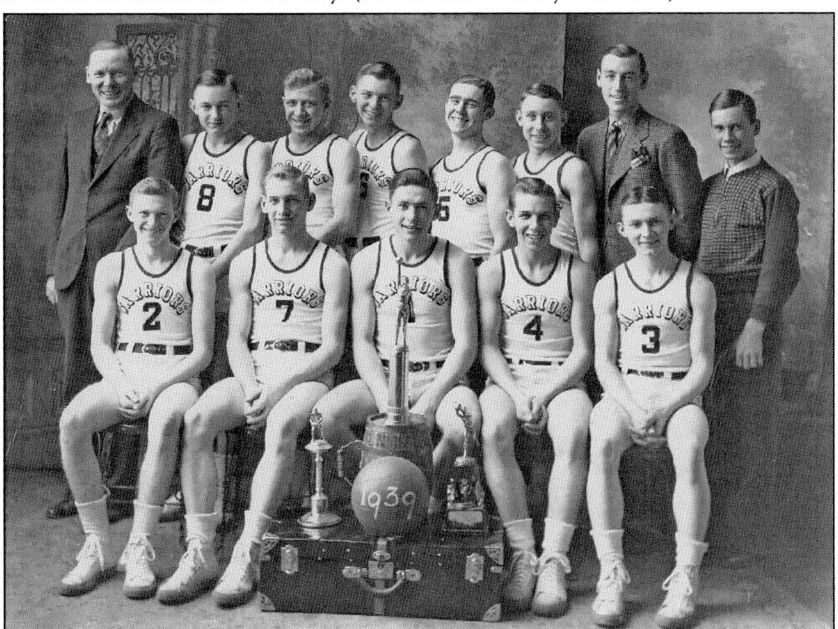

In 1939, the New Winchester High School Warrior basketball team showed off its championship trophies. The team consisted of, from left to right, (first row) George Joseph, Carl Underwood, Richard "Dick" Clark, Harold Lieske, and Ray McVay; (second row) principal Roy Jones, Clifton Moore, Leon Pierson, Roy Jones Jr., Don Buechler, Herbert Cline, coach Amos Shelton, and ? Myers (student manager). (Hendricks County Museum.)

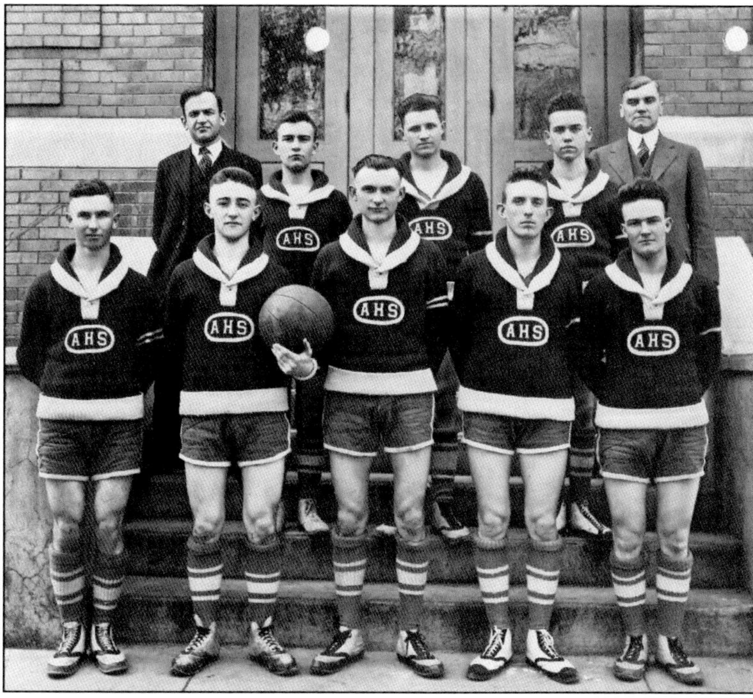

Basketball teams have been important to the community for many years. The sport is part of the Hoosier heritage. How very different are the uniforms worn by these young men from Amo to the ones of today. The players are, from left to right, (first row) Q. Berry, W. Shirley, G. Rhea, C. Crews, and W. Wallace; (second row) F.N. Jones, R. Lisby, J. Booty, W. Fuson, and coach J.W. Wright. (Guilford Township Collection–Plainfield Library.)

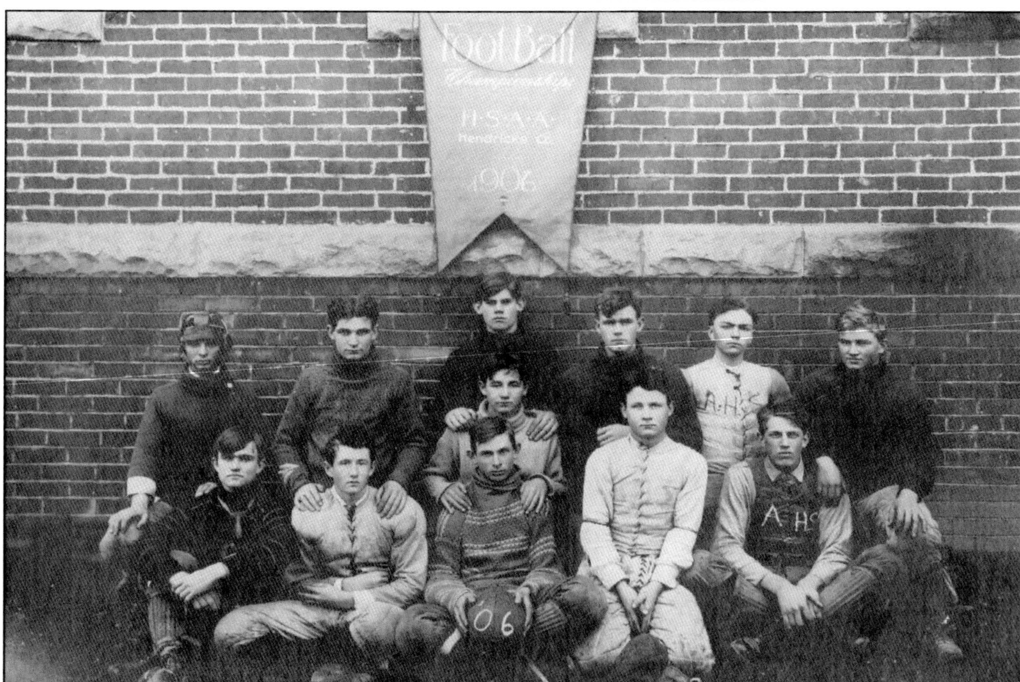

These 1906 Amo football players proudly display their Indiana High School Athletic Association championship banner. The players are, from left to right, (first row) Bob Ewing, Joe Steers, Drassa Pruitt, Glendon Kelley, and Henry Vickery; (second row) Vern McAnnich; (third row) Wesley Lambert, Forest Kelley, Mervyn Hunt, Frank O'Neal, Thomas Masters, and Sam Cooprider. (Hendricks County Museum.)

In 1907, girls' basketball players at Amo High School included, from left to right, Alice Cox, Mary Snyder, Ila Johnson, Ruby Halfhill, Vera Hodson, and Mary Hunt. There was no gym at the time, and all games were played outside. As with the boys' teams, the mode of dress was much different than today. (Hendricks County Museum.)

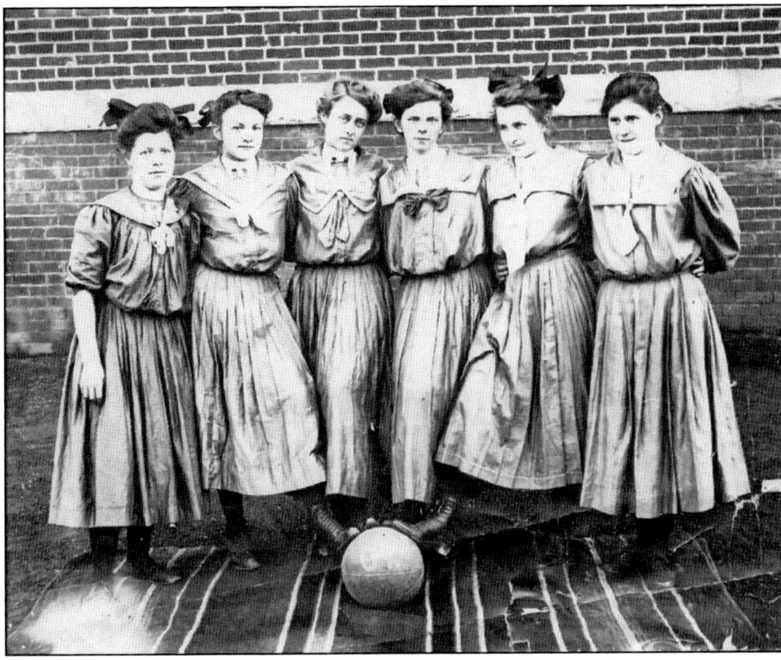

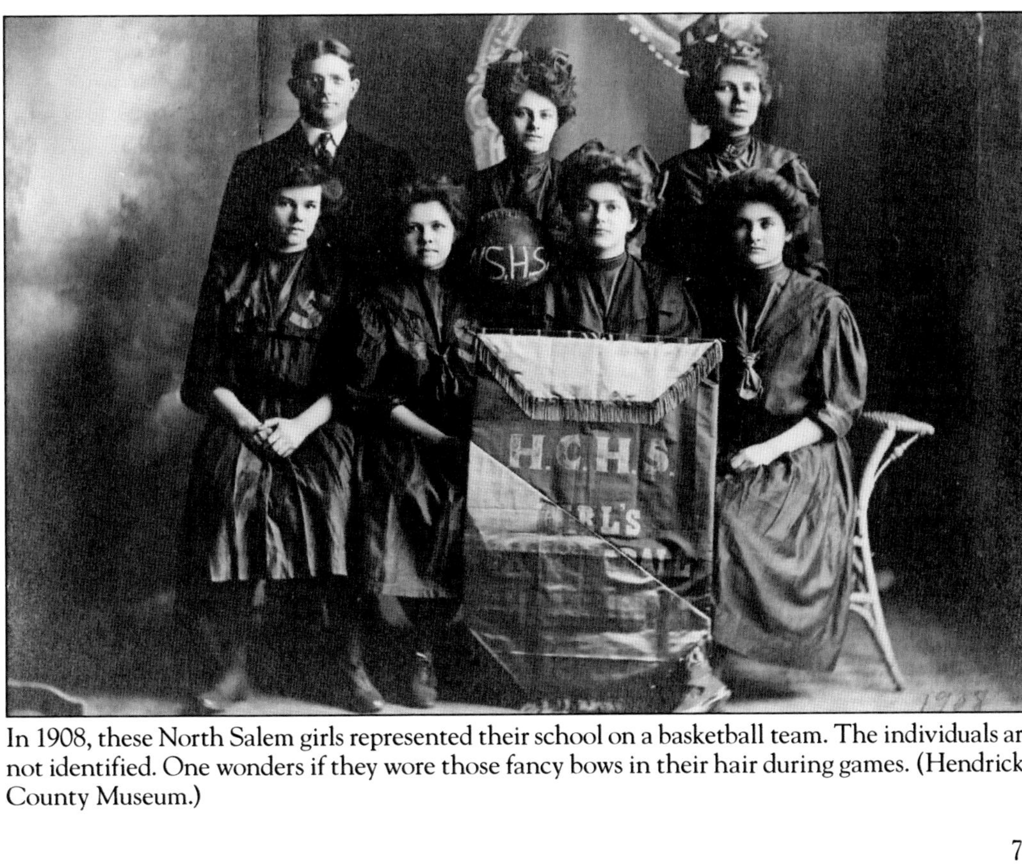

In 1908, these North Salem girls represented their school on a basketball team. The individuals are not identified. One wonders if they wore those fancy bows in their hair during games. (Hendricks County Museum.)

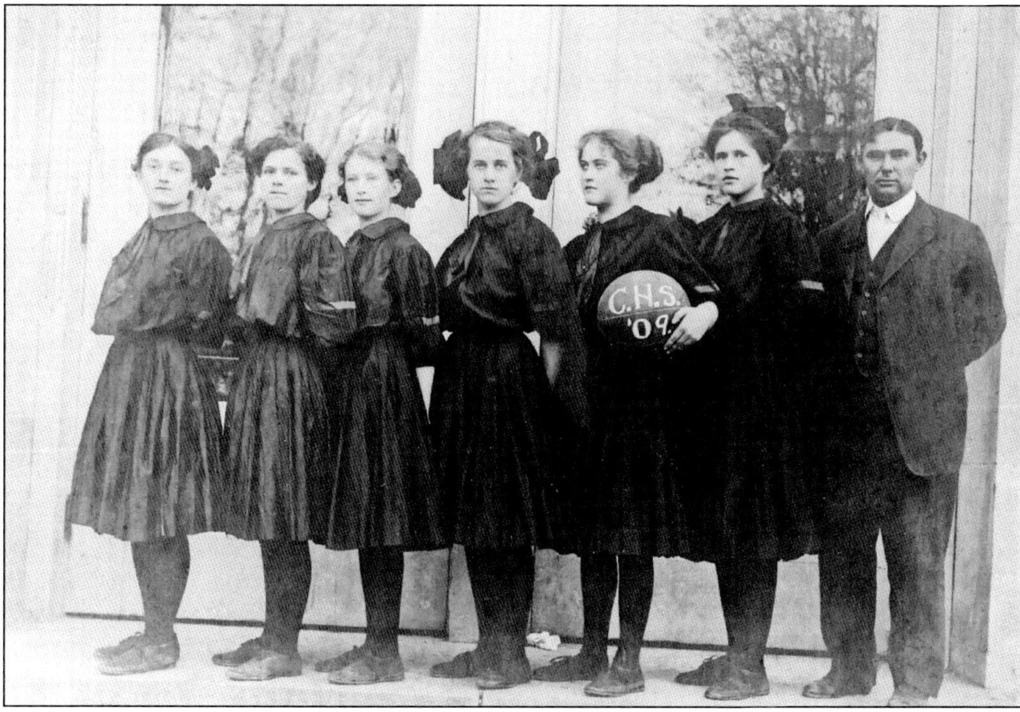

These young ladies on the 1909 Clayton basketball team also enjoyed the sport. Note the fancy uniforms. The players and coach are unidentified. (Guilford Township Collection–Plainfield Library)

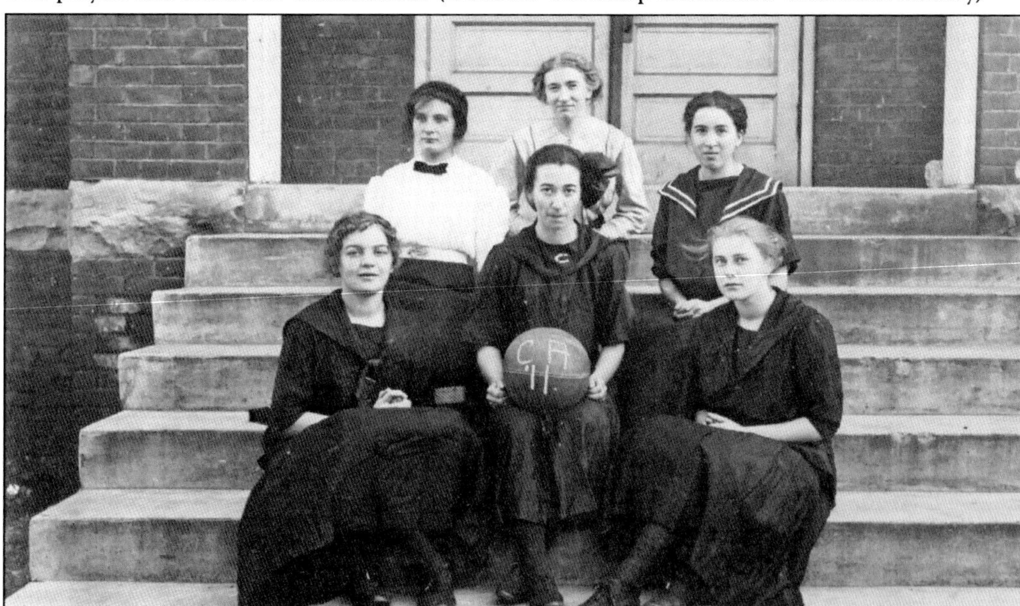

Central Elementary, located in Plainfield, sits on the south side of US 40 where the Central Academy once stood. The Central Academy was dedicated in 1882. Sitting in this 1911 picture are, from left to right, (first row) Doris Herringlake, Helen Hanna, and Nell Mills; (second row) Ora McClain, teacher M. Doan, and Agnes Lamont. Within a few years, the Western Yearly Meeting of Friends closed the school. (Guilford Township Collection–Plainfield Library.)

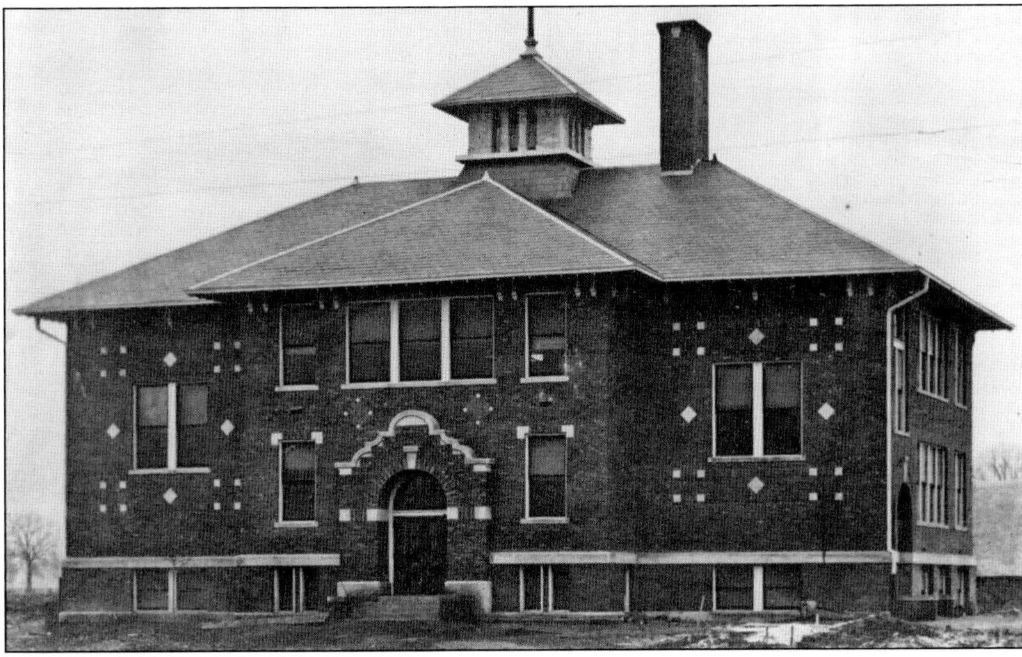

New Winchester is located in Marion Township at the intersection of US 36 and SR 75. The school faced SR 75 and was a vital part of the community. The school was built in 1908. The last graduating class was in 1963, after which it was consolidated with the Danville School System. (Harley Sheets.)

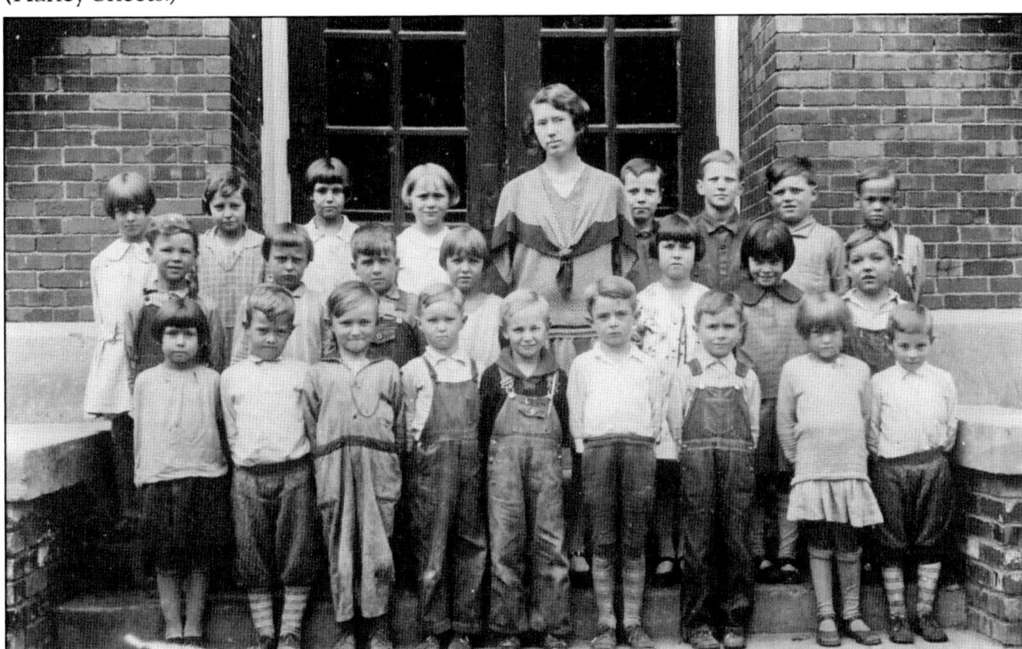

This 1928 class picture features students at the New Winchester School in Marion Township. The only one identified is Ray McVay, who is standing in the first row, third from the left. (Hendricks County Museum.)

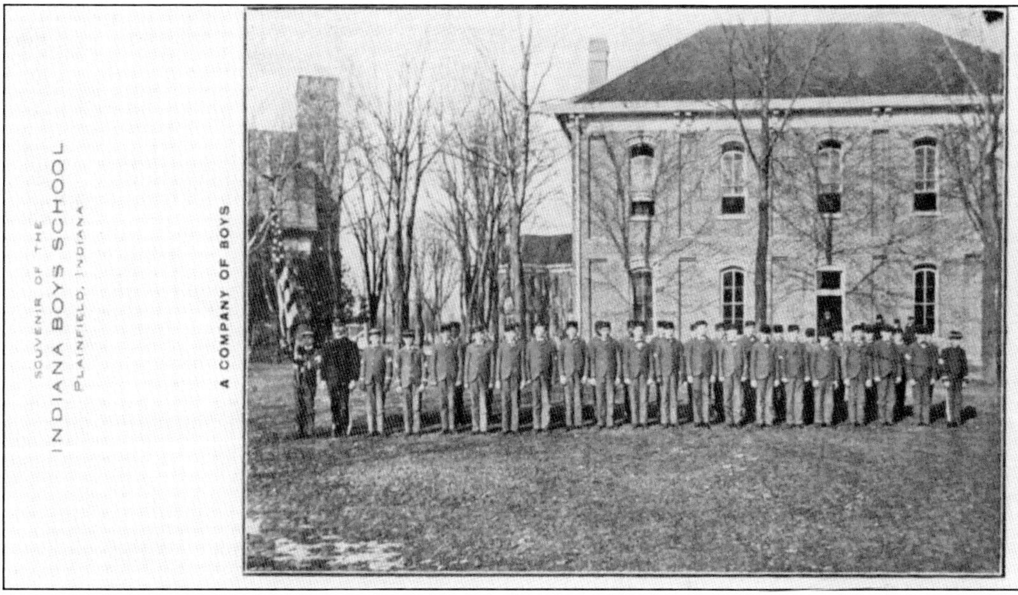

In Plainfield, what began as the House of Refuge had many names over its lifetime. Land was purchased, and in 1868, the first boys were admitted. The boys were housed there and provided instruction in life skills. Shoe making, tinwork, blacksmithing, baking, barbering, printing, farming, gardening, and other vocations were taught. In the 1890s, the Indiana Reform School for Boys became a semimilitary institution. This is apparent from the uniforms the boys are wearing in the postcard above. It dates from after 1901, when the name was changed to the Indiana Boys School. The picture below, also taken after 1901, shows the crowded condition of the establishment. (Both, Joseph Seiter.)

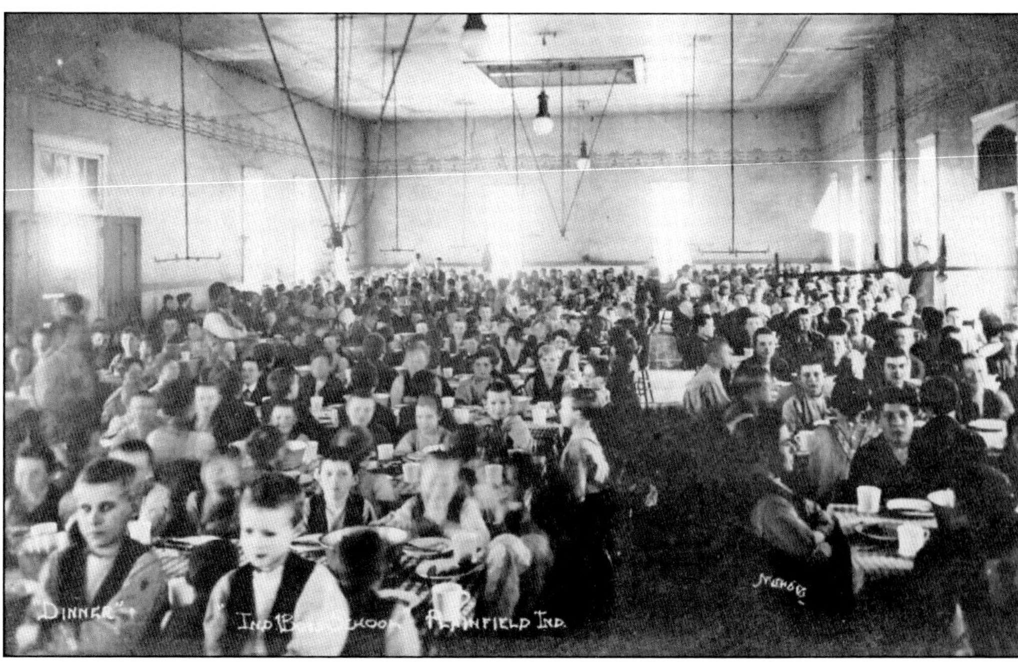

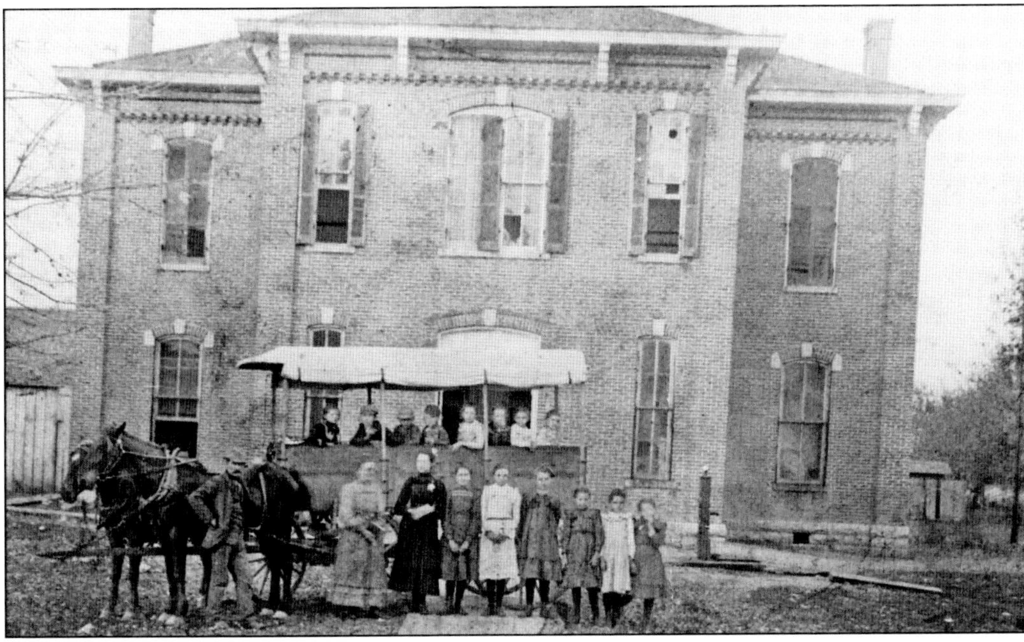

In 1901, this group of students arrived at Pittsboro No. 6 School, located at 220 East Main Street, in an open wagon. William Mayhew is the driver. From left to right, the children are (first row) Alcie Ridgeway, Nora Ridgeway, Hazel Rawlings, Mabel Elmore, Edith McClung, Ruby Rawlings, and Minnie McClung. In the wagon are Dana and Josie Thompson, Claude Kennedy, Roy Elmore, Lottie Ridgeway, Jennie Rawlings, and Gladys Elmore. (Hendricks County Museum.)

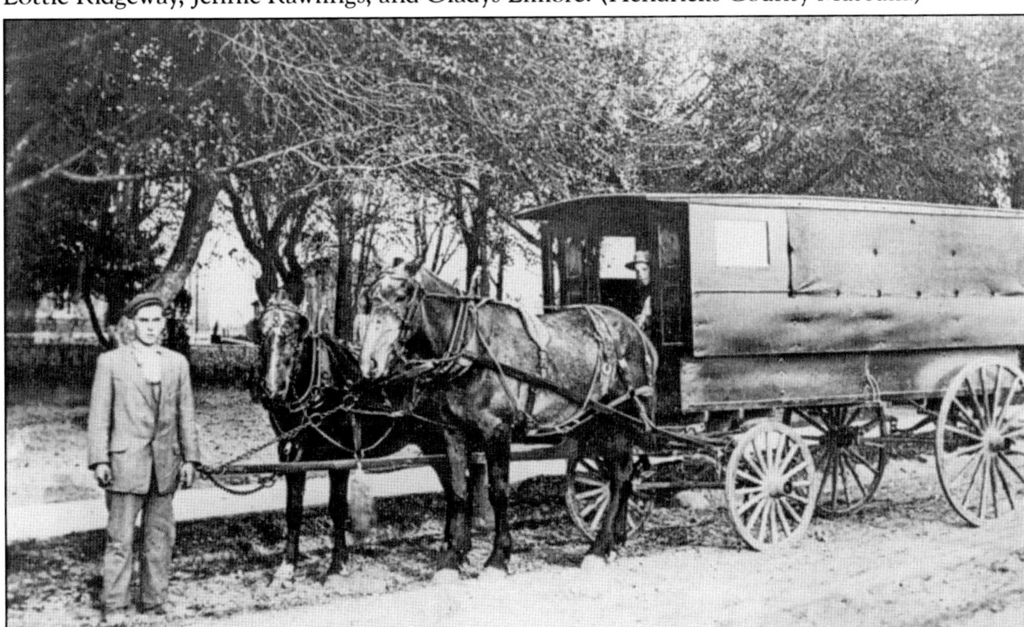

Charles Olsen manufactured school wagons, or hacks, in Pittsboro. The company made the wagons in four lengths, nine, ten, twelve, and fourteen feet, and produced as many as 125 wagons a year. One year, Olsen shipped 50 wagons to North Dakota. Arthur Veatch, son of Jasper Newton Veatch, is the driver of this Olsen school wagon around 1913. (Judy Pingel.)

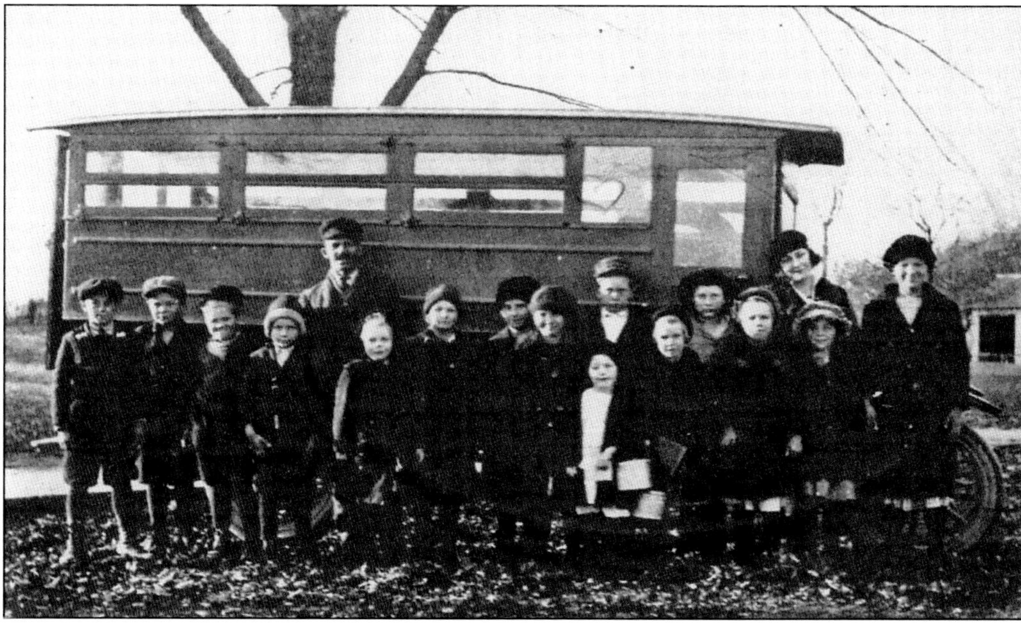

This motorized school bus is thought to have been the first one in Clay Township. The students are, from left to right, Harry Lambert, James Layman, Forest Layman, Ralph Burgess, driver O.Z. Stayton, Maxine Osborne, Lucille Kersey, Lois Rudd, Marverine Smith, Gertrude Smith, Max Burgess, Marjorie Hargrave, ? Burgess, Laura Belle Layman, Mary Bernice Layman, Elizabeth Walton, and Emma Louise Layman around 1920. (David Kersey.)

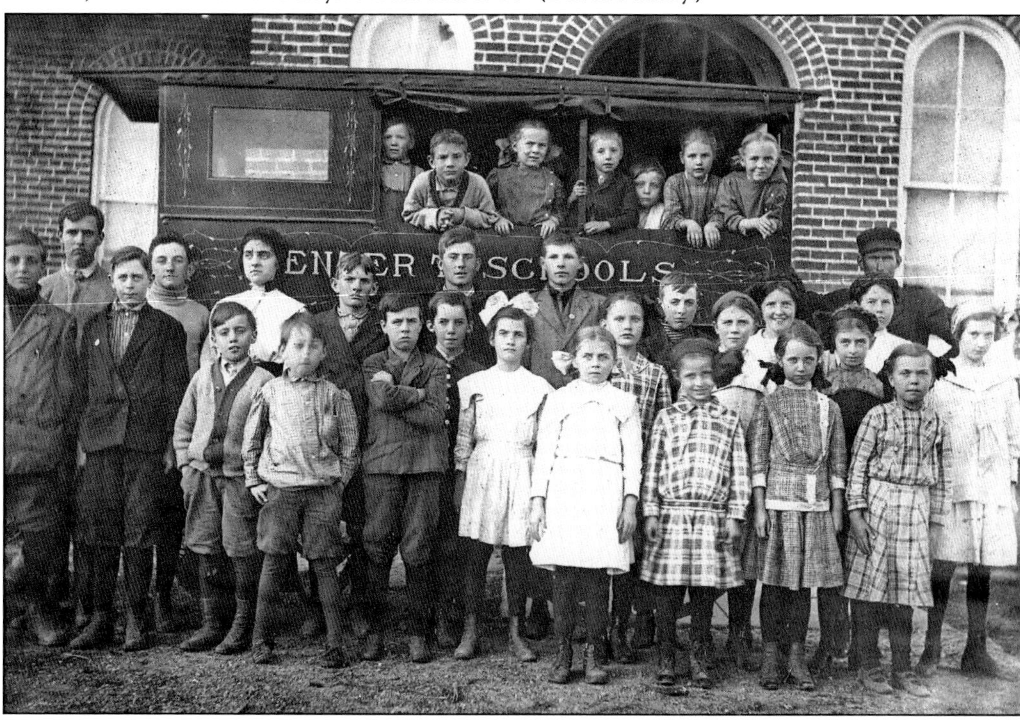

The Danville Center Township school hack was quite ornate. It would have taken an expert to do the pin-striping and lettering on this hack. The students are not identified. (Judy Pingel.)

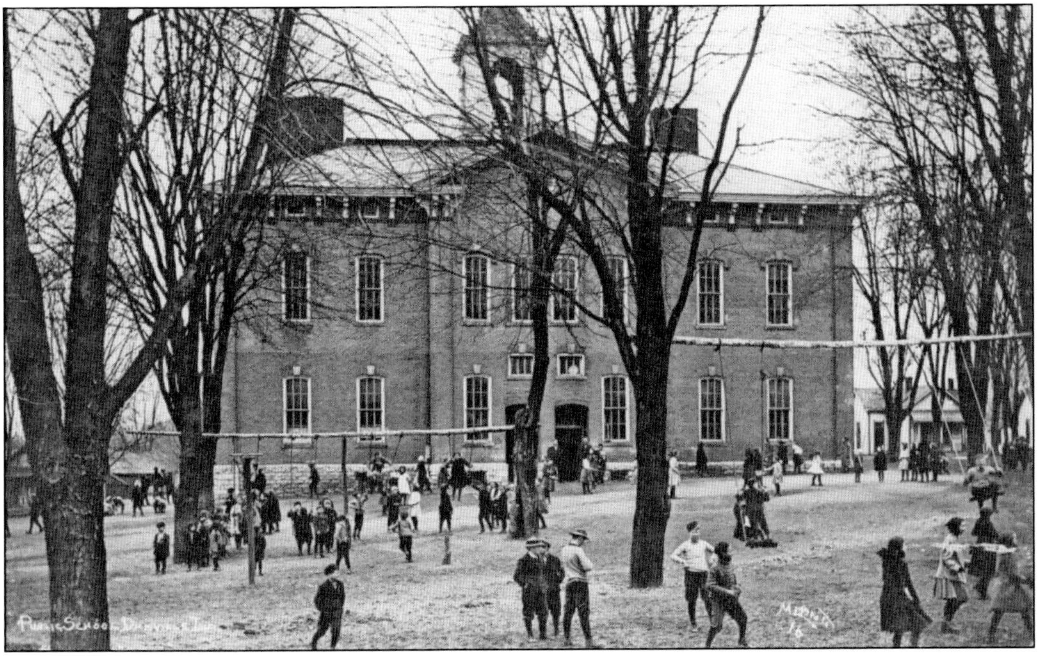

In 1916, the Danville school was located on South Washington Street. It was named the Mattie Keeney School after a respected teacher. The students are enjoying outside recess. The school sat where the north parking lot of the County Government Center is currently located, and the bell from the school is displayed in front of the building. (Bonnie Eggers.)

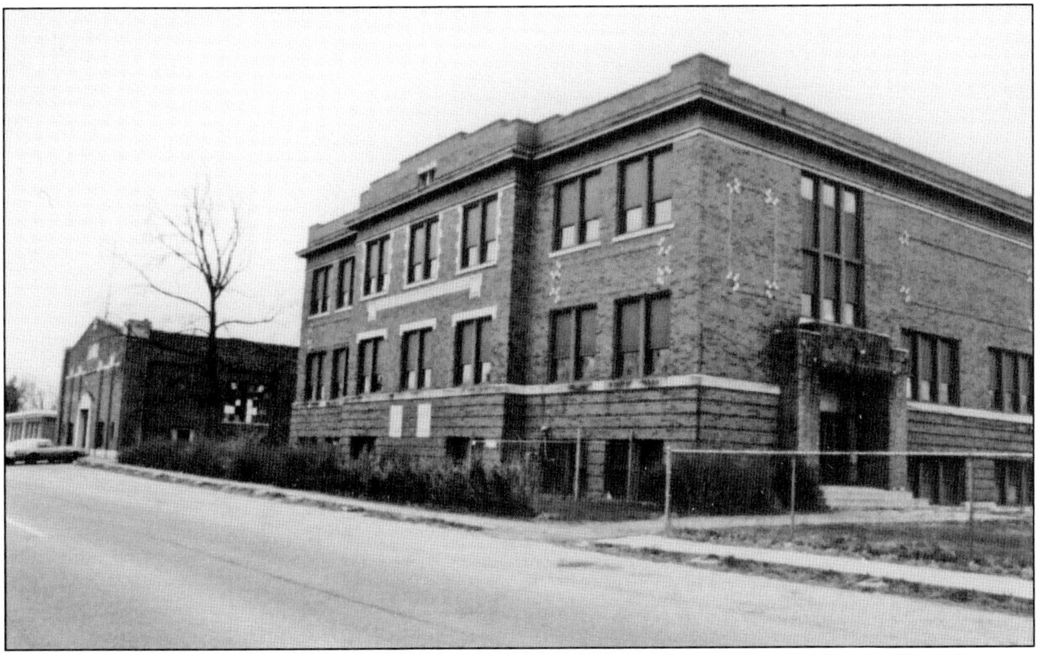

The former Brownsburg gym and school were located on College Avenue. The College Avenue gym was used in the movie *Hoosiers*. They kept the purple and white colors and the bulldog in the center circle. In the movie, it was used for the high school sectional game of the mythical Hickory Huskers. (Brownsburg Public Library.)

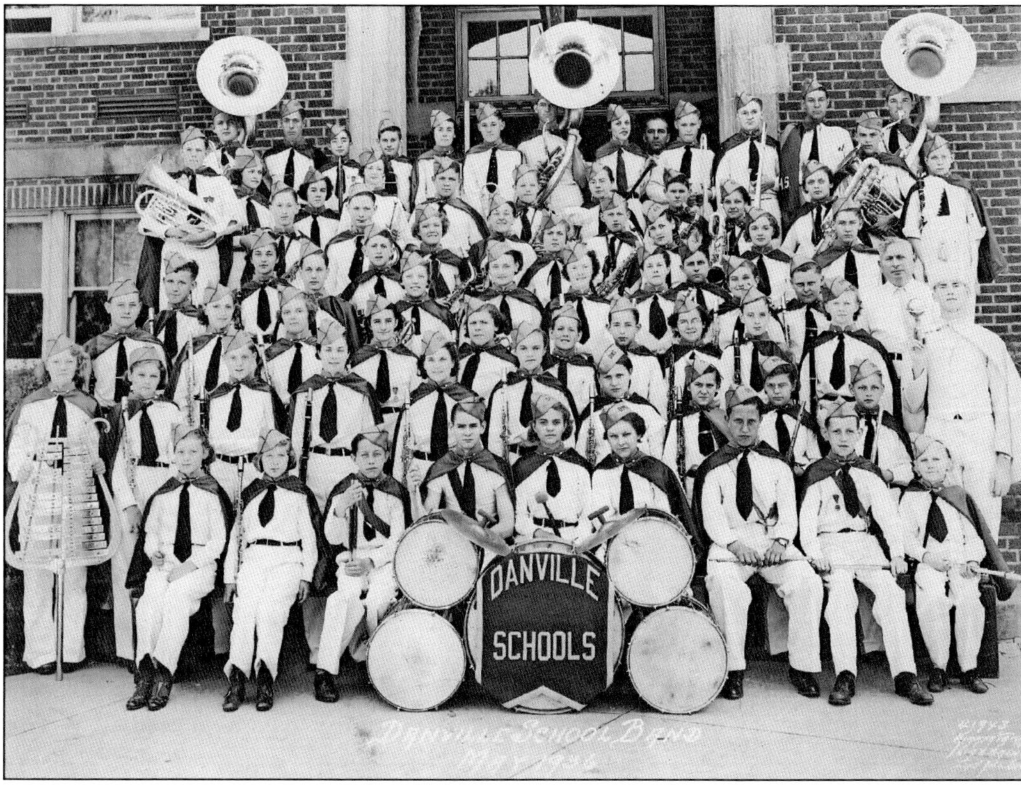

These Danville band students had their picture taken in May 1936. The story has been told how Charles Baker, of Baker and Son Funeral Home, organized a band in Danville. He made arrangements for the boys and girls to receive instruments and instruction on how to play them. When the Danville School hired a band director, in 1932, Charles turned over all his instruments to the school. (Kerry Trout.)

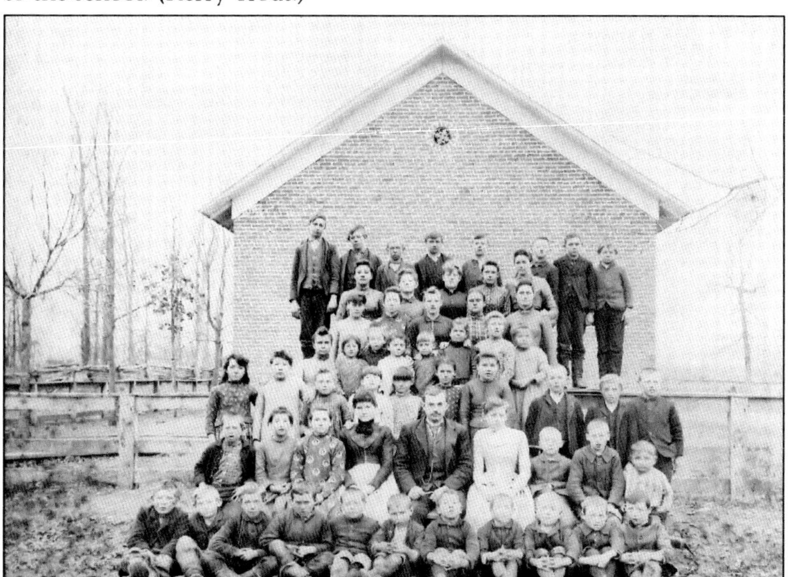

Union Township once had several one-room schools. The Hamilton School was the oldest one, and records show that it was open from 1894 to 1901. Eldora Nelson and Chester Parker were two teachers who taught at Hamilton School. (Hendricks County Museum.)

Cartersburg High School was the first accredited high school in Liberty Township. It was built in 1897 and was considered to be a beautiful building. Students enjoyed having a school close to home. As a result of school consolidation, Cartersburg students were sent to Clayton High School. As with most communities, the loss of their school was deeply felt. The school building was razed in 1964. (Guilford Township Collection–Plainfield Library.)

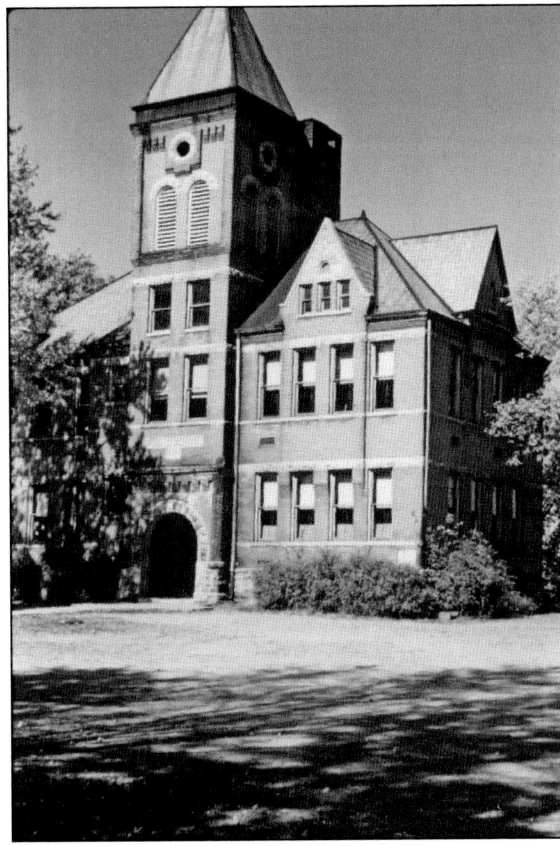

In August 1914, the *Hazelwood Weekly Visitor* wrote about the Hazelwood School: "It is a structure of magnificent proportions or will be when completed. It is a two story and basement building and will be thoroughly modern throughout in all of its departments and furnishings. The basement will consist of two commodious class rooms, one for the agricultural department and the other for the department of domestic science, a gymnasium, furnace rooms, coal bins and boys' and girls' commodious toilet rooms." (Phyllis Parsons.)

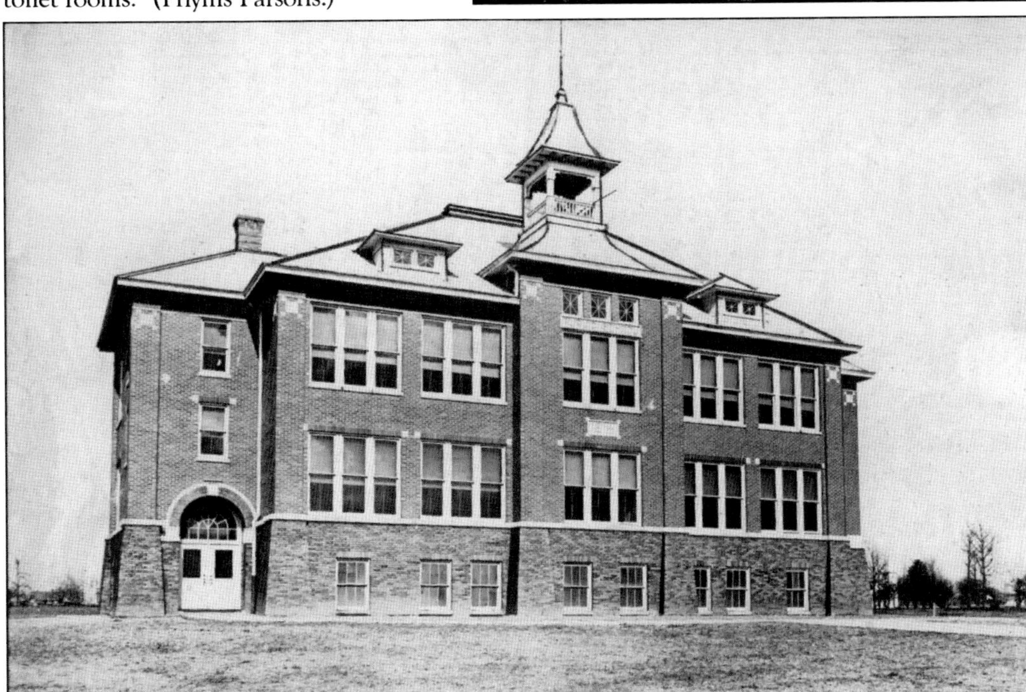

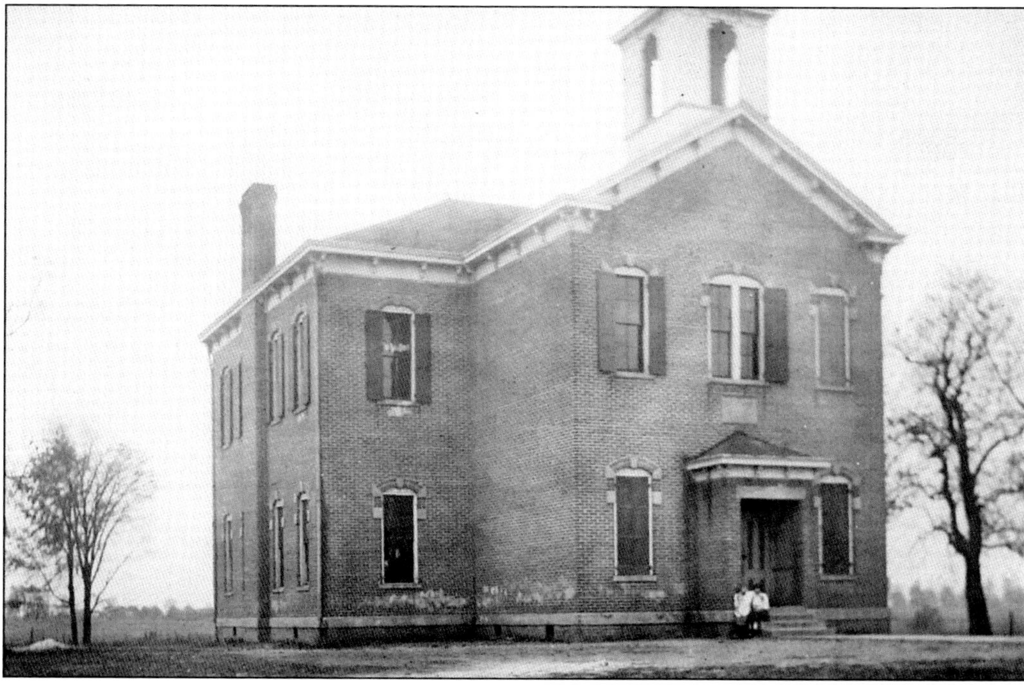

This is the old academy building in Belleville. It stood on the west side of town on the south side of US 40. It was replaced in 1889 by another brick school that looked similar. There is no longer a school building in Belleville. (Guilford Township Collection–Plainfield Library.)

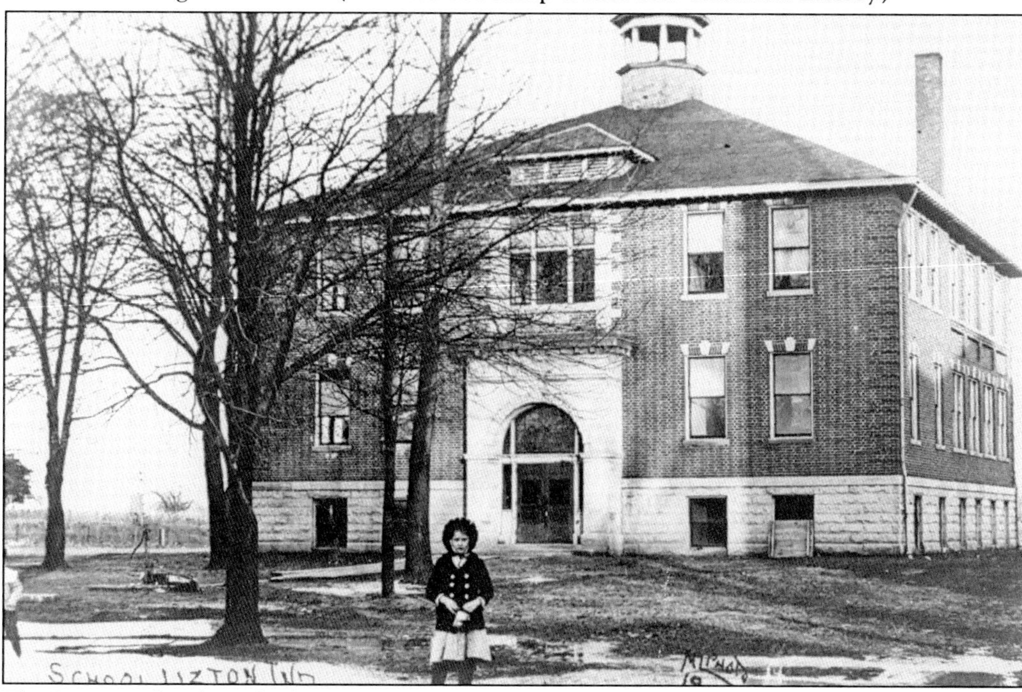

The Lizton School was built in 1905 and served as both a grade school and a high school until Lizton became part of the North West Hendricks School District. Today, the former school is an apartment building. (Hendricks County Museum.)

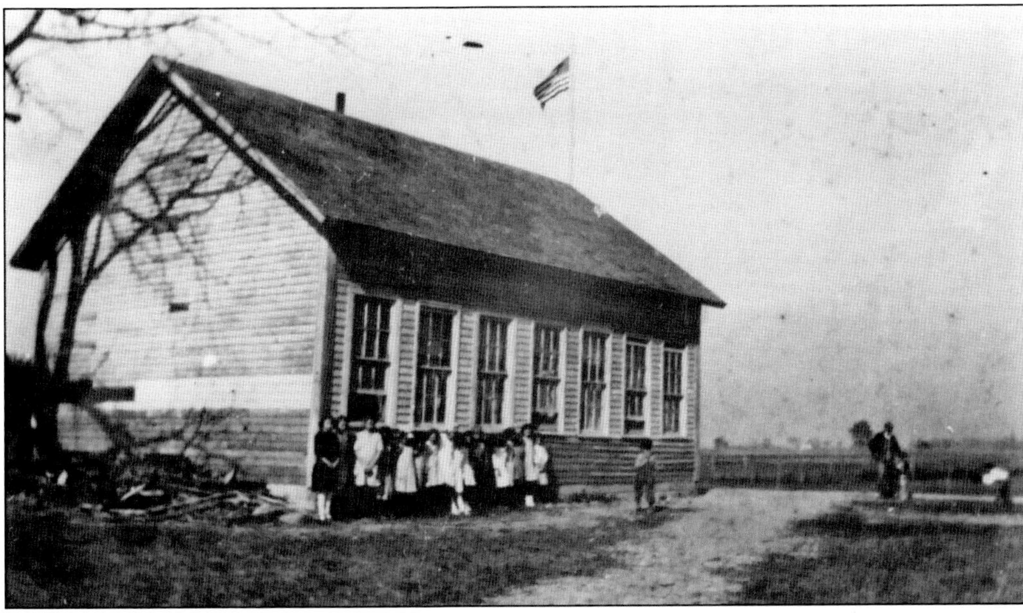

Brown Township was named after James Brown, who settled in the area in 1824. The township was rural, having no railroads, few roads, and no towns. It did, however, have schools for the children of the area. This is a group of students standing outside the Brown Township School No. 5 around 1917–1920. (Guilford Township Collection–Plainfield Library.)

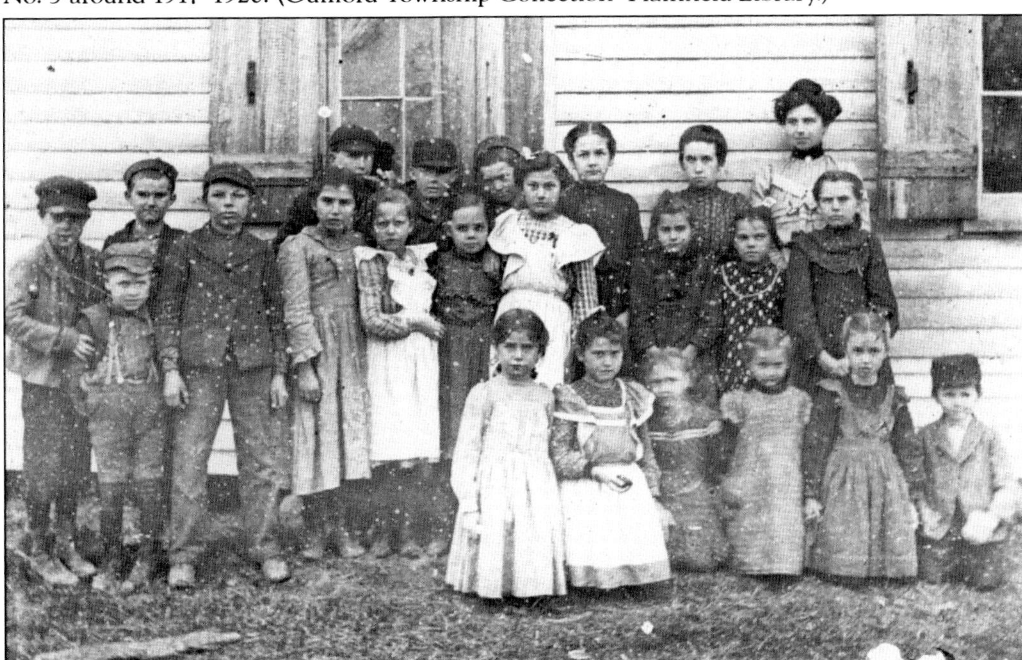

This picture shows the students of Sambo School in Brown Township. The school was previously called Watson and Arbuckle. A legend says that during the Civil War, a cave near the school was used as a stop on the Underground Railroad. Although the name Sambo would be unacceptable today, it was possibly a code for escaping slaves. It was located on SR 267, south of CR 875 North (Mahoney Road). (Hendricks County Museum.)

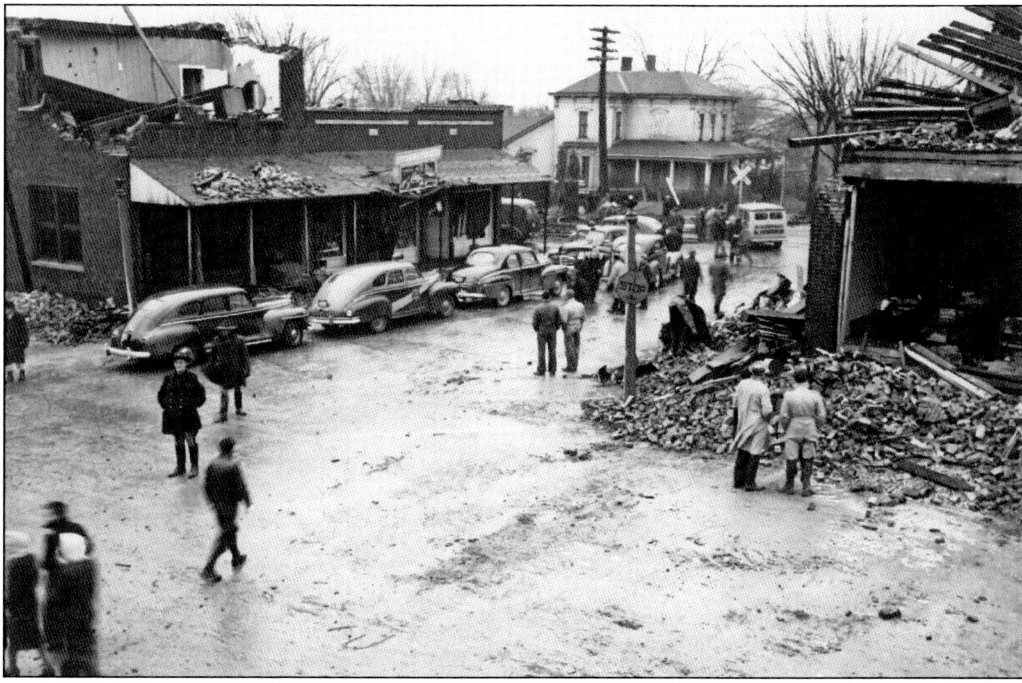

This is another scene of the damage caused by the March 26, 1948, Good Friday tornado that went through Coatesville. A state police officer stands in the intersection while citizens and authorities view the damage. (Hendricks County Museum.)

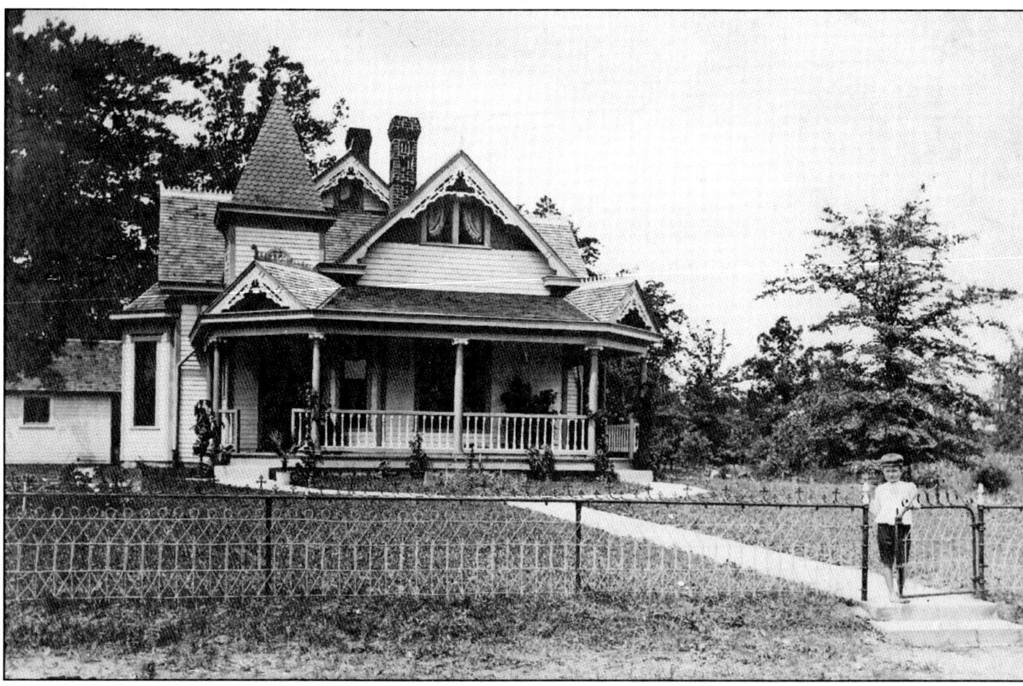

The young boy standing by the gate at the beautiful home of his parents, Ethor and Ida Milhon, is Emory Milhon. Emory was born in 1886. The house is located in Hazelwood and is still in use today. (Phyllis Parsons.)

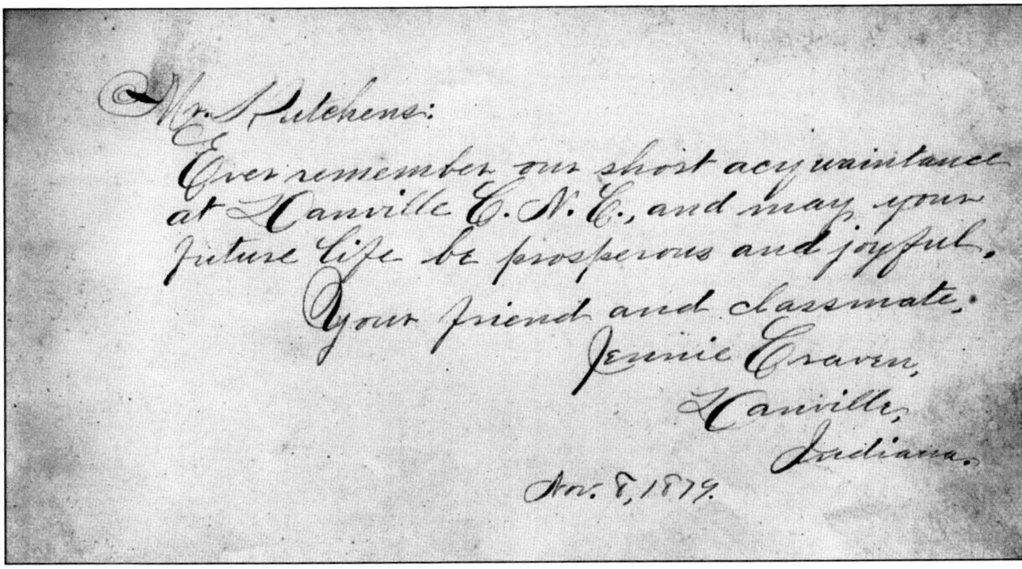

Mr. Hutchens:
Ever remember our short acquaintance at Danville C. N. C., and may your future life be prosperous and joyful.
Your friend and classmate:
Jennie Craven,
Danville,
Indiana.
Nov. 8, 1879.

In 1879, Jennie Craven (1862–1954) penned these words in a Central Normal College classmate's autograph book. The classmate was Clarence Lincoln Hutchins (1860–1933). The beautiful necklace and flowers accentuate Jennie's youthful appearance while a student at Central Normal College. In 1889, Jennie married Samuel Ralston, whom she met when both were students at Central Normal. In 1913, she became the first lady of Indiana when Samuel was elected governor of the state. Jennie was born in Hendricks County. (Above, John Hutchins; right, Phyllis Parsons.)

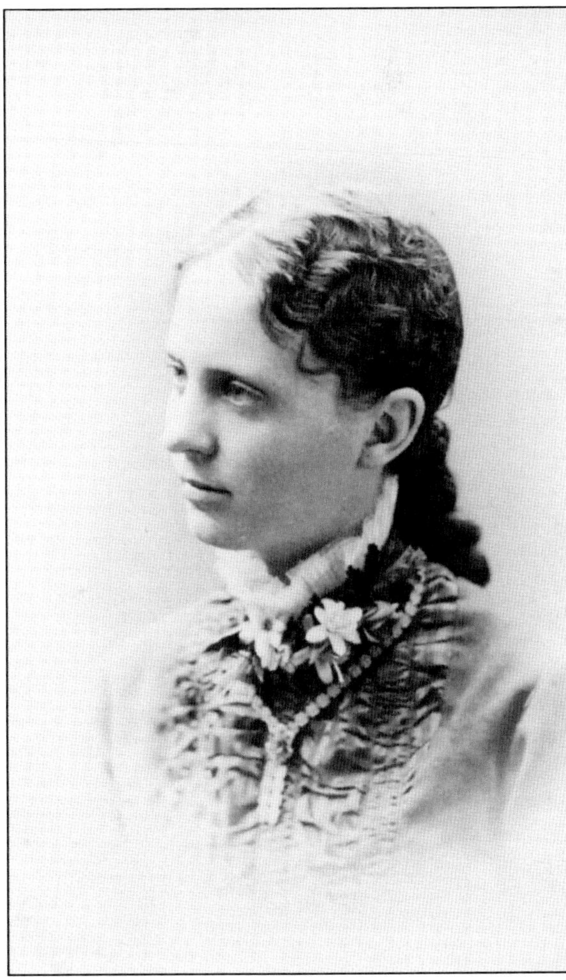

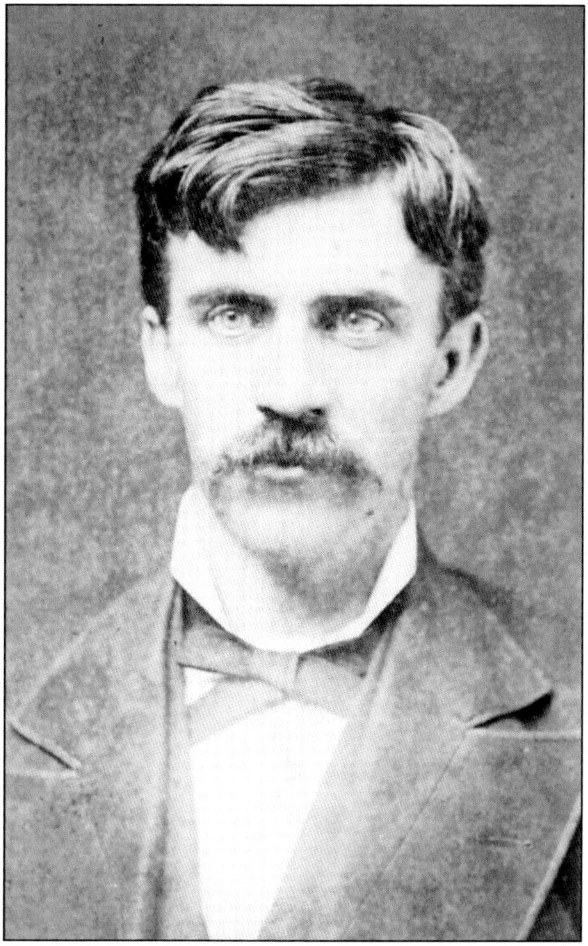

Franklin Pierce Adams (1852–1882) served as principal of Central Normal College. Later, this title was changed to president. On May 20, 1880, he wrote this message to Clarence Lincoln Hutchins, a student at Central Normal College. As Adams was nearing the end of his young life, he asked that his wife, Ora, be appointed president of the college. Although it was highly unusual at that time for a woman to be a college president, Ora was appointed and served in the position until 1889, when she married James A. Joseph and asked to be relieved of her duties. The trustees were very happy with the job she did. (Both, John Hutchins.)

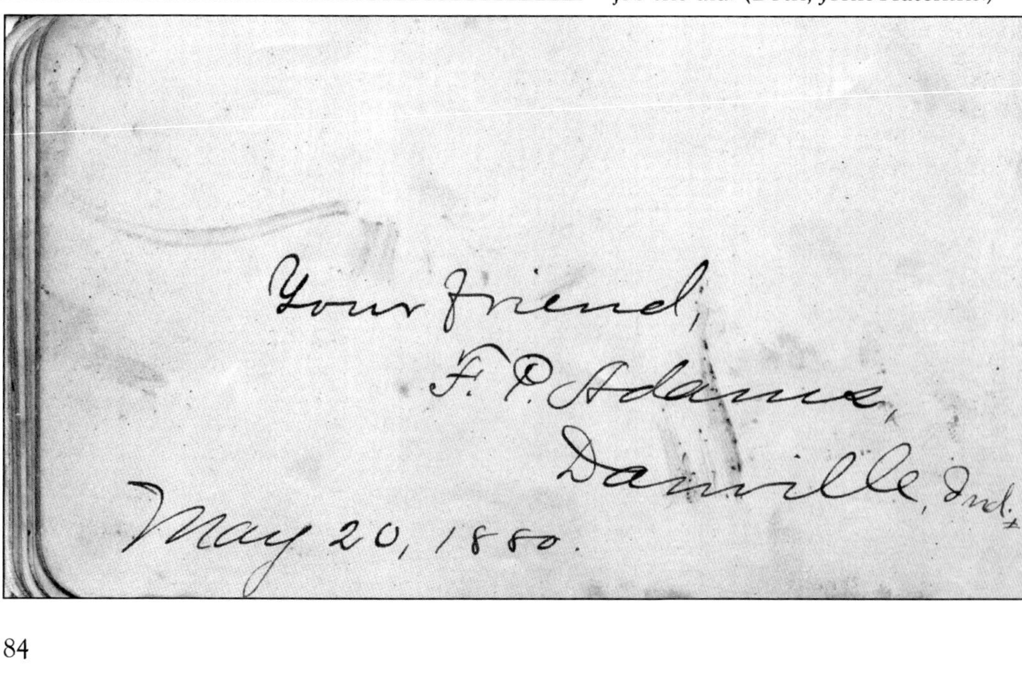

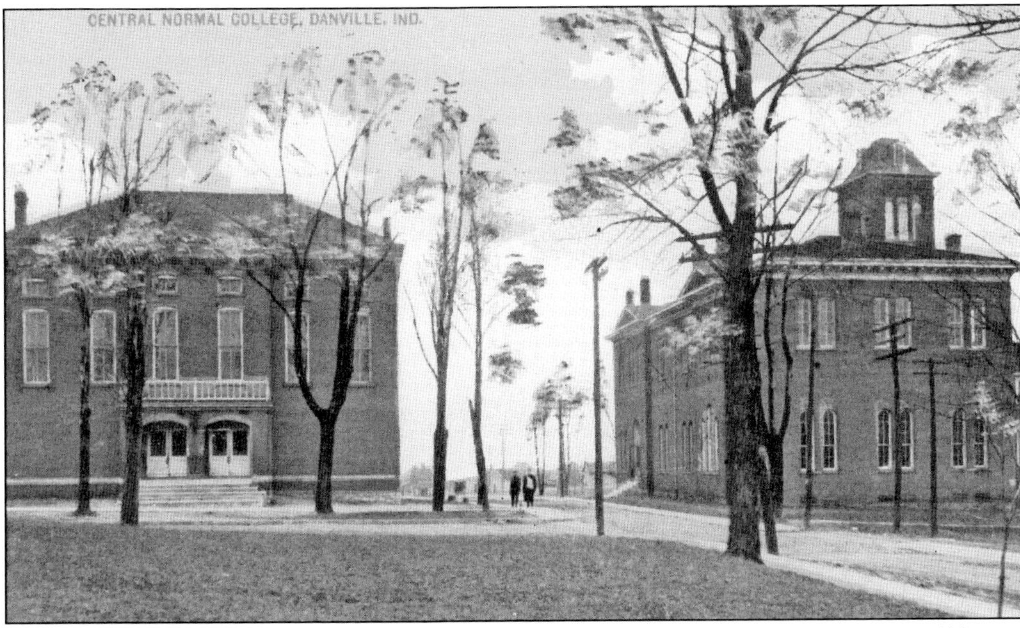

Central Normal College was moved from Ladoga to Danville in 1878 and became a well-known teachers' training college. The two buildings on the Central Normal College campus in this picture are Recitation Hall (left) and Chapel Hall. Recitation Hall was the former Danville Academy building. It housed the bookstore, library, and classrooms and was heated by coal-burning stoves in each room. (Bonnie Eggers.)

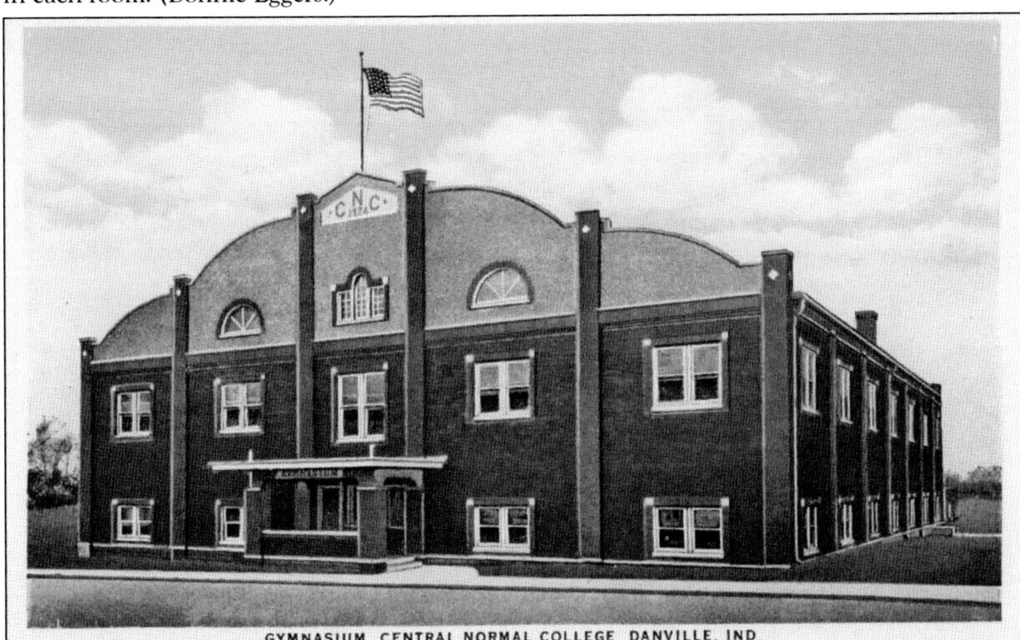

The first Central Normal gymnasium was built in 1924. A fire destroyed the gymnasium in 1936. Eight male students were living in the gym, but they were able to get out safely. As they did when the first gym was built, students again helped with its construction. In 2012, it is used by the Town of Danville as part of the town hall and as a community recreation center. (Phyllis Parsons.)

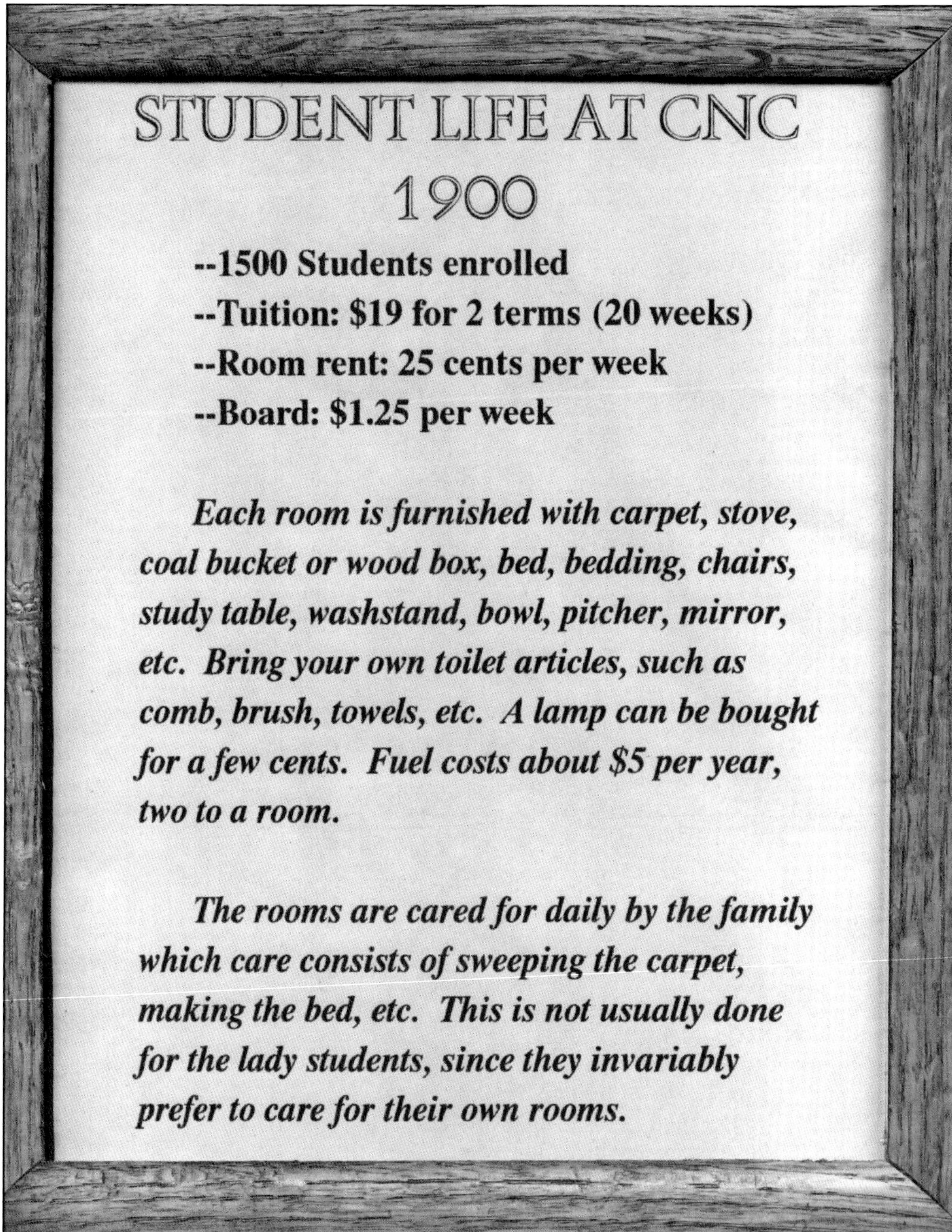

There were no dormitories at Central Normal College, so most of the students rented rooms from families in Danville. This 1900 poster advises students of their educational costs and responsibilities. (Hendricks County Museum.)

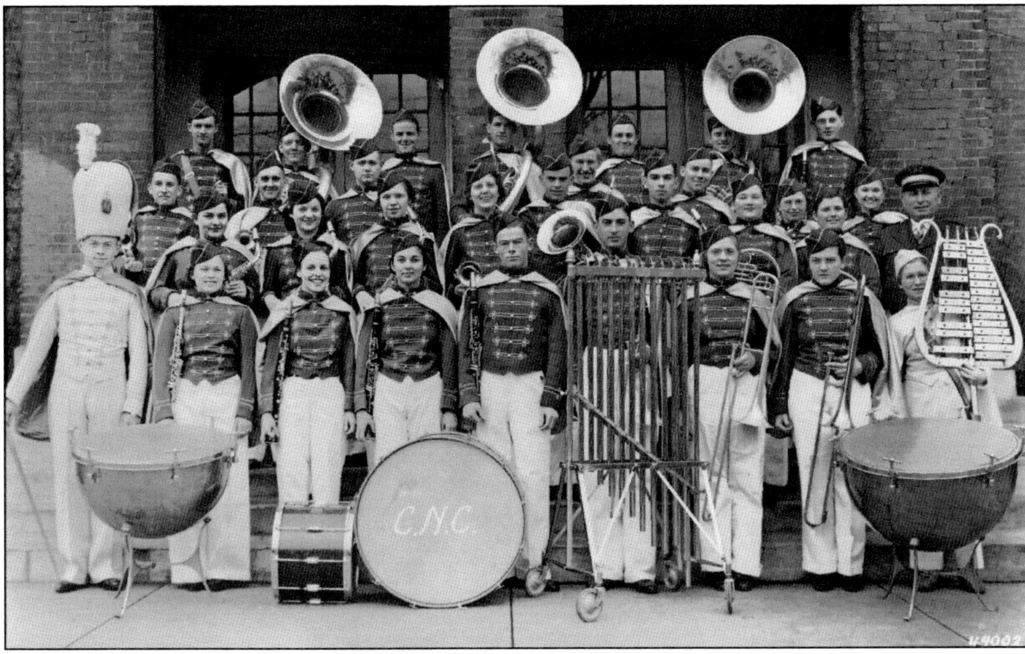

The Central Normal College band played at many of the college's activities. (Hendricks County Museum.)

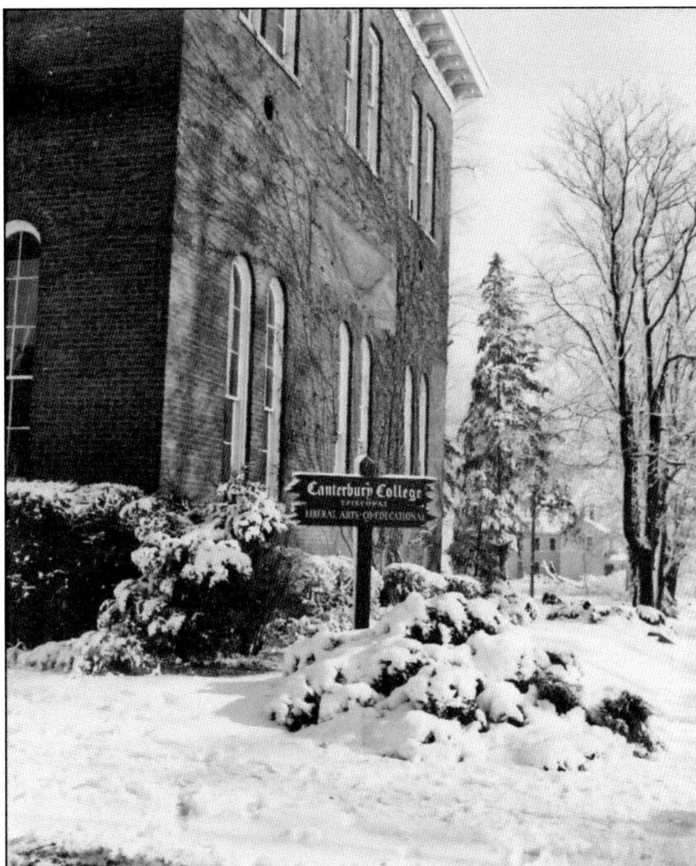

In 1946, the Northern Diocese of the Episcopal Church purchased Central Normal College. It was renamed Canterbury College. The signs on the lawn show the new college name. Due to financial problems, Canterbury College was closed in 1951. (Hendricks County Museum.)

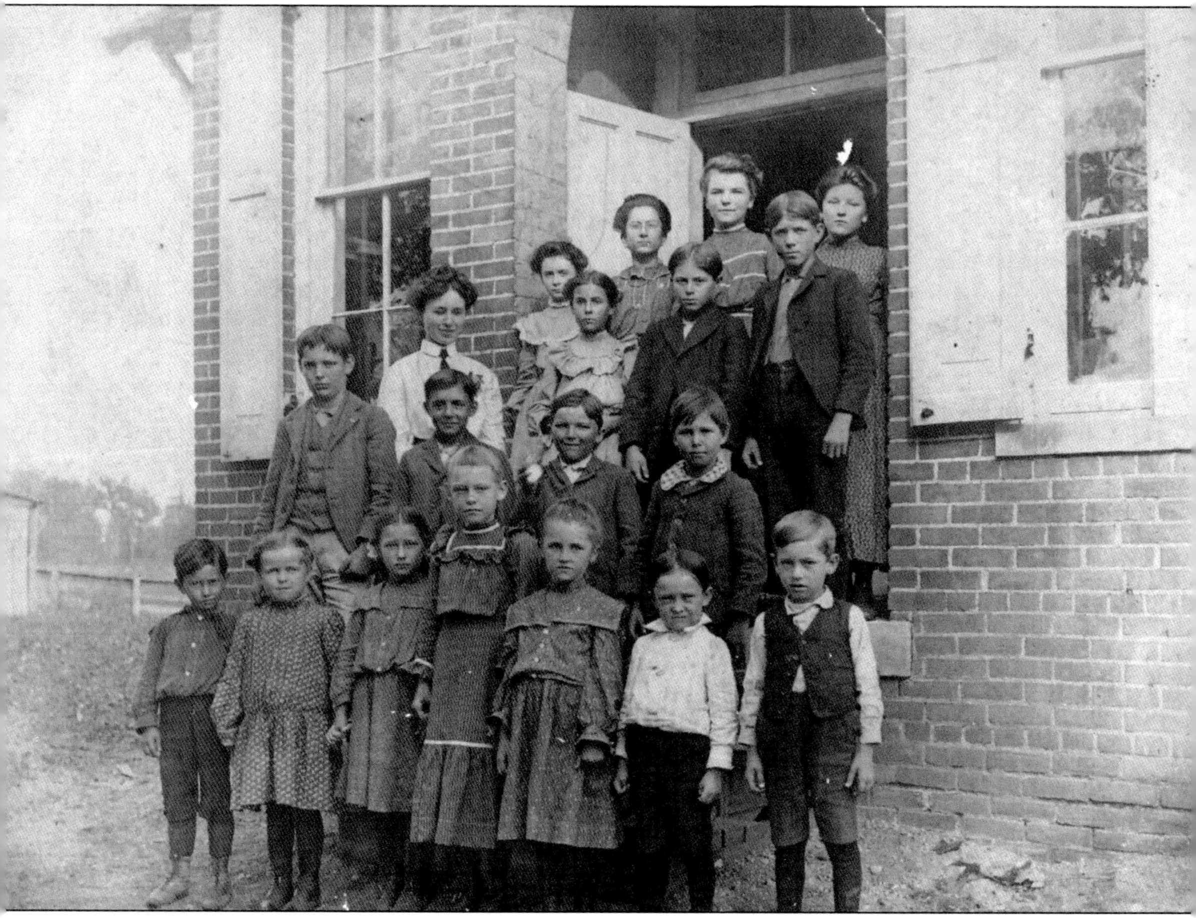

The Scott schoolhouse was in Liberty Township on CR 100 West, south of US 40. It is now a private residence. The students pictured here around 1901 are, from left to right, (first row) Benjamin Franklin Short, Carol Edmondson Whicker, Marcia Short Raber, Marjorie Callahan, and three unidentified; (second row) unidentified, Jim Busby, and two unidentified; (third row) teacher Frances Payton, two unidentified, and Lawrence Mabe; (fourth row) two unidentified, ? Rushton, and Alta Rushton. (Hendricks County Museum.)

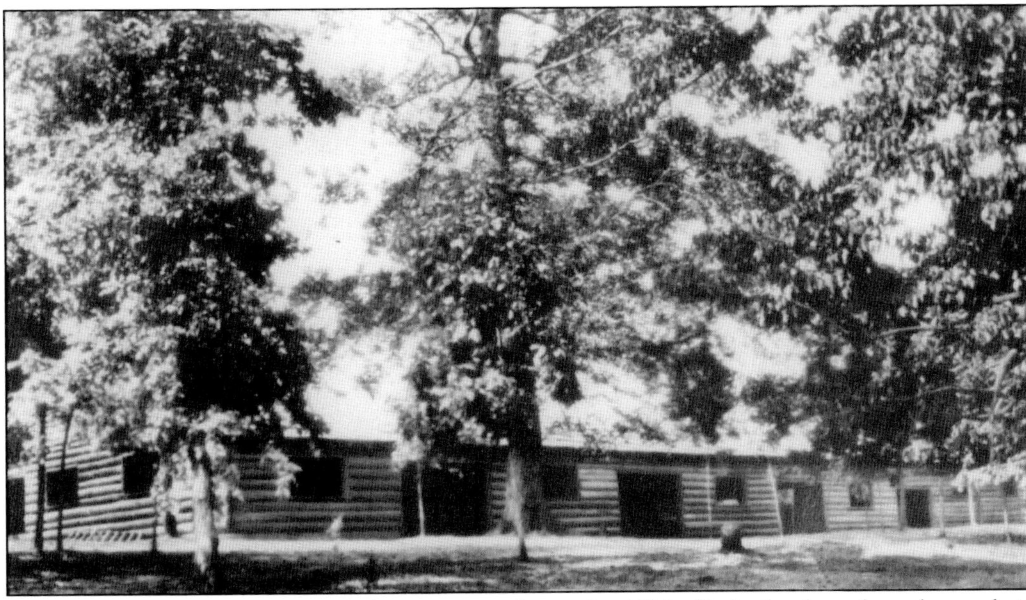

E. Howard Cadle was a nationally known revivalist in the 1930s. He built a large log tabernacle in the woods at the east edge of Belleville in 1936. Hundreds of people came to hear the preaching. Famous gospel quartet groups provided music. B.R. Lakin, a well-known minister, preached many services at the tabernacle. Later, Cadle built the famous Cadle Tabernacle in Indianapolis. (Phyllis Parsons.)

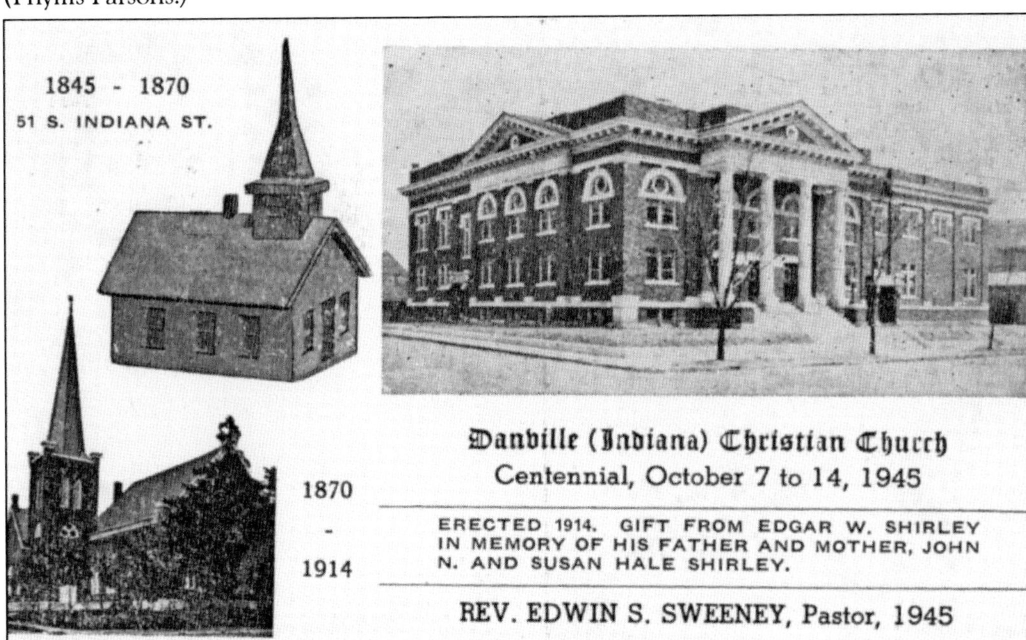

The Danville Christian Church had three buildings. The first was a small frame structure located on the east side of South Indiana Street, just south of Main Street. It was built in 1845 and used until 1870. The second church was a brick building, which was used from 1870 to 1914. The current large brick building is located on the north side of West Main Street. (Hendricks County Museum.)

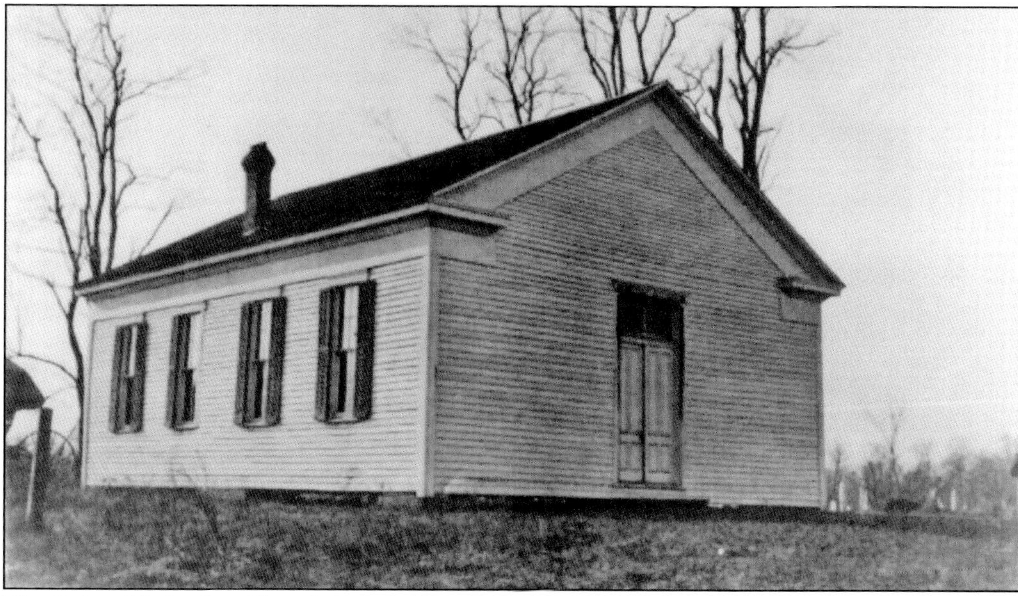

The Salem Methodist Church is the oldest church in Hendricks County still on its original site. It was built in 1829 and is typical of the old frame churches that were built in the county. The church was remodeled about 1882, and a basement was added later. In 1977, the Belleville Bible Church bought it, and members still meet there to worship God. (Above, Phyllis Parsons; below, Guilford Township Collection–Plainfield Library.)

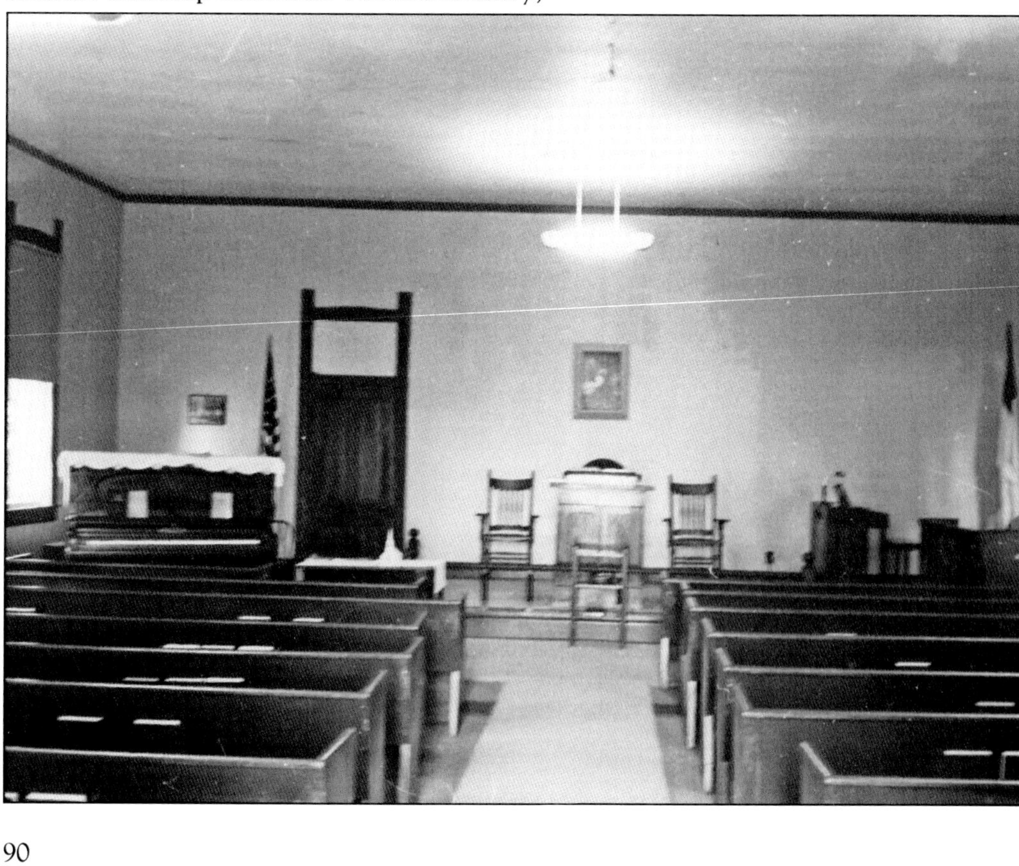

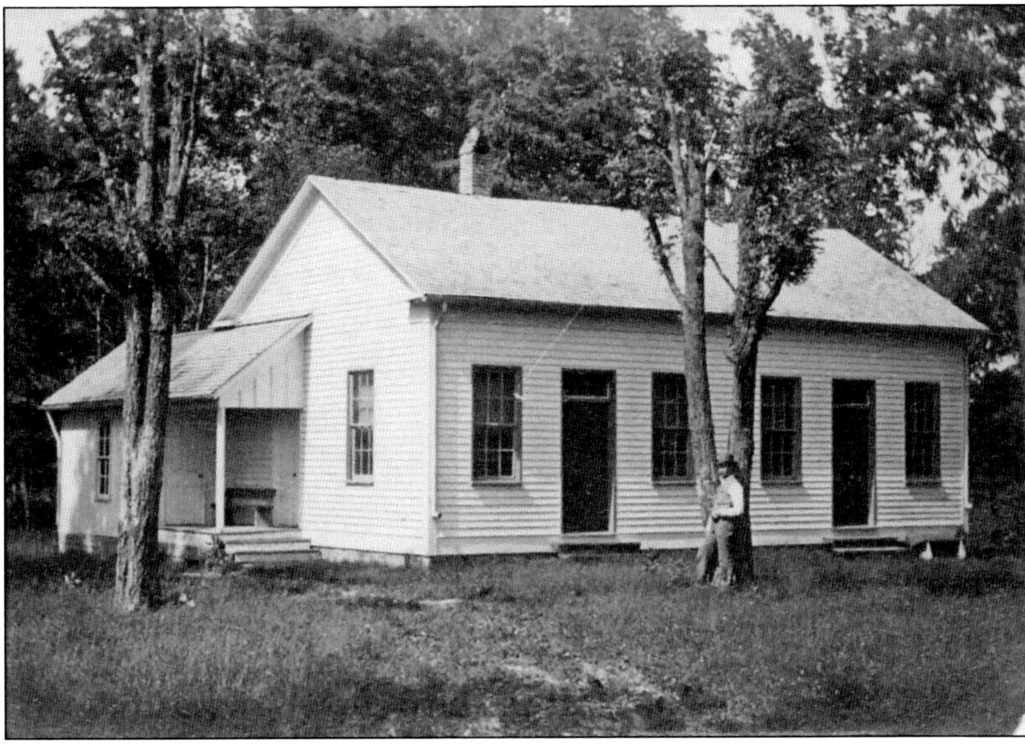

The North Branch Friends Meetinghouse sat in southern Liberty Township. Photographer J.P. Calvert captured this moment of Eli Hadley standing by a tree. The meetinghouse was later torn down, and the lumber was used to build a house in the neighborhood. (Guilford Township Collection–Plainfield Library.)

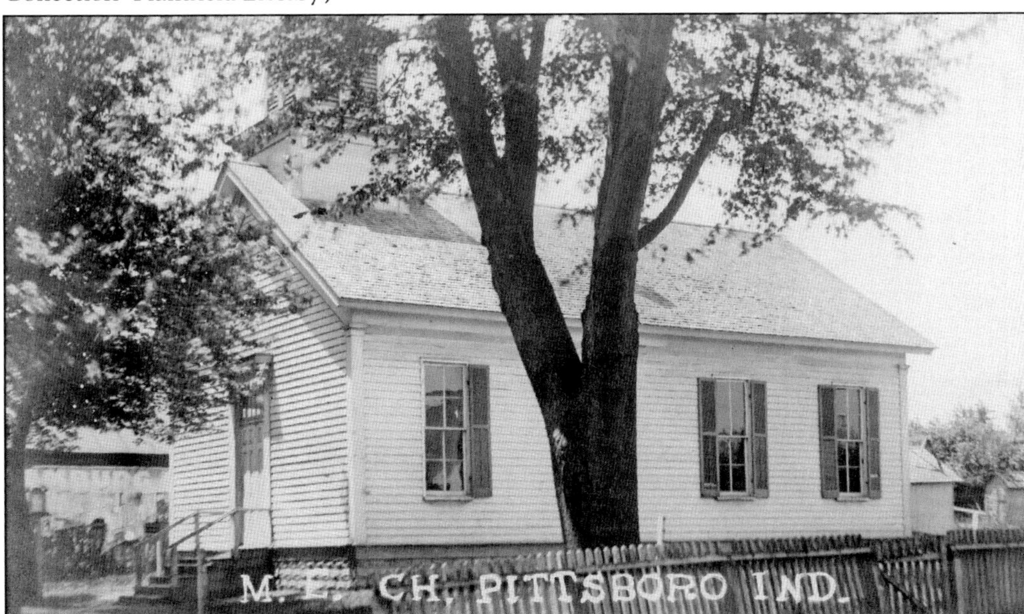

This is an early picture of the Pittsboro Methodist Church. Although this building was abandoned many years ago, the congregation itself continues to meet for worship. (Bonnie Eggers.)

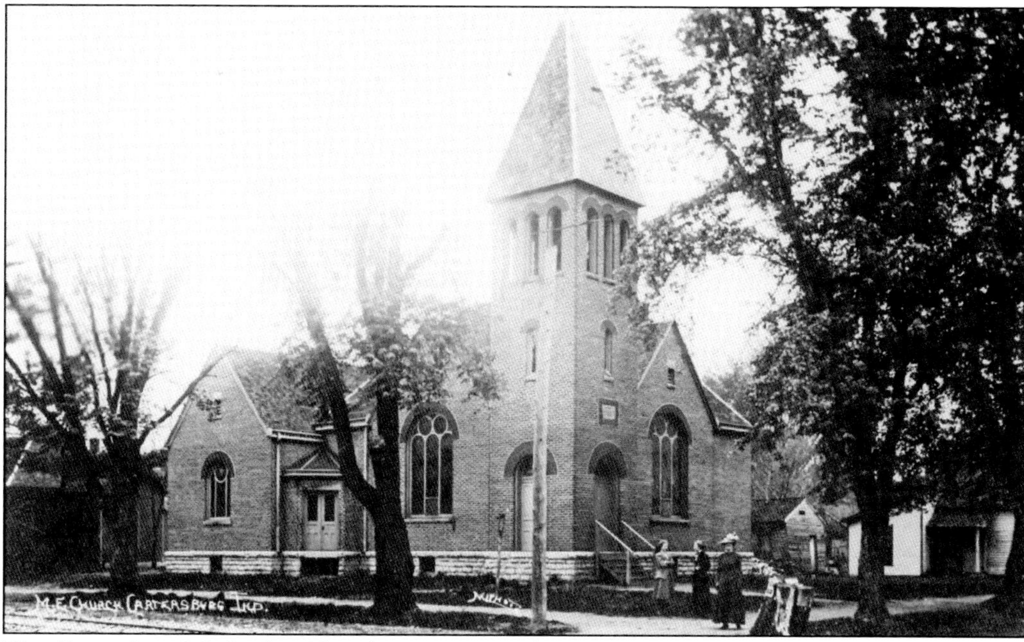

The Cartersburg Methodist Church was organized in the winter of 1856–1857 and was housed in a frame structure. In 1894, land was donated to build a new brick building. In the late 1960s, when the congregation began to dwindle, the Methodist Church closed the church. It was a sad day for people of the community when they watched the demolition of their beloved church, which many of their forefathers helped to build. (Guilford Township Collection–Plainfield Library.)

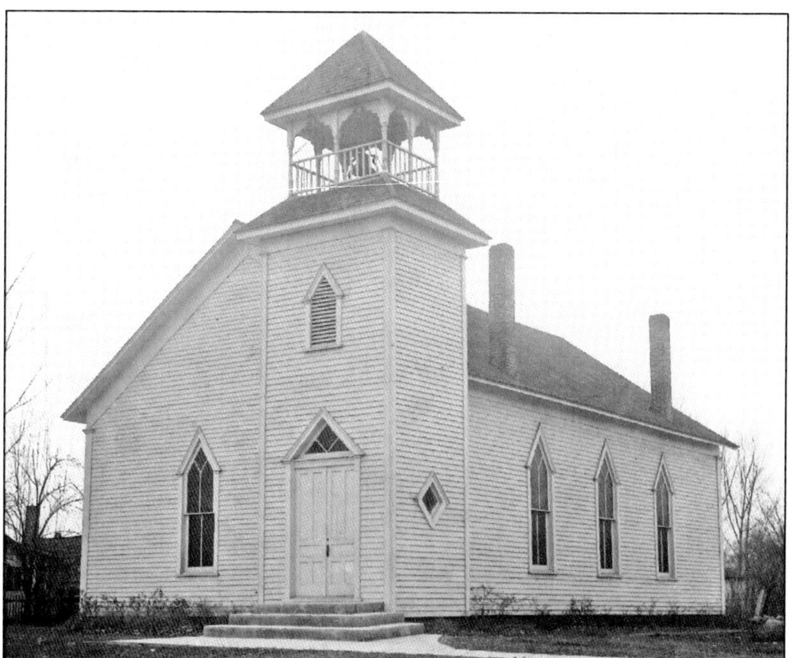

The Amo Methodist Church is still standing but looks much different today. It was remodeled in 1917. They turned the building one half a turn to face Pearl Street and put brick on the frame structure. (Guilford Township Collection–Plainfield Library.)

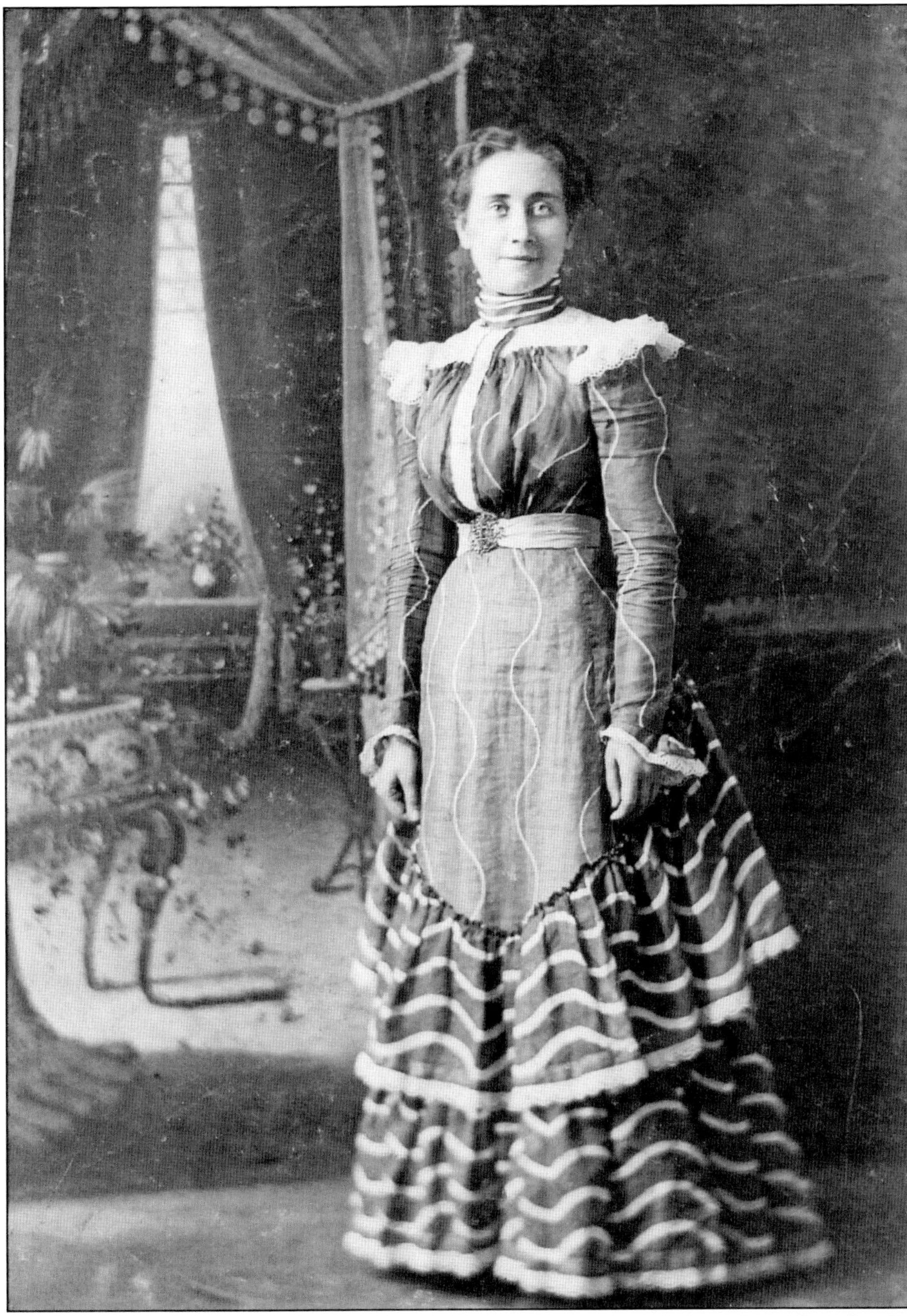

Mary "Ottie" Roberts (1872–1944) was a direct descendant of Brownsburg town founder William Harris. Ottie served on the first Brownsburg library board and was appointed as its first librarian. (Hendricks County Museum.)

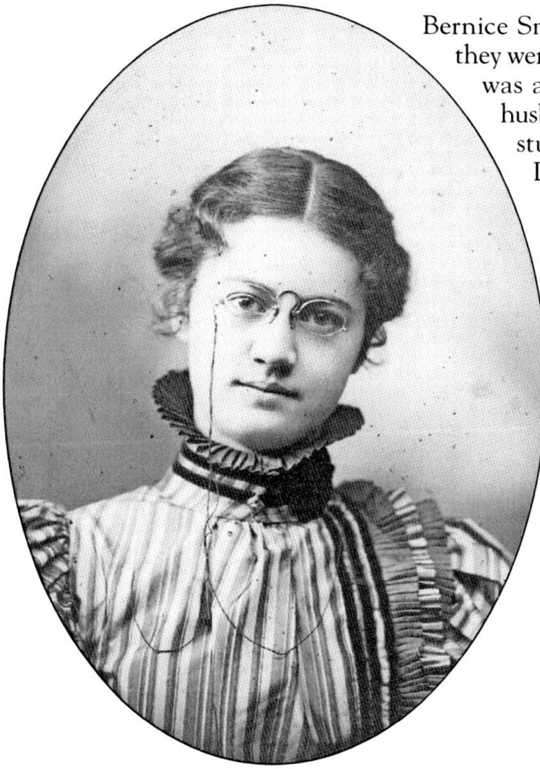

Bernice Smith (1876–1953) married Joseph Ferree, and they were the parents of Joseph and Katherine. Bernice was a graduate of DePauw University. After her husband's death in 1930, she took classes in library studies. In 1931, at the age of 55, she became the Danville librarian. Bernice served the Danville community in this capacity until her death in May 1953. (Hendricks County Museum.)

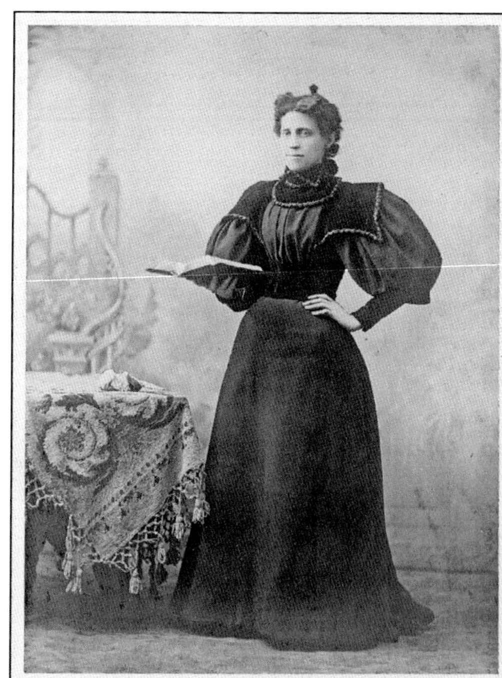

Rella Cromwell (1861–1921) lived in Reelsville, Putnam County. She was a minister who traveled to communities in nearby counties, including Hendricks, to preach. She was the first woman minister at the Coatesville Methodist Episcopal Church. In 1910, she was preaching at a church in Indianapolis. Her evangelical travels took her to Kansas and other parts of the country. This picture was taken in March 1896. (Hendricks County Museum-Mary Lou Knetzer Kress, Picture Album.)

Five

Gatherings and Celebrations

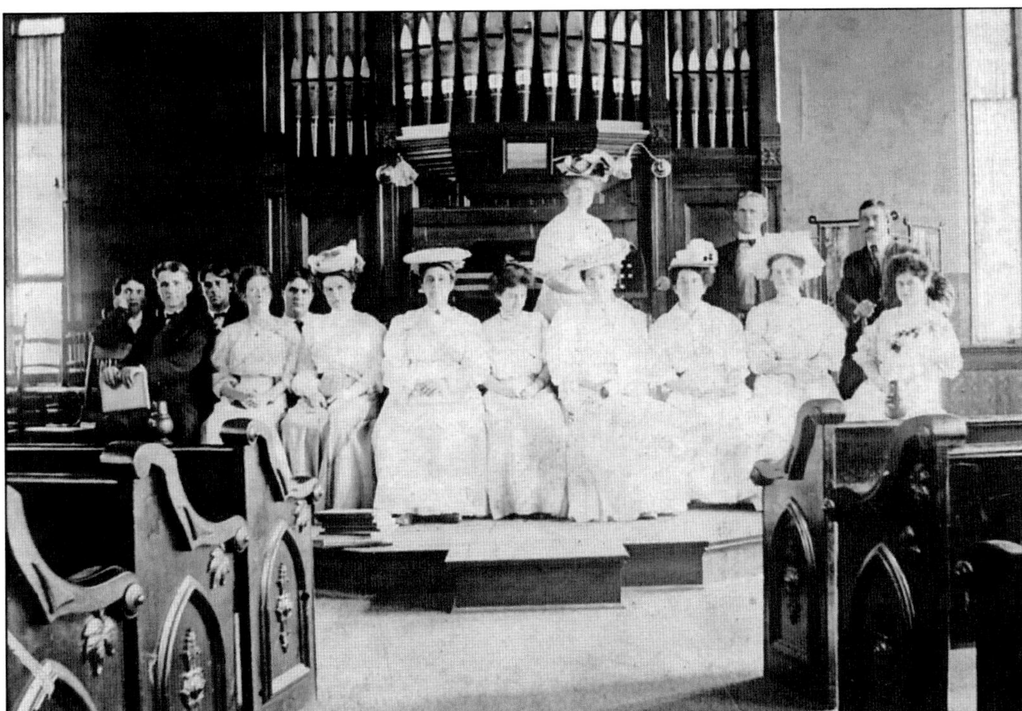

The men and women of early Hendricks County were hardworking and yet got together for the happy and the sad times of life. This group of men and women are in their Sunday best for an activity at the Danville Methodist Church on South Washington Street. They are seated in front of the pipes of the church's large organ. On August 11, 1989, a fire destroyed this building. (Hendricks County Museum.)

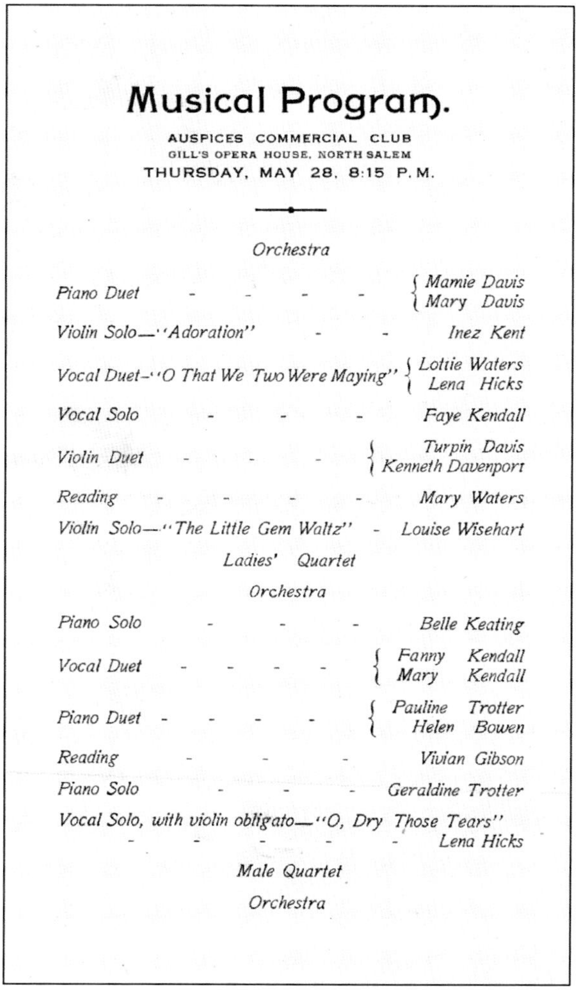

Musical Program.

AUSPICES COMMERCIAL CLUB
GILL'S OPERA HOUSE, NORTH SALEM
THURSDAY, MAY 28, 8:15 P.M.

Orchestra

Piano Duet - - - - *Mamie Davis, Mary Davis*

Violin Solo—"Adoration" - - *Inez Kent*

Vocal Duet—"O That We Two Were Maying" *Lottie Waters, Lena Hicks*

Vocal Solo - - - *Faye Kendall*

Violin Duet - - - - *Turpin Davis, Kenneth Davenport*

Reading - - - - - *Mary Waters*

Violin Solo—"The Little Gem Waltz" - *Louise Wisehart*

Ladies' Quartet

Orchestra

Piano Solo - - - *Belle Keating*

Vocal Duet - - - - *Fanny Kendall, Mary Kendall*

Piano Duet - - - - *Pauline Trotter, Helen Bowen*

Reading - - - *Vivian Gibson*

Piano Solo - - - *Geraldine Trotter*

Vocal Solo, with violin obligato—"O, Dry Those Tears" - - - - - - *Lena Hicks*

Male Quartet

Orchestra

The Auspices Commercial Club hosted its musical at Gill's Opera House in North Salem. William G. Gill constructed the building, which served as the opera house and town hall, in 1891. Gill was born in Virginia. He erected many structures in Eel River Township, including banks, a brick school house, and concrete bridges. In 1914, William Gill was still operating the opera house. (Jamie Neal.)

This group of men made up the Brownsburg concert band about 1903. (Brownsburg Public Library.)

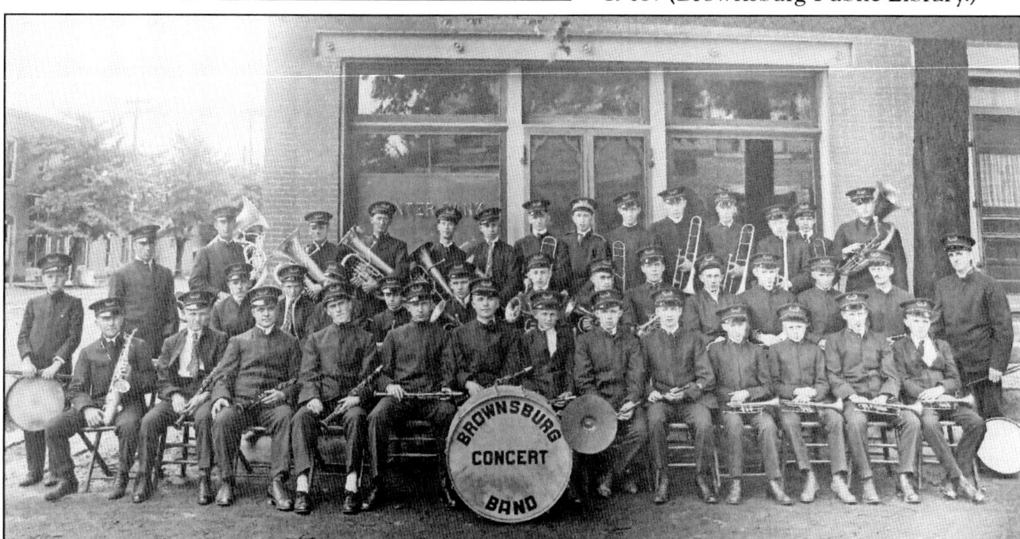

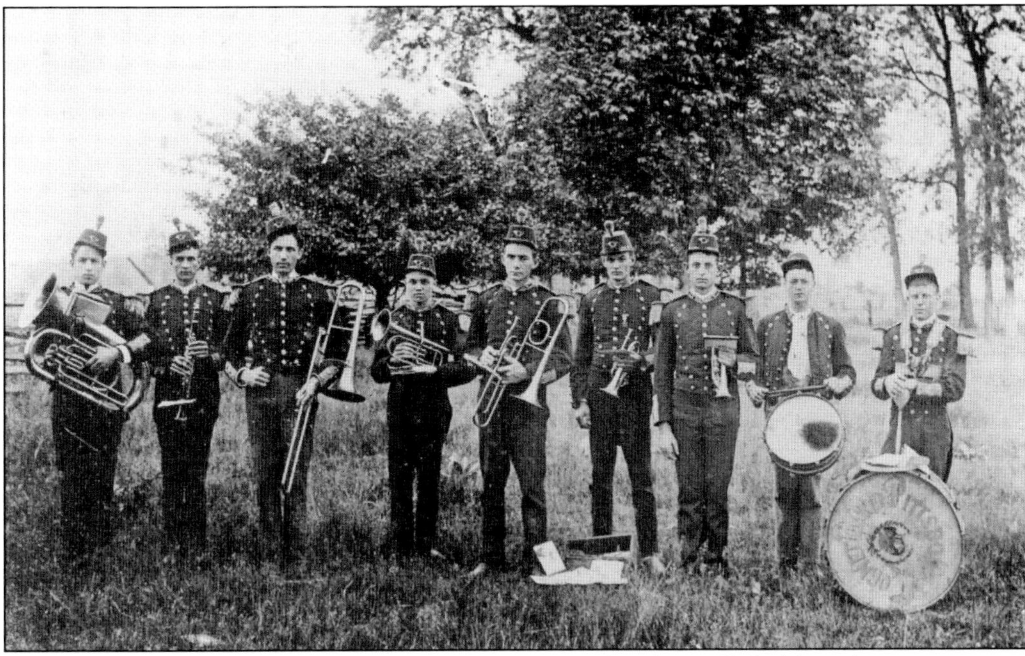

The men in this 1885 Pittsboro band are fully uniformed and proudly holding their instruments. Band members are, from left to right, Chester Weaver, Sherman Waters, Hollis Weaver, Charles Cox, Charles Richardson, John Waters, Urban Weaver, Virgil Watson, and Harry Stillinger. (Hendricks County Museum.)

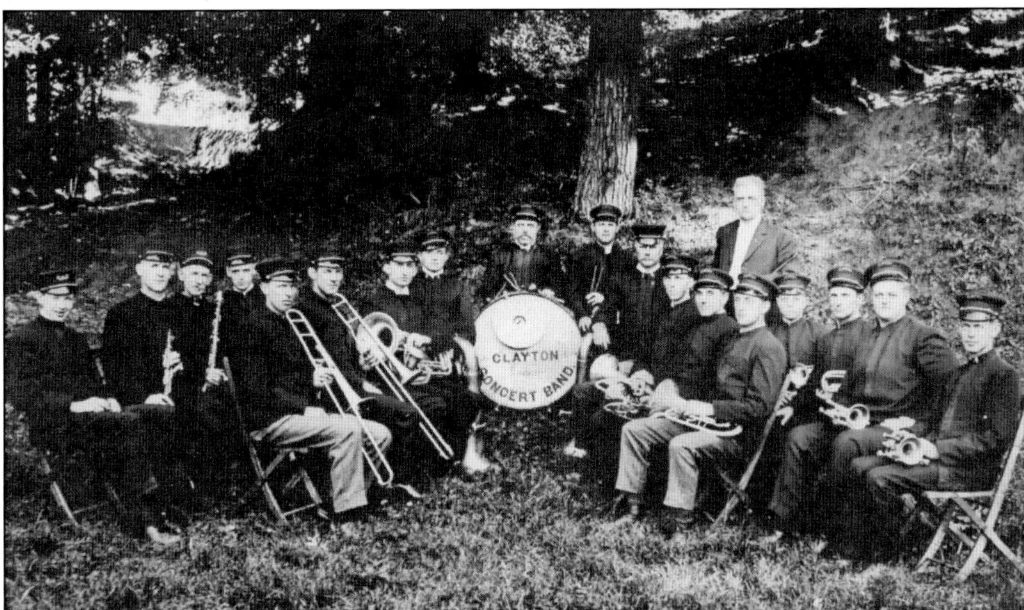

Here is the Clayton concert band around 1905. The names of those pictured were listed randomly, and the list only includes 15 out of the 19 people. The band director's name is Rudy, and the other names are Fred McCurdy, Hershel Rynerson, Al Bell, Alva Farquar, Ernest Rynerson, Benchard Carr, Corbin Rushton, Howard Mitchell, Charles Worrell, Charles West, George Wills, Donald Reid, Paul Martin, and Herbert Wills. (Guilford Township Collection–Plainfield Library.)

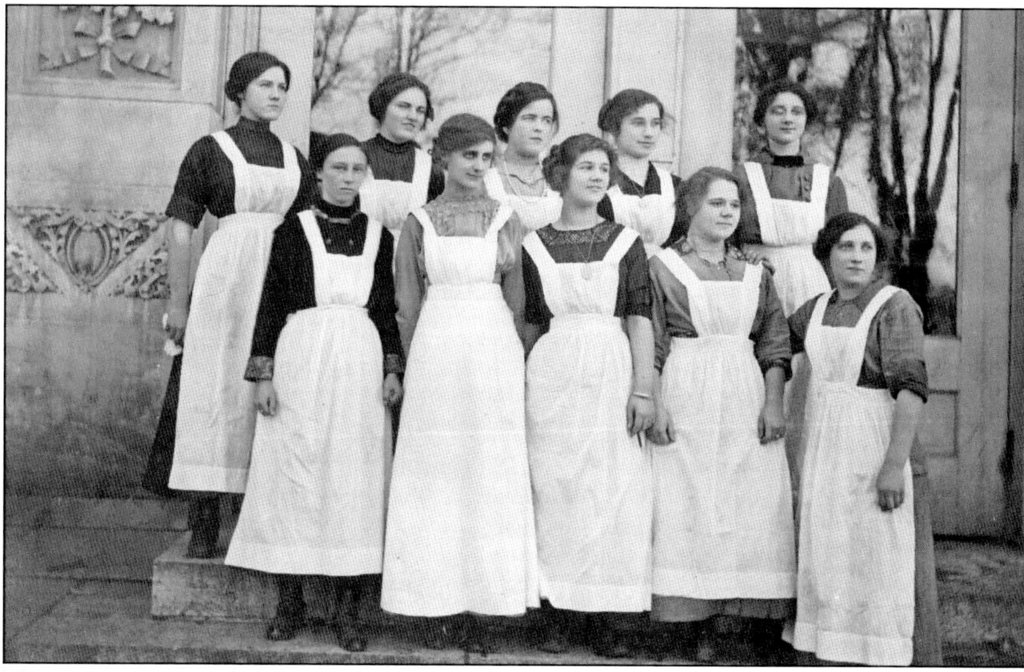

These serious young ladies are students of the domestic science class of Clayton High School. They were being prepared to set up housekeeping, and it looks like the class required a white apron. The students are, from left to right, (first row) Eileen Rushton, Dee Worrell, unidentified, Ruby Riley, and Mary Brooks; (second row) unidentified, Grace Veatch, Carolyn Edmondson Whicker, Marcia Short Raber, and unidentified. The picture was taken about 1915. (Guilford Township Collection–Plainfield Library.)

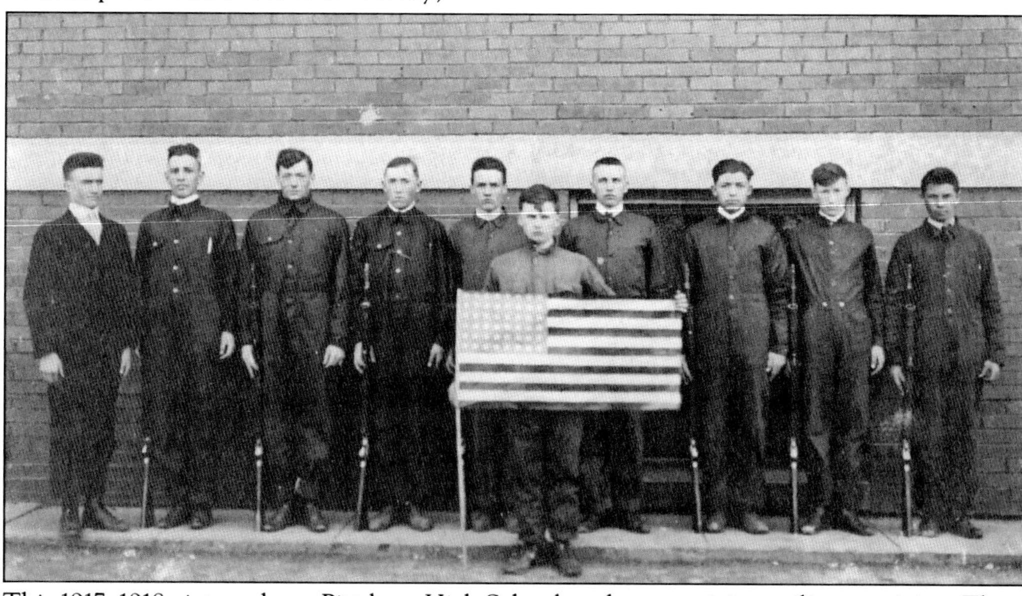

This 1917–1918 picture shows Pittsboro High School students receiving military training. Those pictured are, from left to right, instructor Leo Fitzgerald, Byron Yeager, John Halfaker, Henry Halfaker, Paul Robbins, Kenneth Overstreet (with flag), Lowell Keeney, Harold Delong, Marvin Weaver, and Fred Bowman. (Hendricks County Museum.)

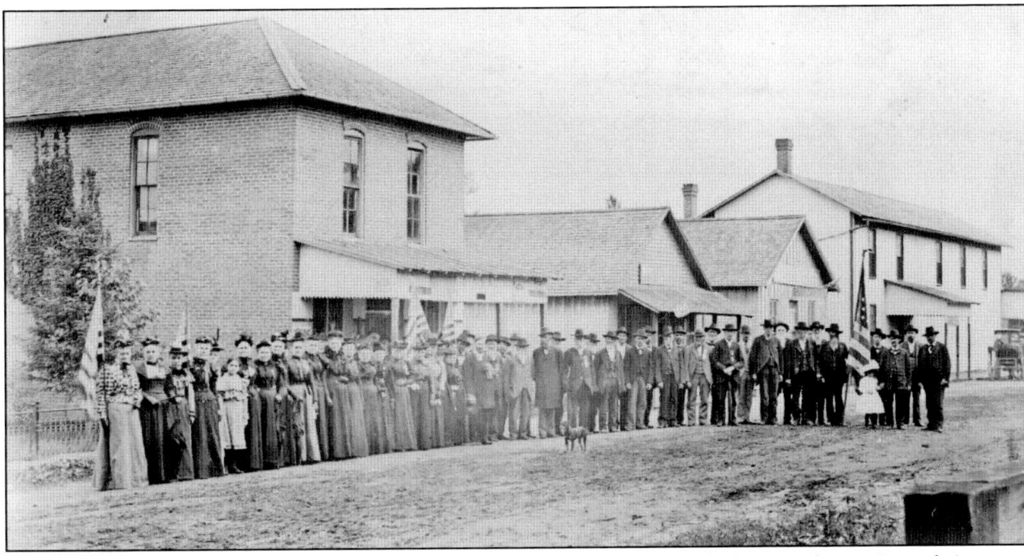

Men and women stand proudly as the Women's Relief Corps and the Pittsboro Grand Army of the Republic unit join together in front of the Junket Building in Pittsboro. Upon the soldiers' return from the Civil War, they formed the Grand Army of the Republic (GAR). The men in the picture below represent the Thomas Ashby Post of the GAR at Pittsboro. They are, from left to right, (sitting) Marshall Holtsclaw and Luke Dillon; (first row, standing) James Smoot, Mel Phillips, Dudley Parker, W.D. Lewis, Captain Wilson Henry Ward, A.C. Weaver, William Tout, Simon Weddle, John Bell (with John Allen Bell), and Ellis Weaver; (second row) Lewis Davis, Frank Ray, Calvin Warrick, Henry Kirk, Jessie Lacy, and Deloss Parker; (third row) James Hatfrell, Marion Watson, C.P. Cox, Monroe Wills, Steward Wills, John Smith, Sam Janes, Lee Ashby, James Pebworth, and Jack Smith. (Both, Hendricks County Museum.)

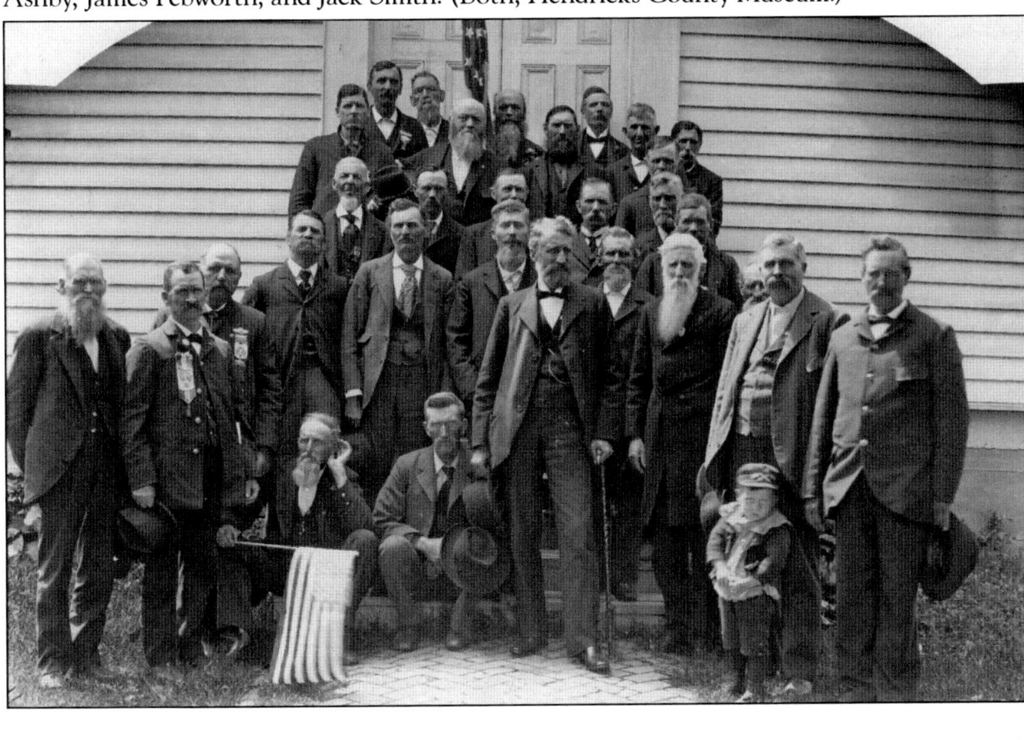

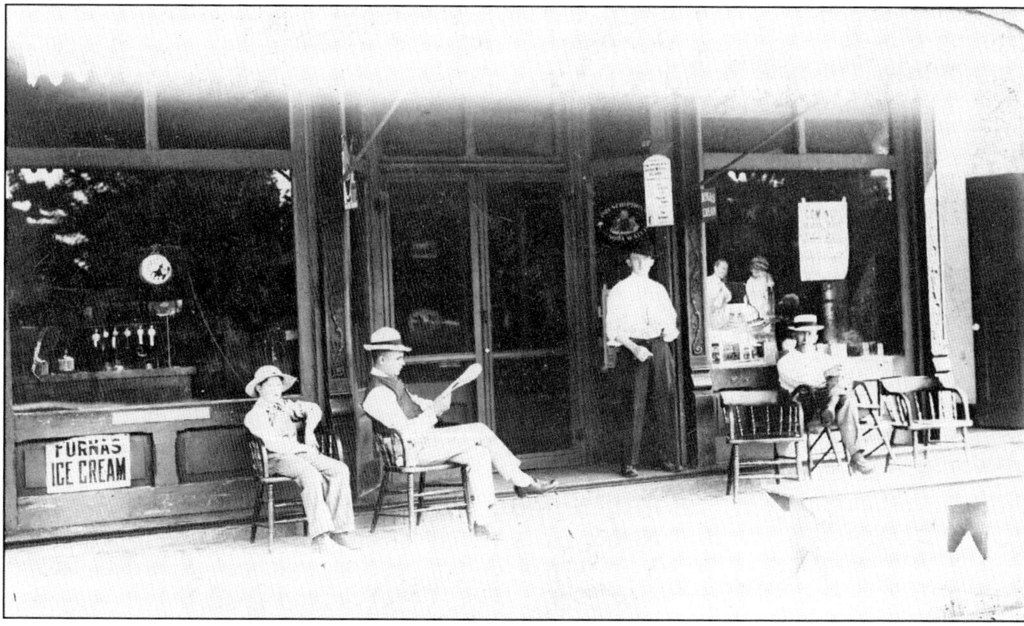

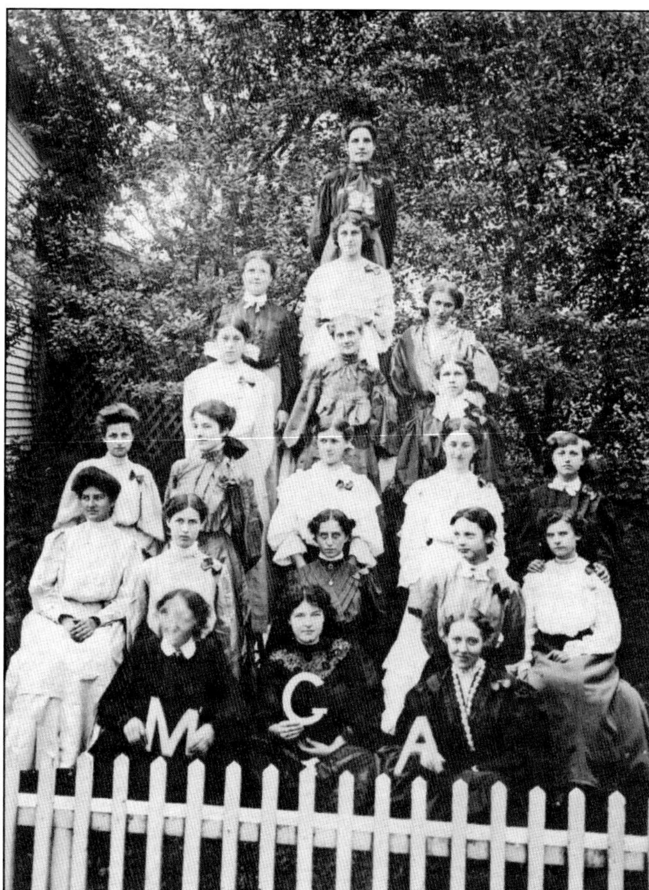

These two pictures represent summer days in Hendricks County. Hats were a part of the attire for these gentlemen on a lazy day in North Salem in the picture above. One man stands at the entrance to the store while the others relax in their chairs. The boy also seems to be enjoying his time of relaxation. At left, these unidentified Pittsboro girls formed a club in 1900, and the following poem describes it: "The girls have organized a club they call the 'M.G.A.,' / and each one is wondering what to them those letters say. / Many opinions have been told as to what those letters mean, / but so careful is the secretary that the books have ne'er been seen. / But coming back to the name, it matters not one cent, / for anyone with eyes can see it's 'Merry Girls Amusement.' " (Above, Bonnie Eggers; left, Hendricks County Museum.)

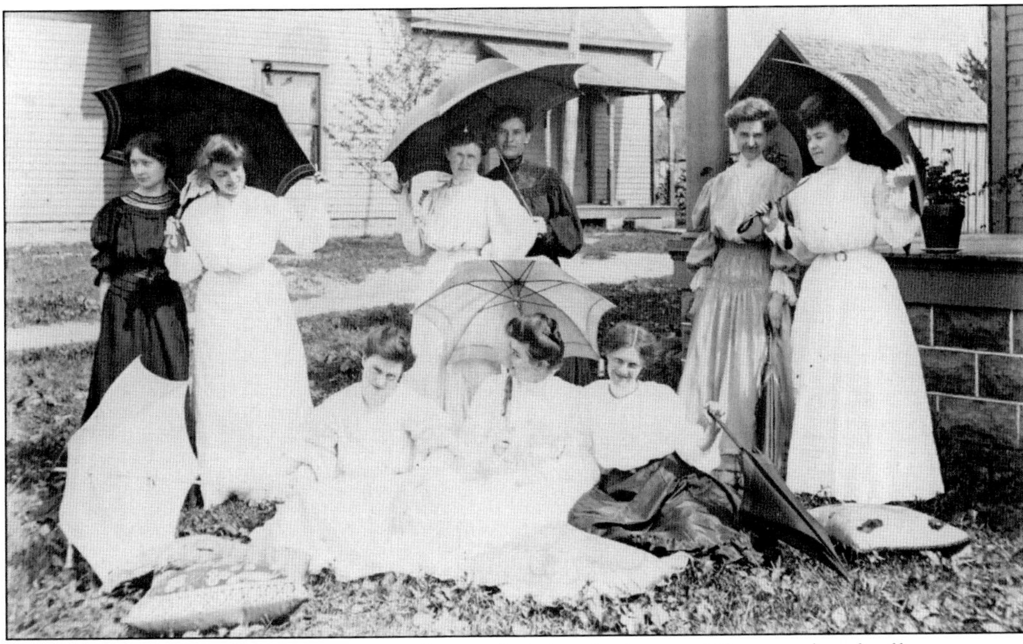

These young ladies enjoyed a summer day in their lovely dresses. They used umbrellas to protect them from the sun. The date given is July 2, 1905. The location is unknown, as are the names of the ladies. (Guilford Township Collection–Plainfield Library.)

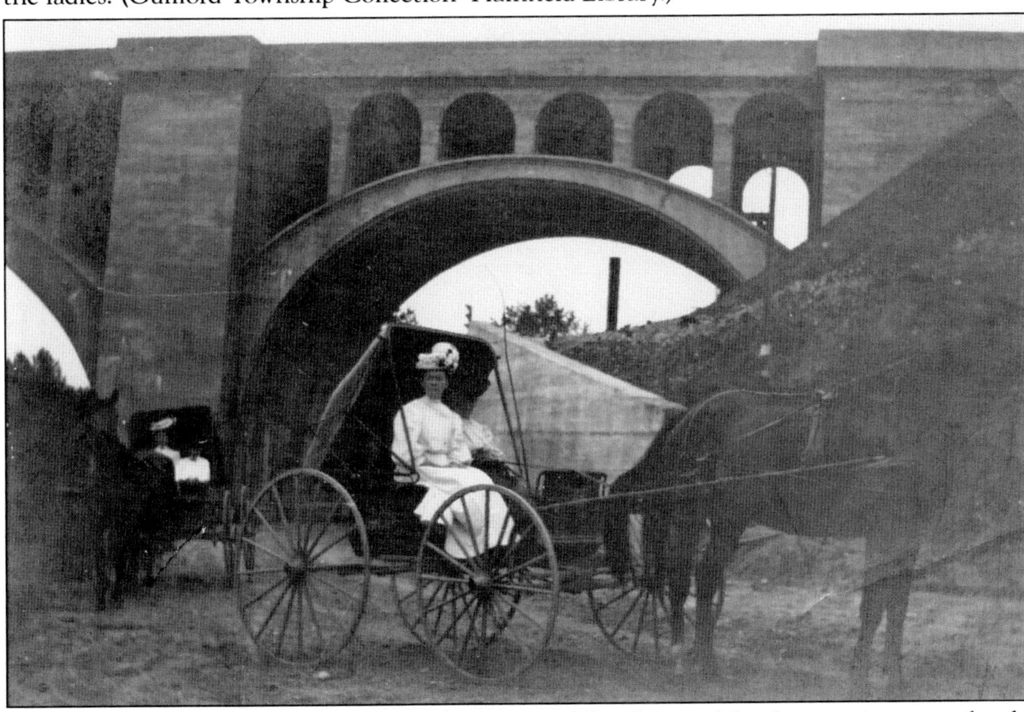

It seems to be a grand day for a ride in the country. The driver of the first carriage must be the photographer. The riders in the second carriage appear to be a woman and a boy. There are two interesting pipe-like structures in the background. This was taken at the Twin Bridges at Danville. (Guilford Township Collection–Plainfield Library.)

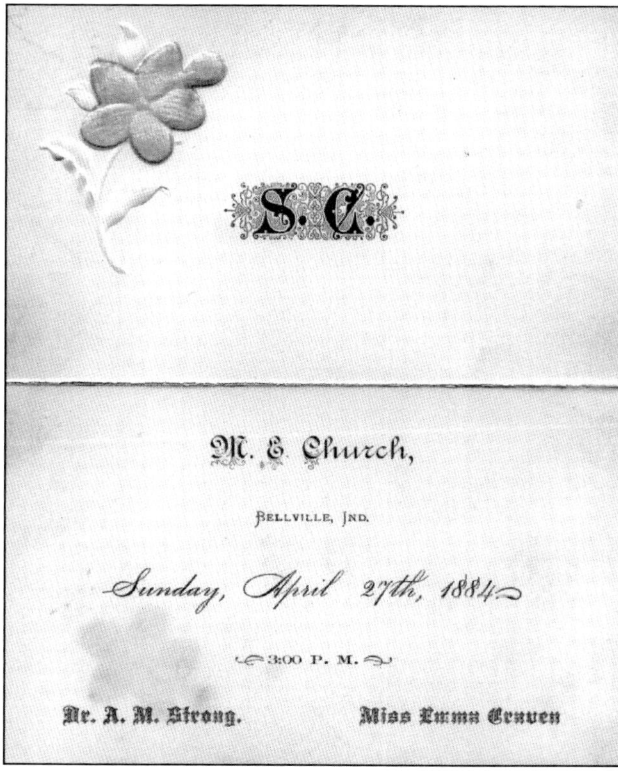

S. C.

M. E. Church,

Bellville, Ind.

Sunday, April 27th, 1884

3:00 P. M.

Mr. A. M. Strong. Miss Emma Craven

On Sunday, April 27 1884, a wedding invitation was extended. Dr. Asa M. Strong and Sarah Emma Craven were to be married in the Belleville Methodist Church. Jonathan F. Woodruff, a minister of the gospel, was to perform the ceremony. Emma and Dr. Strong were together until his death in May 1930. (Hendricks County Museum.)

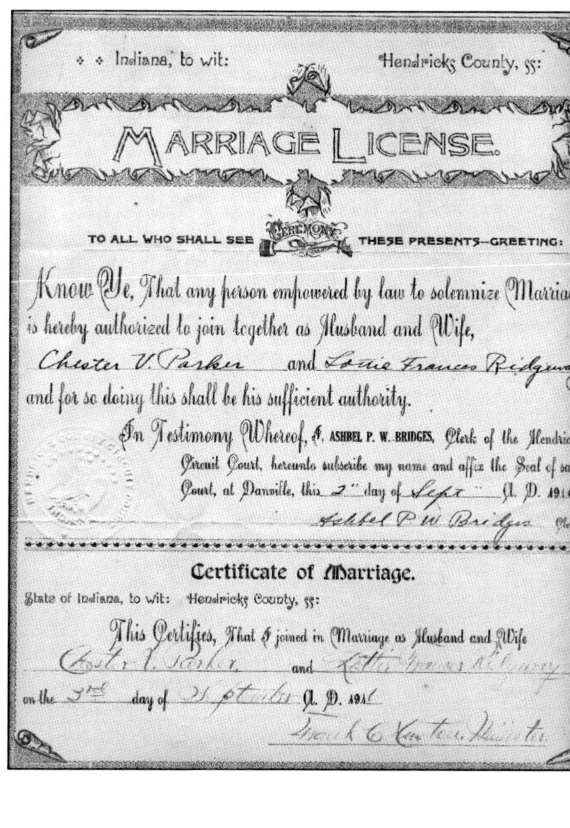

Indiana, to wit: Hendricks County, ss:

MARRIAGE LICENSE.

TO ALL WHO SHALL SEE THESE PRESENTS—GREETING:

Know Ye, That any person empowered by law to solemnize Marriage is hereby authorized to join together as Husband and Wife, Chester V. Parker and Lottie Frances Ridgeway and for so doing this shall be his sufficient authority.

In Testimony Whereof, I, ASHBEL P. W. BRIDGES, Clerk of the Hendricks Circuit Court, hereunto subscribe my name and affix the Seal of said Court, at Danville, this 2nd day of Sept A. D. 1916

Ashbel P. W. Bridges Clerk

Certificate of Marriage.

State of Indiana, to wit: Hendricks County, ss:

This Certifies, That I joined in Marriage as Husband and Wife Chester V. Parker and Lottie Frances Ridgeway on the 3rd day of September A. D. 1916

Chester and Lottie Ridgeway Parker lived in the Pittsboro area. Parker received his teaching degree from Central Normal College in Danville. He taught in a one-room school, called Hamilton, in Union Township. Their children were Ruth, Margaret, and Robert. Parker served in the Indiana House of Representatives from 1934 to 1940. He later opened a tax service business in Pittsboro and was elected county auditor in 1952. (Hendricks County Museum.)

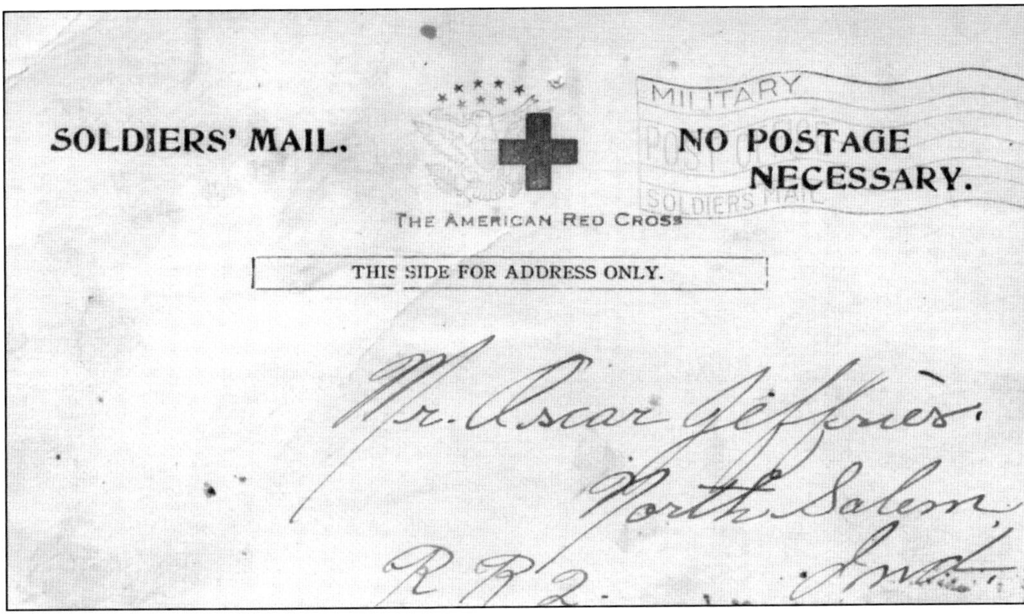
SOLDIERS' MAIL.

NO POSTAGE NECESSARY.

THE AMERICAN RED CROSS

THIS SIDE FOR ADDRESS ONLY.

Mr. Oscar Jeffries.
North Salem,
R R 2. Ind.

It was a happy time for Oscar Jeffries of North Salem when he received the news that his younger brother Ora had arrived safely overseas. Ora was 24 years old, single, and worked as a farmer from Rockville, Indiana, when he joined the service during World War I. The Red Cross assisted soldiers by providing cards and free postage to send news home. It was such a blessing for families to hear from their loved ones in the service. (Both, Hendricks County Museum.)

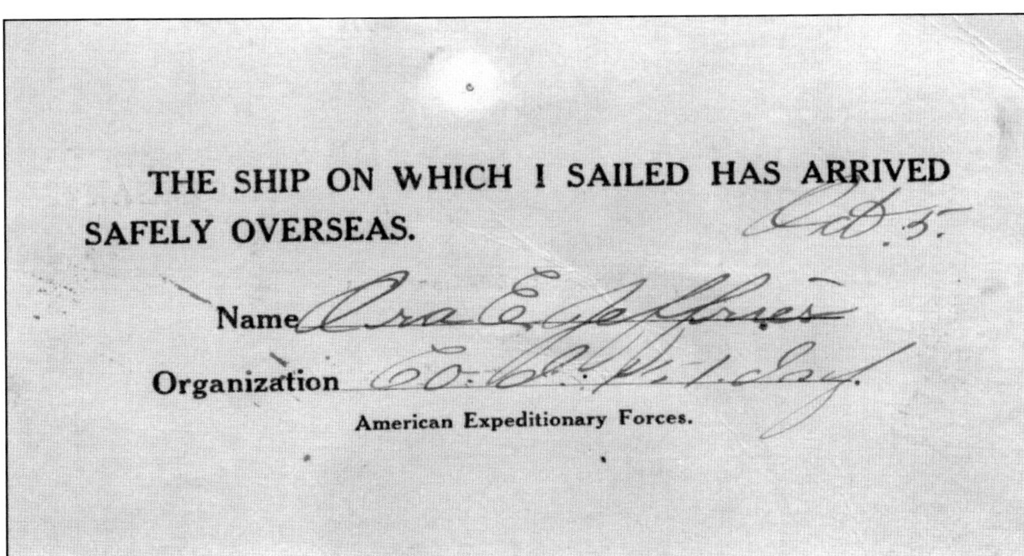
THE SHIP ON WHICH I SAILED HAS ARRIVED SAFELY OVERSEAS. Oct. 5.

Name Ora E. Jeffries

Organization Co. C. 4th Inf.

American Expeditionary Forces.

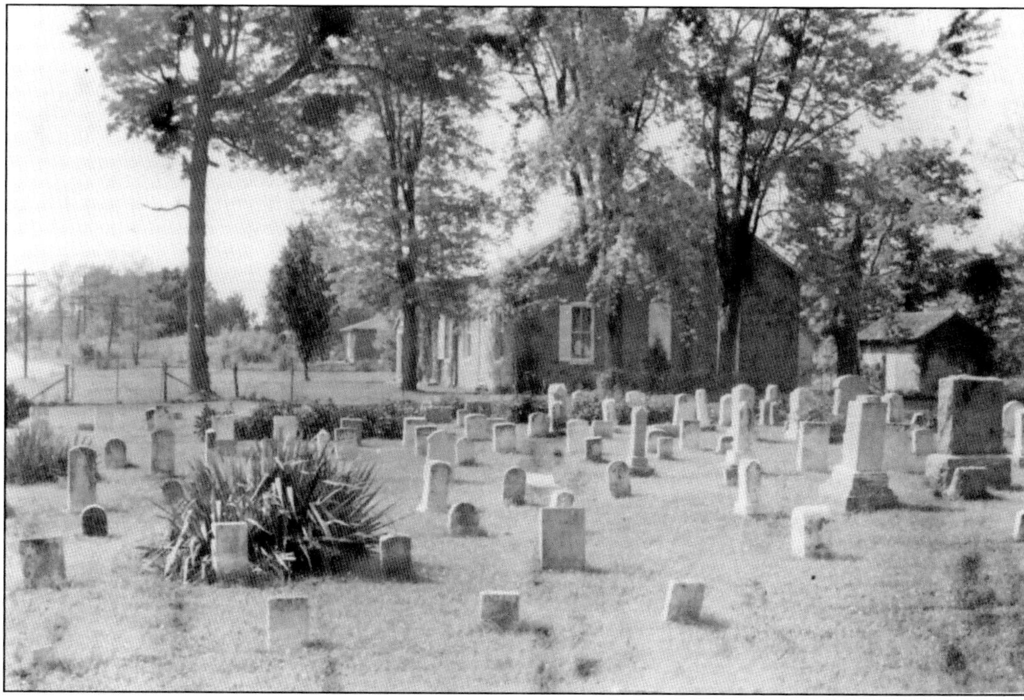

The Sugar Grove Friends Meetinghouse is still standing in Guilford Township. The church got its name from a sugar camp located nearby. Little has changed there, except for additions to the cemetery, and a visit brings back memories of a time past. The meetinghouse is still used for special services. (Guilford Township Collection–Plainfield Library.)

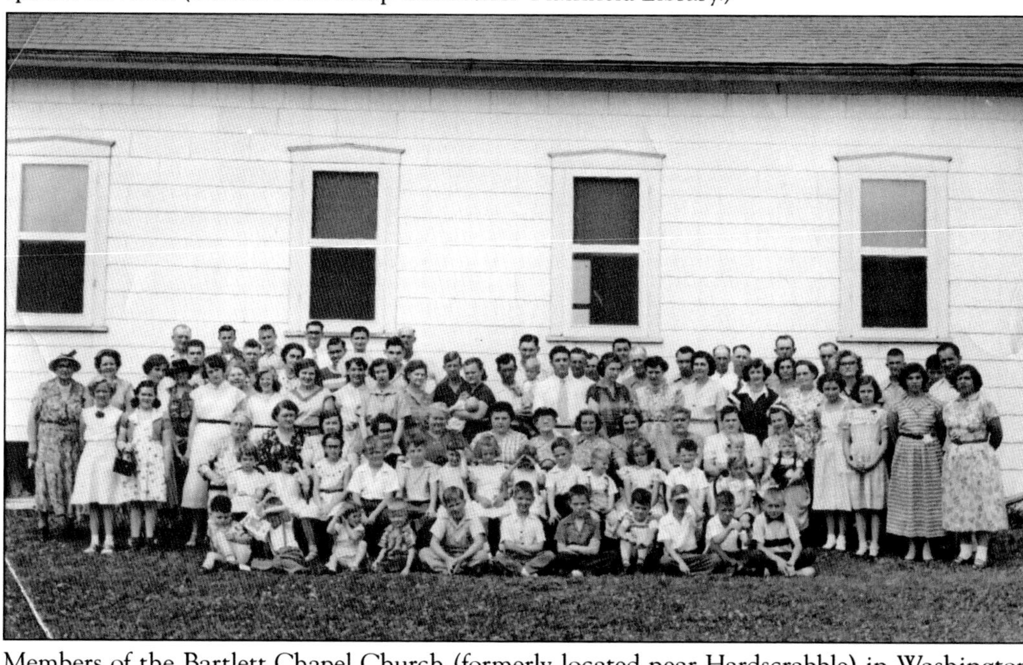

Members of the Bartlett Chapel Church (formerly located near Hardscrabble) in Washington Township proudly gathered together for a group photograph. This picture was taken in the 1950s. (Sue Covey Wood.)

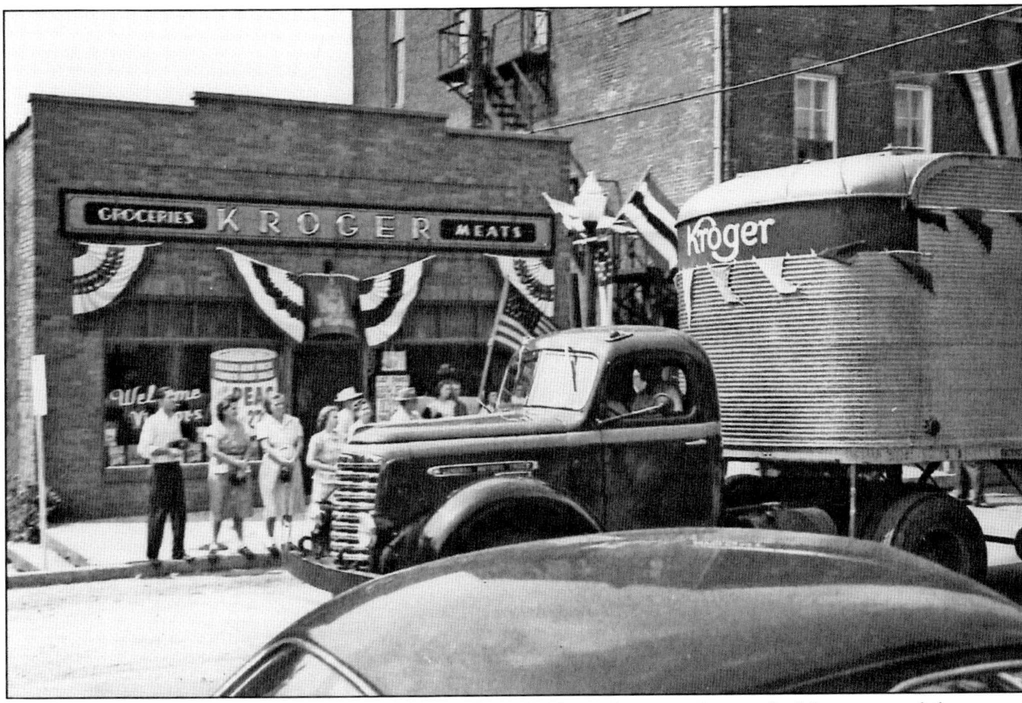

The Brownsburg Centennial was celebrated in 1948, and a parade was held as part of the event. The Kroger grocery truck passes by the Kroger store at 25 East Main Street. Both the truck and the store are decorated in patriotic banners. Kroger later moved to a shopping center on the north side of town. In the picture below, two draft horses pull an antique hearse in the same parade. (Both, Brownsburg Library Collection.)

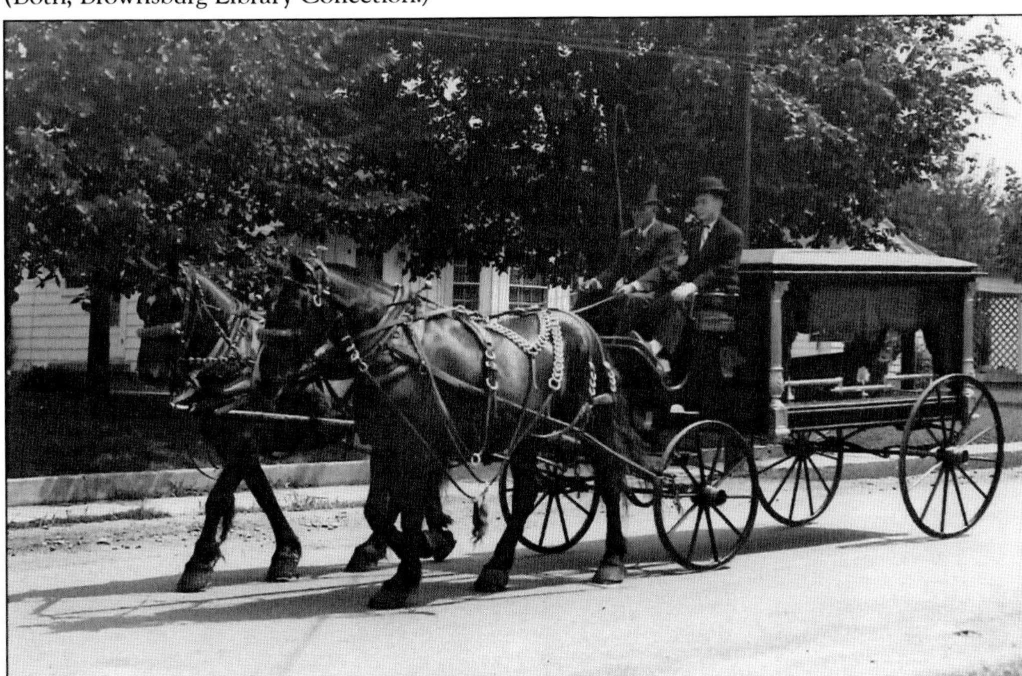

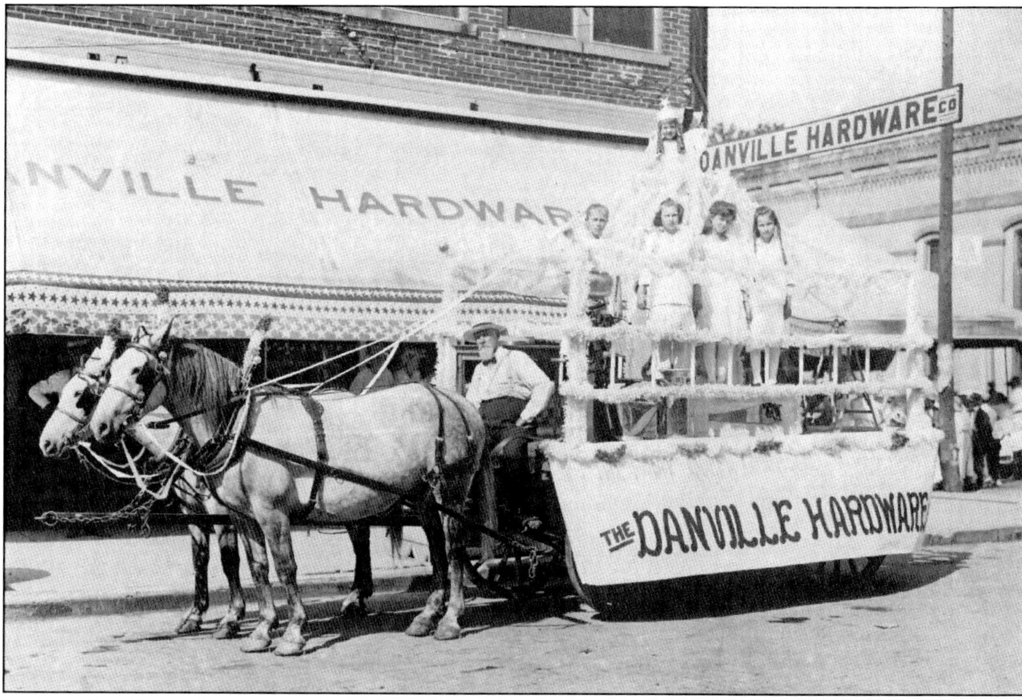

In this 1924 Danville parade, the Danville Hardware float passes by the Danville Hardware store. The hardware store was owned by George Keeney. The girl on the top of the float is Dorothy Gentry. Standing below her on the float are, from left to right, Dora Mills, Ethel Arnold, Elnora Cummings, and Charlotte Tinder. The driver is John McCollum. (Judy Pingel.)

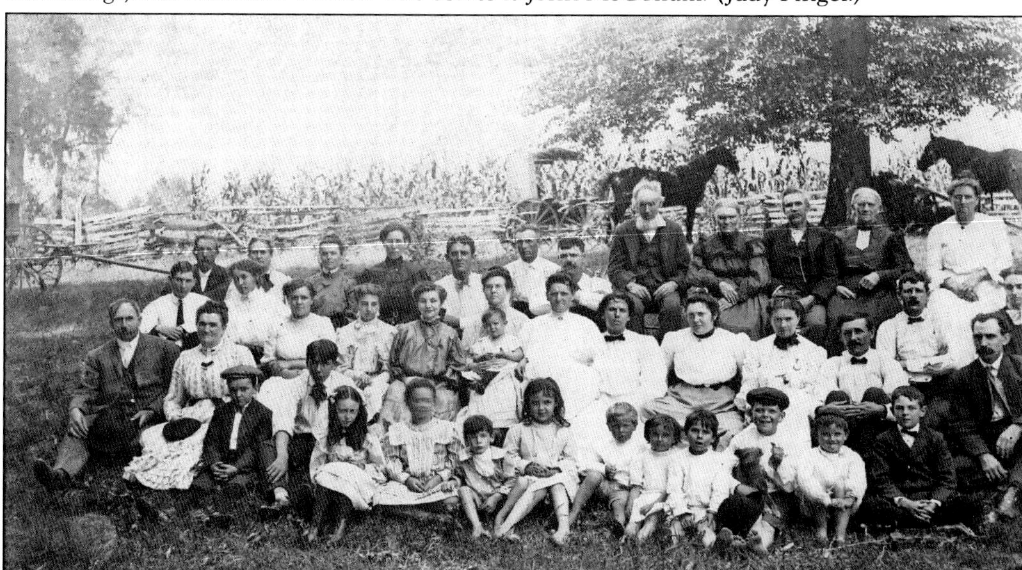

Jehu Rudd was born in 1845 in Indiana and lived in Franklin, Marion, and Clay Townships. He married Sarah Lasley, and they raised a large family. It looks like they got the family together for a reunion. There is a field of corn with a rail fence and a horse and buggy in the background, but those were commonplace to Hoosier ancestors. (Guilford Township Collection–Plainfield Library.)

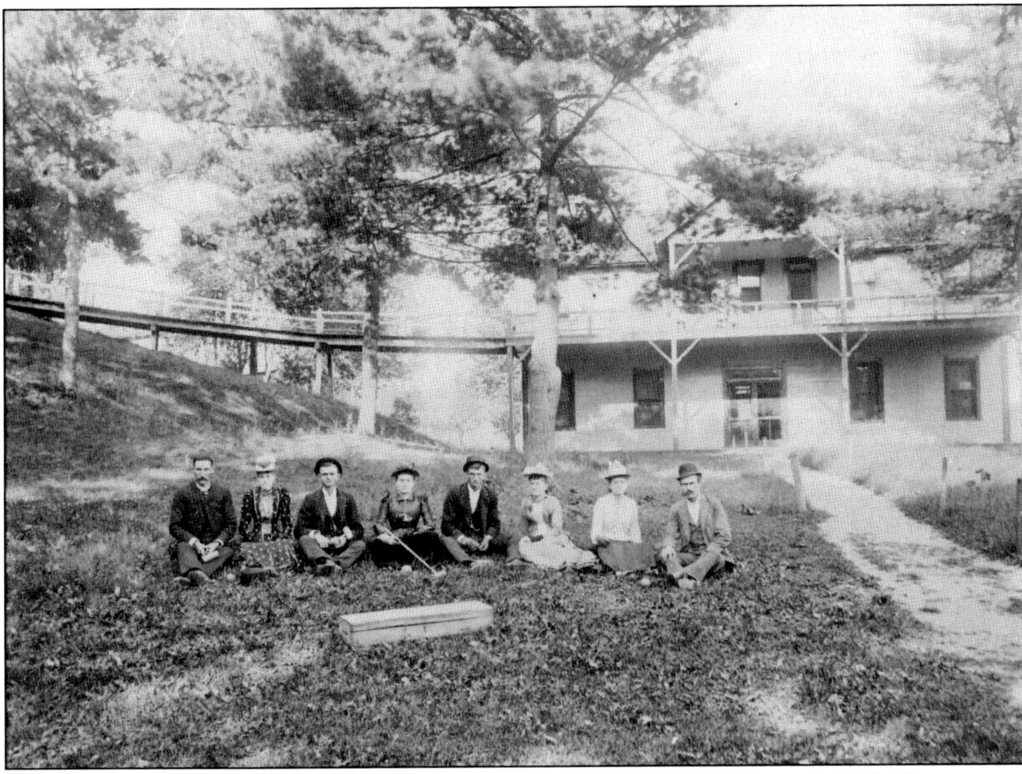

Cartersburg Magnetic Springs was a popular resort from the late 1890s until 1906. Visitors came from all over the country to refresh themselves in the healing waters of the springs. There was a hotel, which was filled during the summer months. Many reunions, banquets, and elegant parties were held at the springs. The hotel was a wooden structure, and in September 1906, a fire destroyed it. The hotel was not rebuilt. The picture below shows Jim McCormick as he drove the Cartersburg Magnetic Springs water delivery truck to Indianapolis and other areas in 1915. The water was delivered for many years after the resort closed. (Both, Hendricks County Museum.)

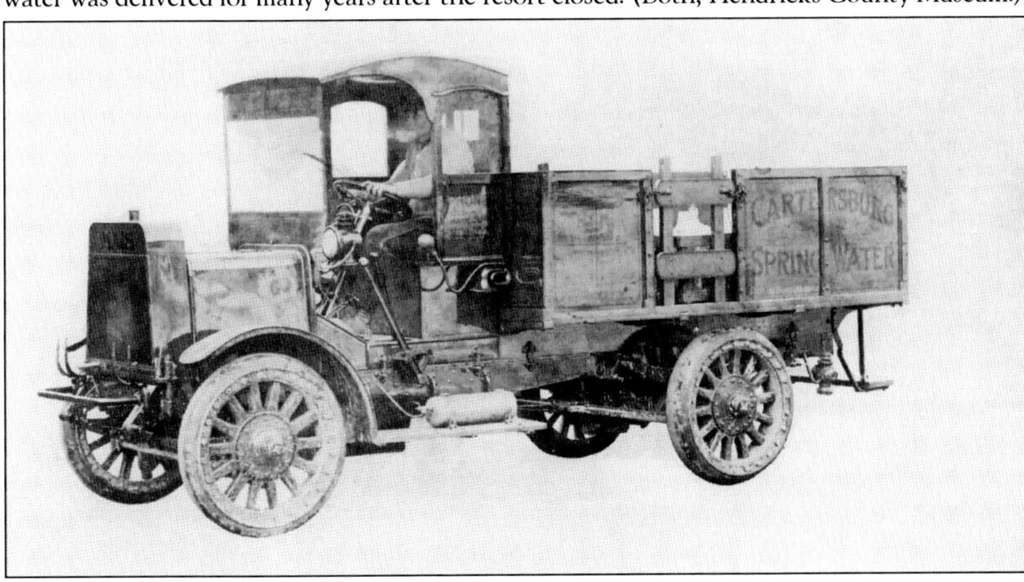

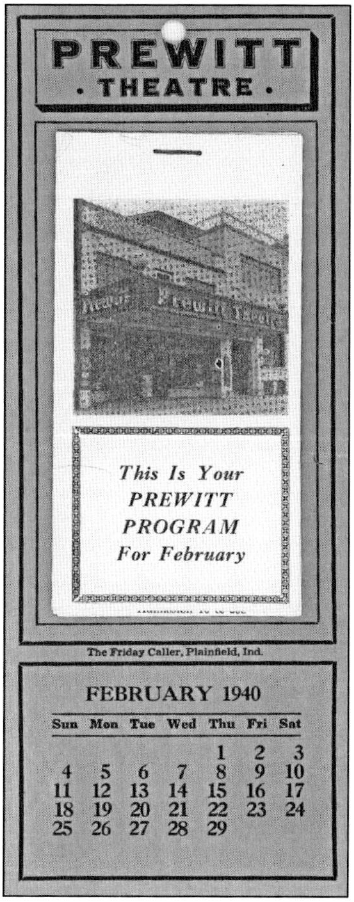

The Prewitt Theatre in Plainfield had its formal opening in November 1927. Prices for movies were 12¢ for children under 12, 15¢ for adults, and 35¢ for a box seat. The Prewitt family lived in an upstairs apartment over the theater. Today, the former movie theater sits idle. (Harley Sheets.)

The drive-in movie was a popular form of entertainment in the 1940s and 1950s. Hendricks County had at least three drive-ins. This poster shows that Coatesville hosted outdoor movie showings at Harlan's Grove. In the late 1950s, Coatesville also had outdoor movies on Saturday nights in the summertime on the street. (Hendricks County Museum.)

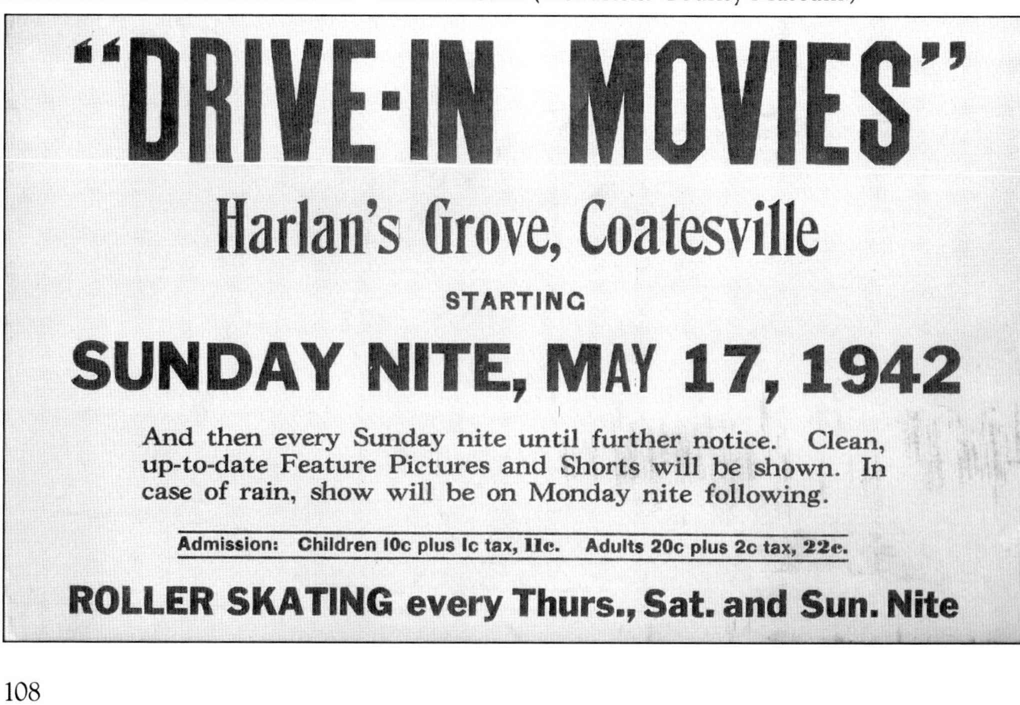

This interesting ad ran in the *Plainfield Messenger* in 1934. John Russell Stair, whose name was misspelled in the ad, flew the plane from the Thomas Harvey Little Field, which was just west of Plainfield. In the picture below, Thomas Harvey Little's son-in-law Dr. Walter Sharer is seated in the plane, ready to fly. He was good friends with Stair. John Stair gave flying lessons to Purdue students and others, and two of his students were Roger Chaffee and John Glenn, who later became NASA astronauts. (Both, Robert Sharer.)

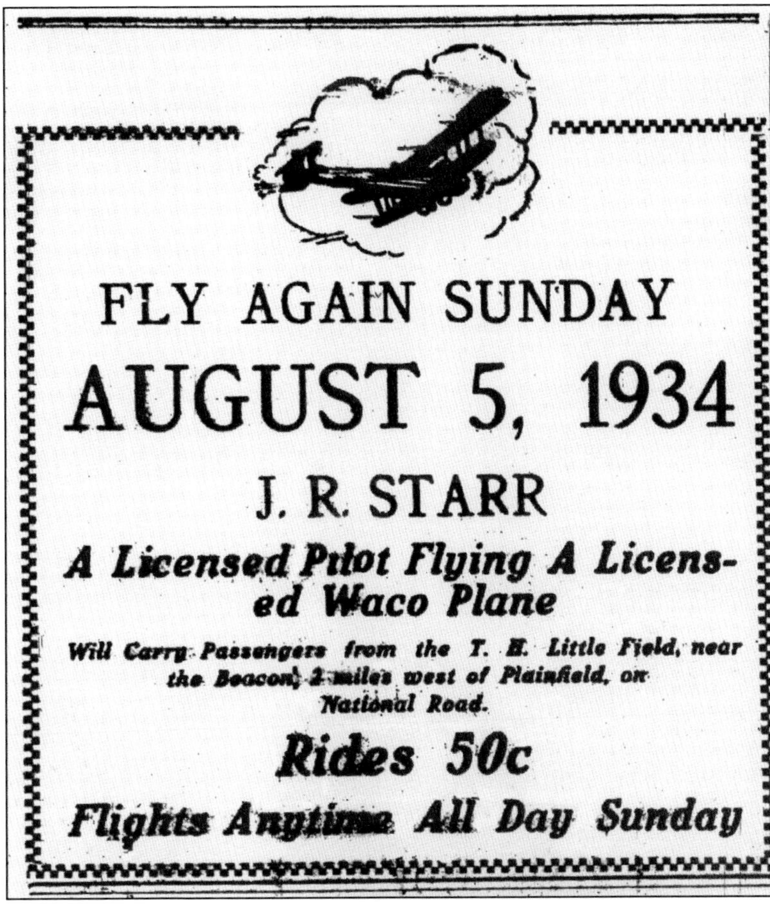

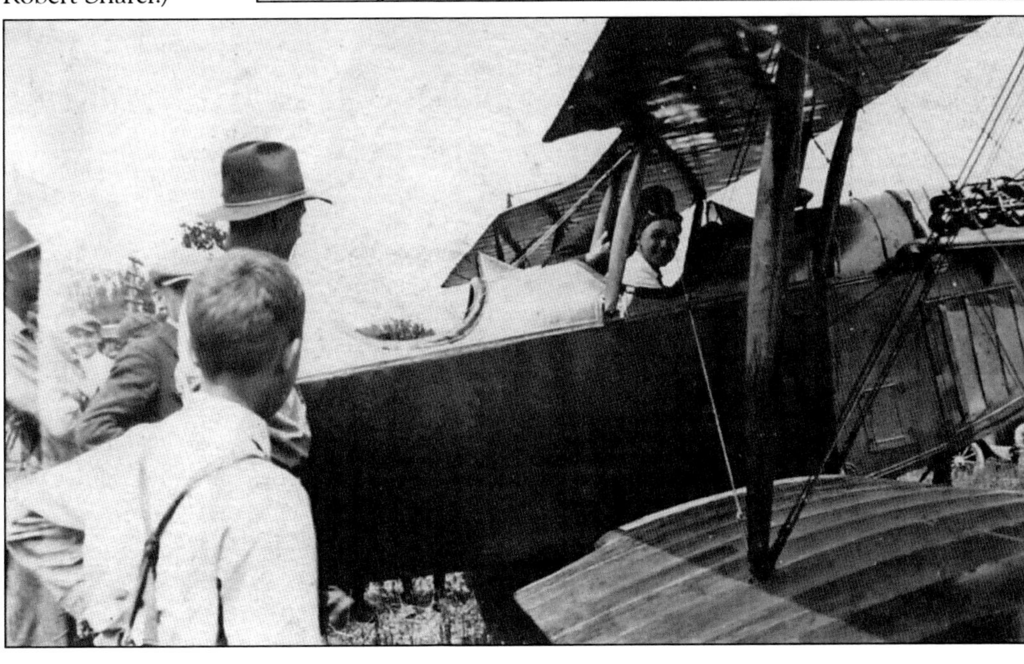

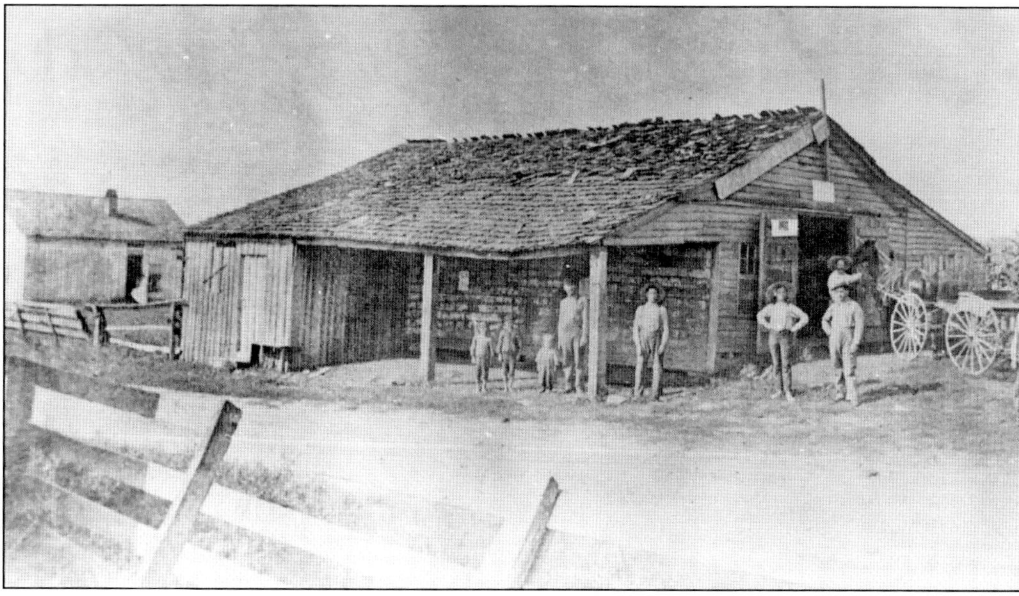

Center Valley was located in Liberty Township. It included the Friendship Regular (Primitive) Baptist Church, a cemetery, a school, a blacksmith shop (above), a general store (below), and a post office. A brick school was built in 1882 and used until 1901. The building still stands and is a private residence today. (Both, Guilford Township Collection–Plainfield Library.)

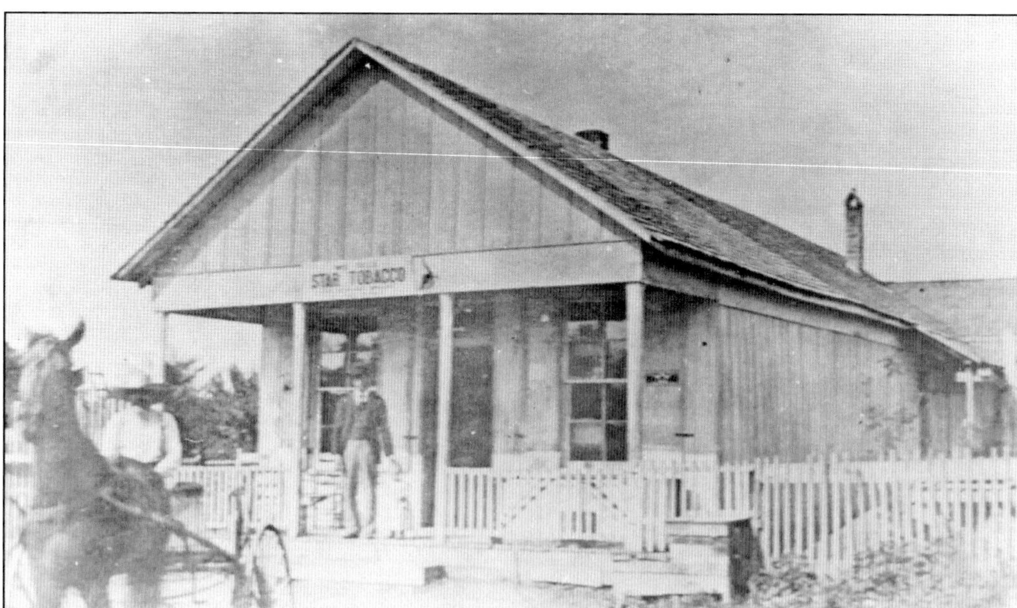

Six

Communities Remembered

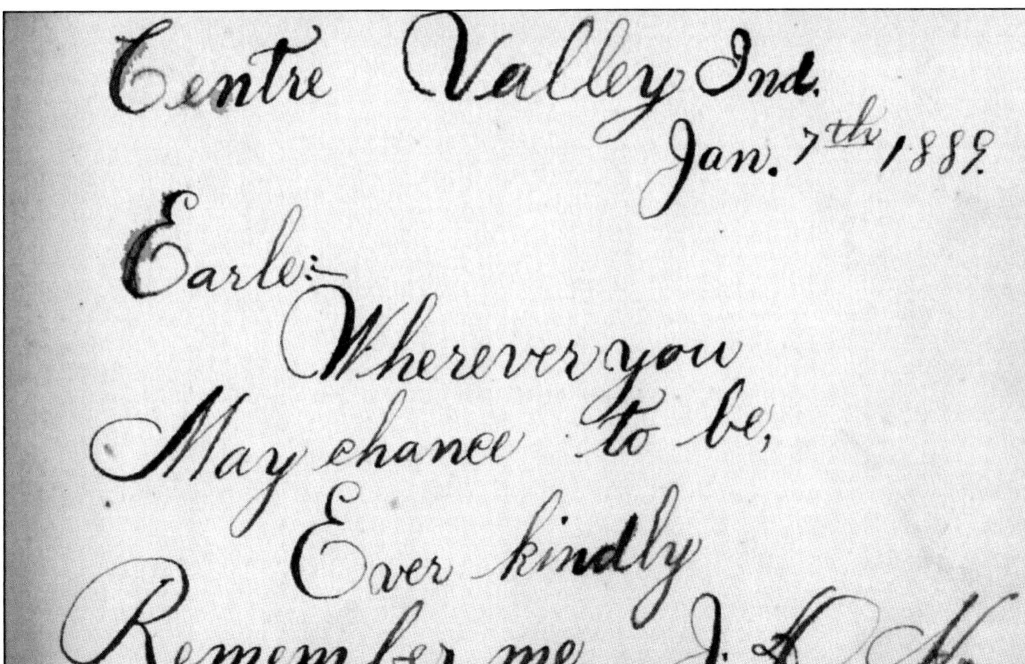

Centre Valley Ind.
Jan. 7th 1889.
Earle:—
Wherever you
May chance to be,
Ever kindly
Remember me. J. L. H.

This final chapter shares some information about communities that have disappeared over time. The first one is Center Valley. The autograph book was a popular way to remember friends. This message was written in 1889 and is addressed to Earle of Centre Valley. Earle's last name was Craven, like many others at Center Valley. (Hendricks County Museum.)

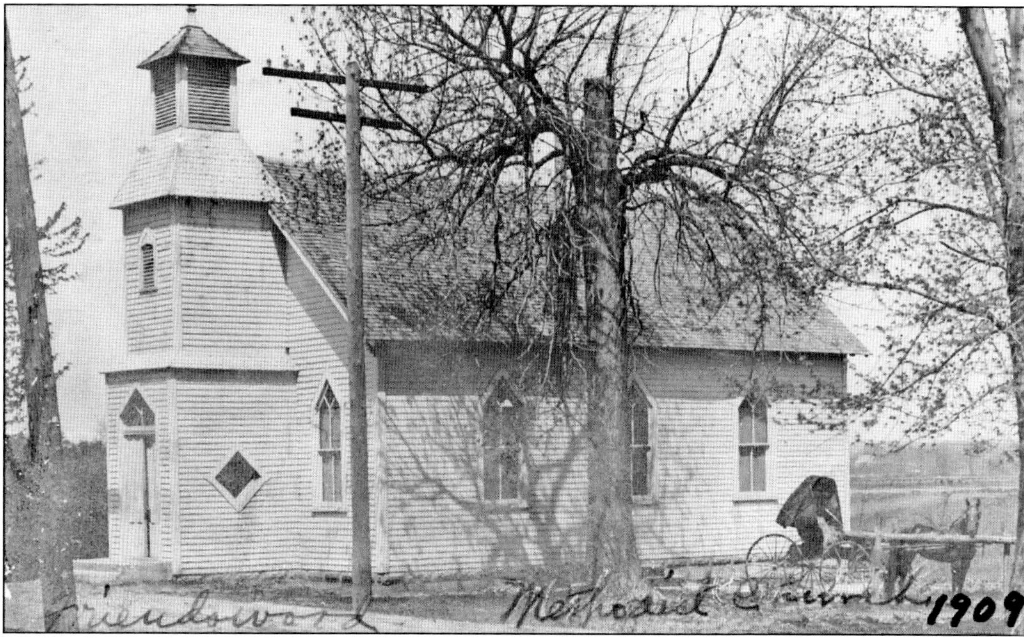

Friendswood, in Guilford Township, was platted in 1871. It had the Kellum & Co. Cheese Factory, a general store, a railroad depot, a sawmill, a gristmill, two blacksmith shops, a wagon shop, and a school. A tollgate was located on a gravel road near Friendswood. The Friendswood Methodist Church is shown in 1909. The minister often served the surrounding churches in addition to his own church. (Guilford Township Collection–Plainfield Library.)

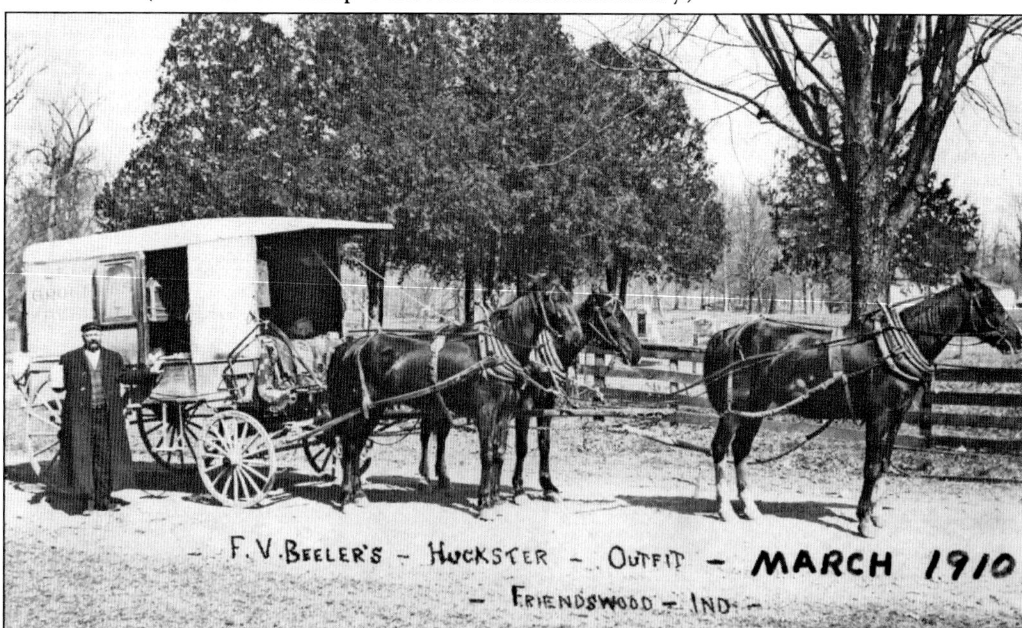

Frederick Beeler (1851–1926) traveled the Friendswood area with his huckster wagon, selling merchandise from his general store door to door. He ran his huckster business from 1876 to 1913. It was a popular form of business for merchants at the time. (Guilford Township Collection–Plainfield Library.)

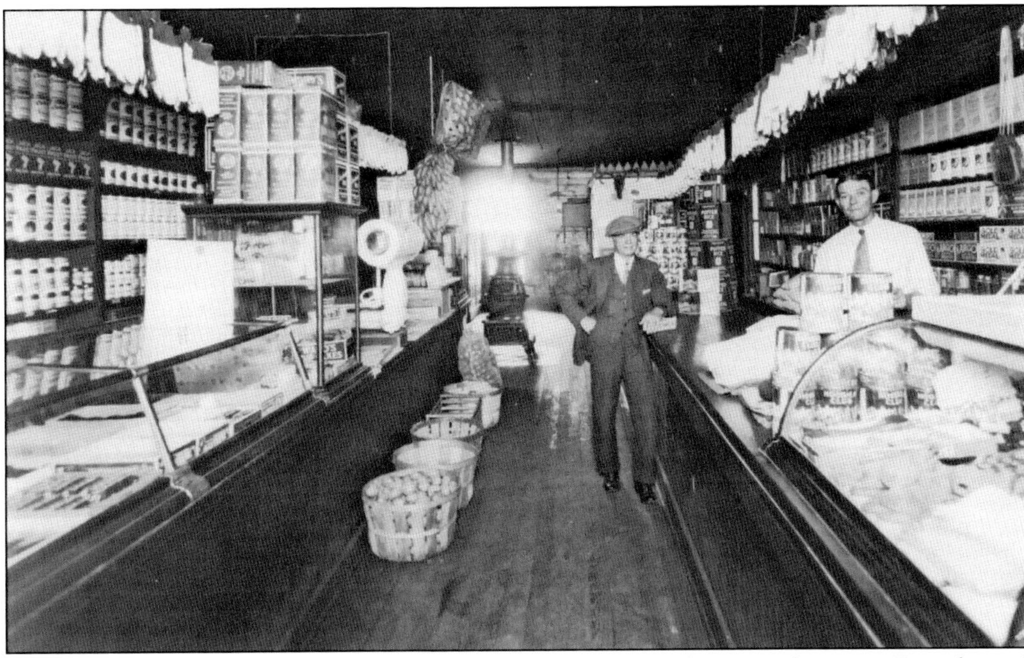

Fredrick Beeler and his wife, Ella Beeler (1858–1948), owned the general store in Friendswood. After Fred's death, Ella continued to run the business. By 1920, their son Charles (1876–1960) was operating the store. Note all the changes that had been made in the Beeler store from 1928 (above) to 1947 (below). (Both, Guilford Township Collection–Plainfield Library.)

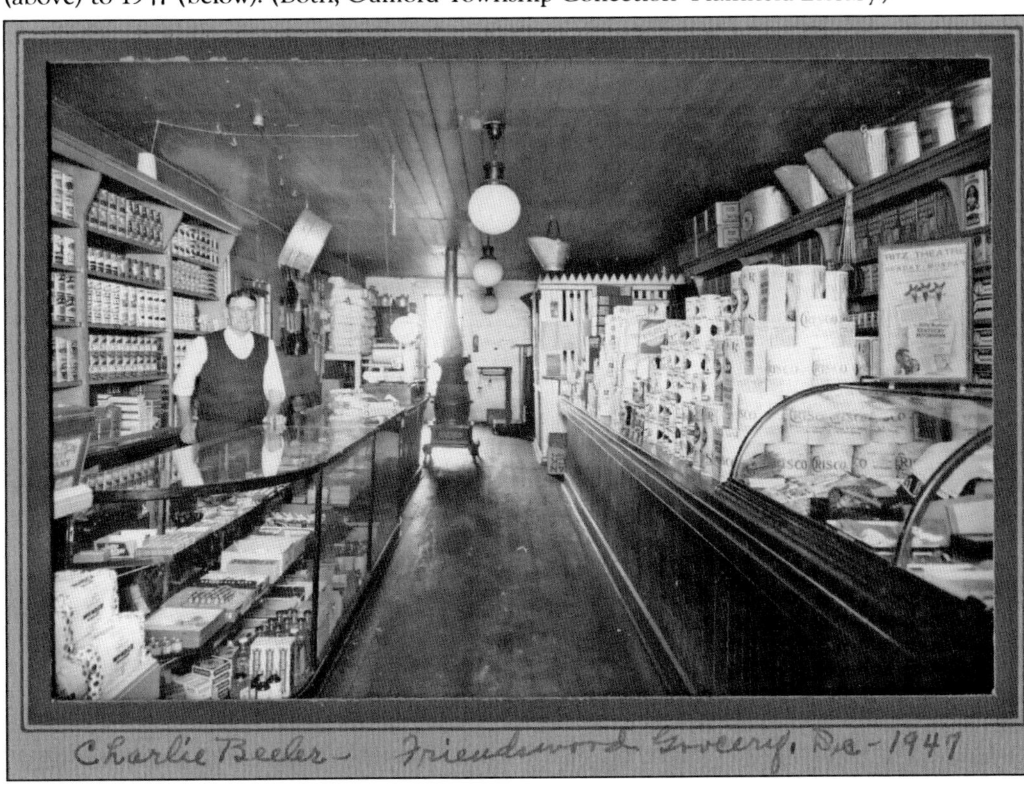

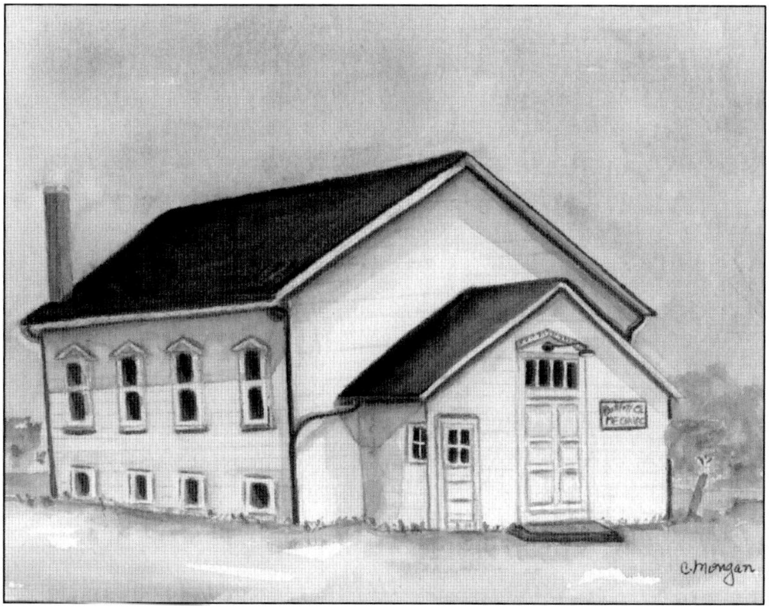

Gale was located in Center Township at old US 36 and CR 300 East. It had a blacksmith, a hardware store, a post office (1882–1906), and the Bartlett Chapel Church. In 1860, the church was a one-room frame building. In 1961, when the congregation relocated a few miles east to Hardscrabble, the original church building became the clubhouse for the Hendricks County Golf Course. (Drawing by Carol Mongan, Bartlett Chapel Church.)

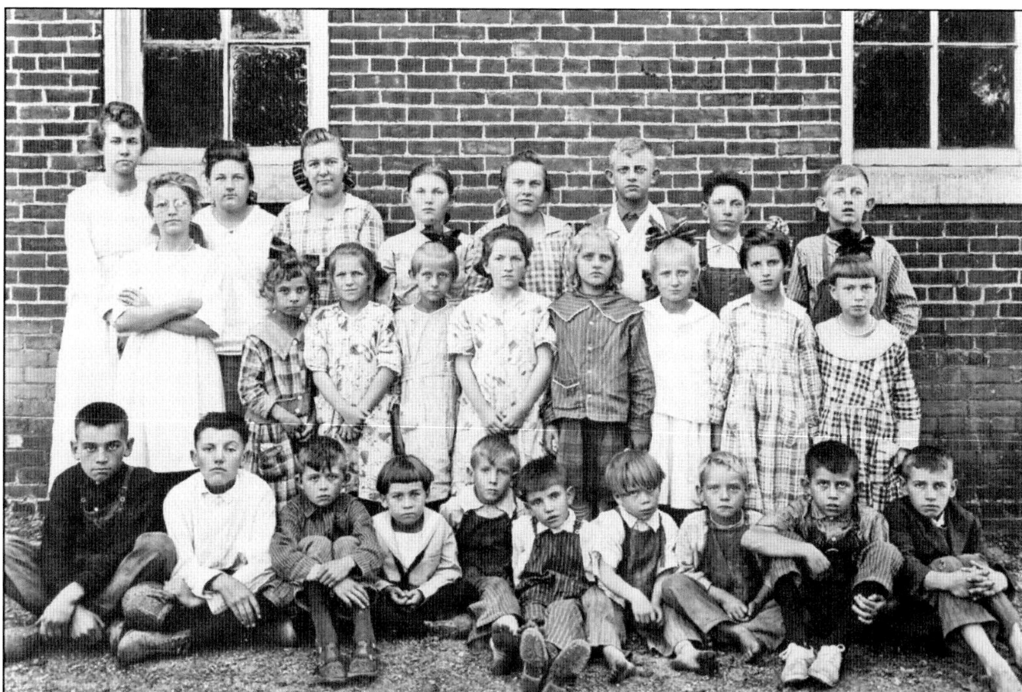

Jordan School was located between Danville and Gale. Students in 1919 are, from left to right, (first row) Orel Carter, Howard Cain, Ivan Gibbs, unidentified, Maurice Brady, Richard Cain, Bryon Stanley, Marion Walter, Aaron Gibbs, and unidentified; (second row) Marguerite Stanley, ? Carter, Pauline Stanley, Marion Gibbs, Esther Stanley, Rita Walters, Maxine Woods, Mary Cain, and Mildred Hughes; (third row) Beulah Brady, Grace Cox, Gertrude Hughes, Eunice Thompson, Dorotha Hughes, Joe Gibbs, Emmett Stanley, and unidentified. (Hendricks County Museum.)

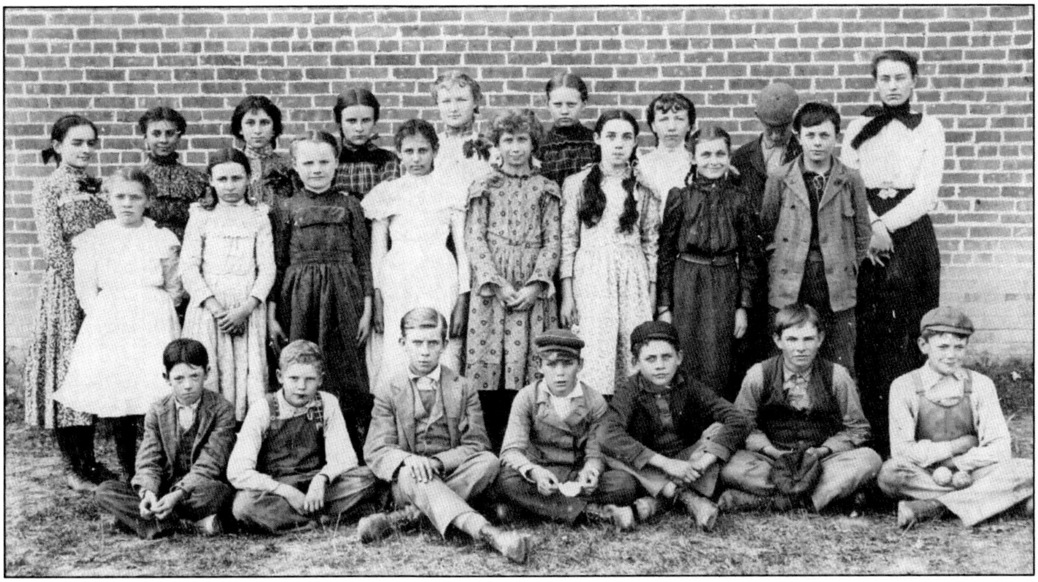

Hadley was first named Mimosa. Located on the northern edge of Clay Township, it was laid out in 1872 along the New York Central Railroad. The Mimosa Post Office was established in 1871 and changed to Hadley in 1874. The post office closed about 1922. These young students attended school at Hadley. (Hendricks County Museum.)

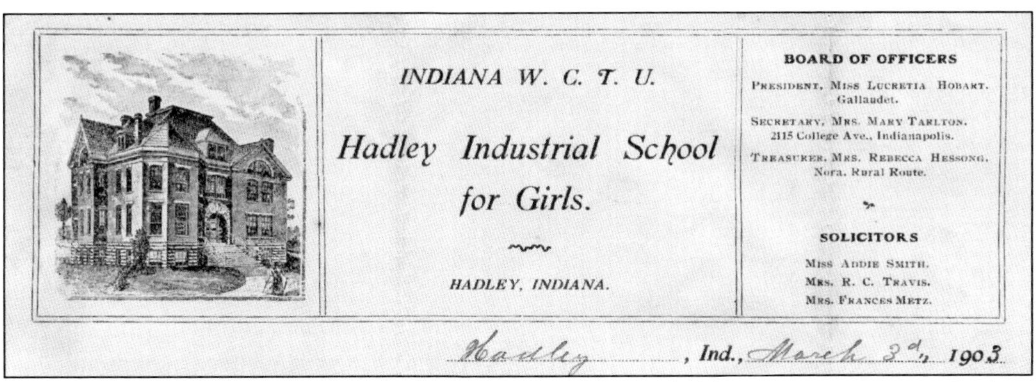

INDIANA W. C. T. U.

Hadley Industrial School for Girls.

HADLEY, INDIANA.

BOARD OF OFFICERS

PRESIDENT, MISS LUCRETIA HOBART.
Gallaudet.

SECRETARY, MRS. MARY TARLTON.
2115 College Ave., Indianapolis.

TREASURER, MRS. REBECCA HESSONG.
Nora, Rural Route.

SOLICITORS

MISS ADDIE SMITH.
MRS. R. C. TRAVIS.
MRS. FRANCES METZ.

Hadley, Ind., March 3d, 1903

The dedication of the Hadley Industrial School for Girls was held on August 17, 1894. Quakers Addison and Martha Hadley founded it to help orphan girls. The school's goal was to provide young ladies with the skills of homemakers. The school lasted 15 years. This was the school's letterhead, showing the brick school; it is dated 1903. (Hendricks County Museum.)

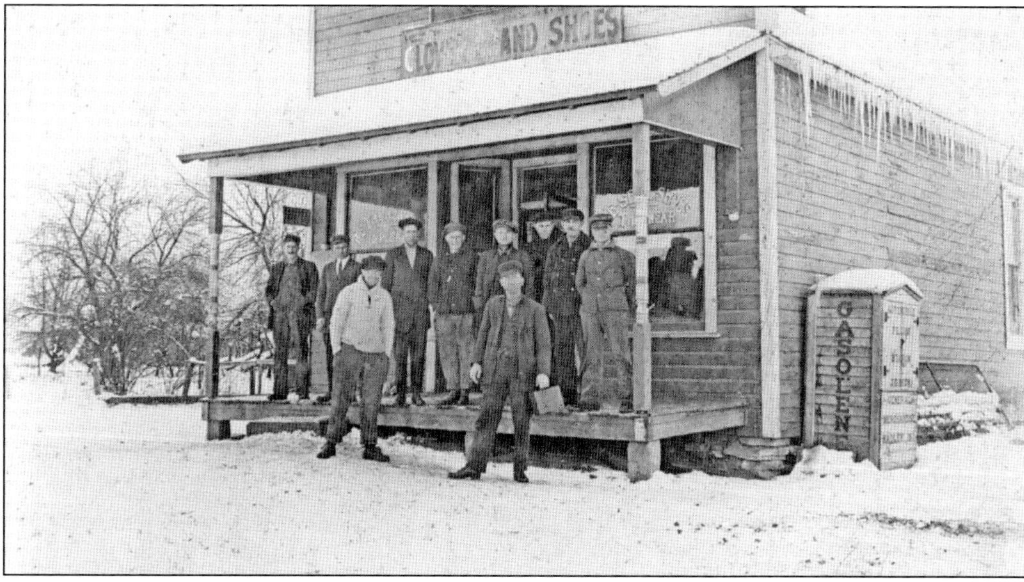

The Hadley General Store displays its motto, "We Try Always to Please," in the window at the right. Over the door, Clover brand shoes are advertised. An article in a newspaper about J.W. Gentry stated that he opened a general store at Hadley in 1896. He later became county sheriff. The grocery was a casualty of the terrible tornado that ripped through the county on Good Friday 1948. (Bonnie Eggers.)

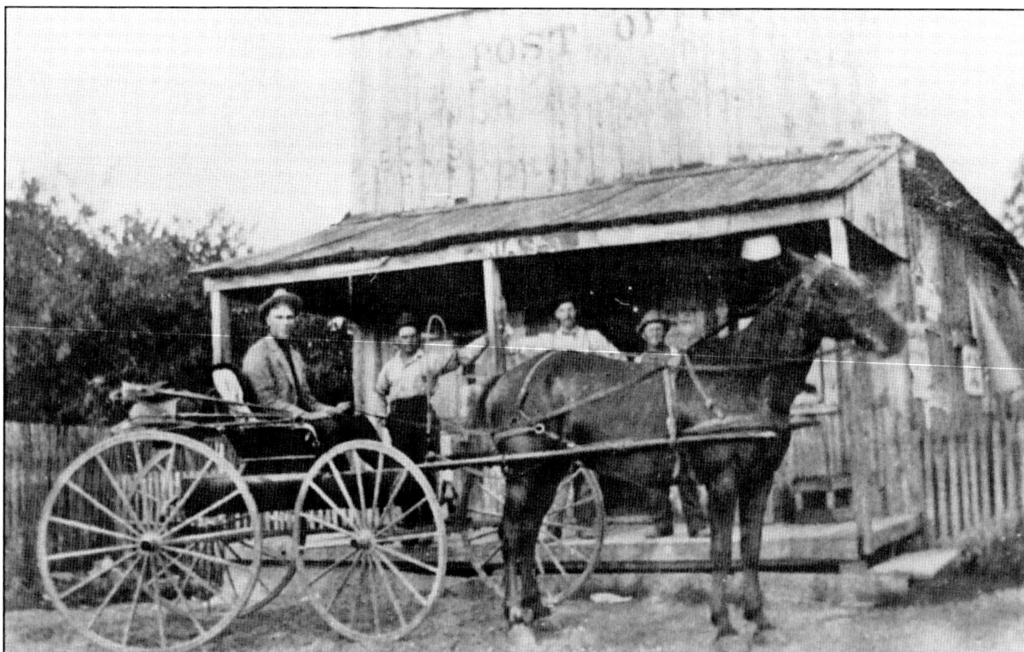

Joppa was a lively settlement and trading center in the southwest corner of Guilford Township. During the Civil War, it had a sawmill, a general store, a blacksmith shop, and a wagon factory. The Joppa Post Office's first postmaster was Joshua Cook. The office was established February 1880 and closed October 1893. It was reestablished in June 1897 and was active until February 1903. (Guilford Township Collection–Plainfield Library.)

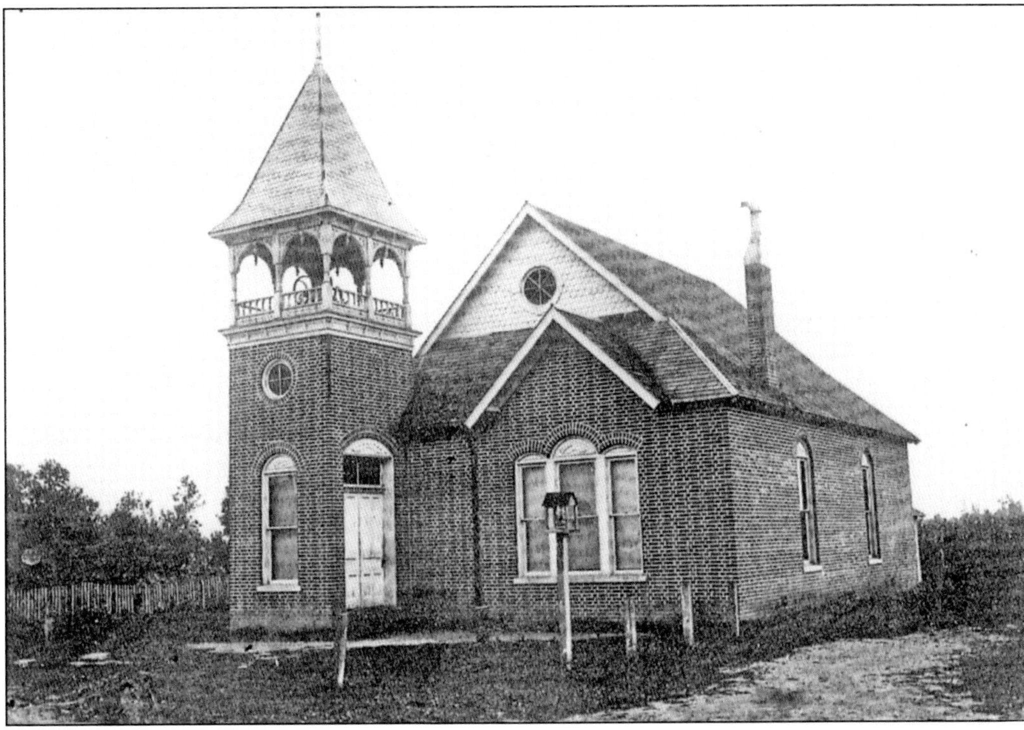

Maplewood is approximately two miles south and two miles west of Pittsboro. Maplewood had a tile and brick factory, a grain elevator, a Christian church, a school, and a post office. The post office operated between 1881 and 1912. The Maplewood Church was the hub of the area from 1885 to 1998. When the church disbanded, the building took on a new life by becoming the home for the Hendricks County Theatre. The picture above shows how the building once looked, and the picture below shows the building as it looks today. (Both, Hendricks County Museum.)

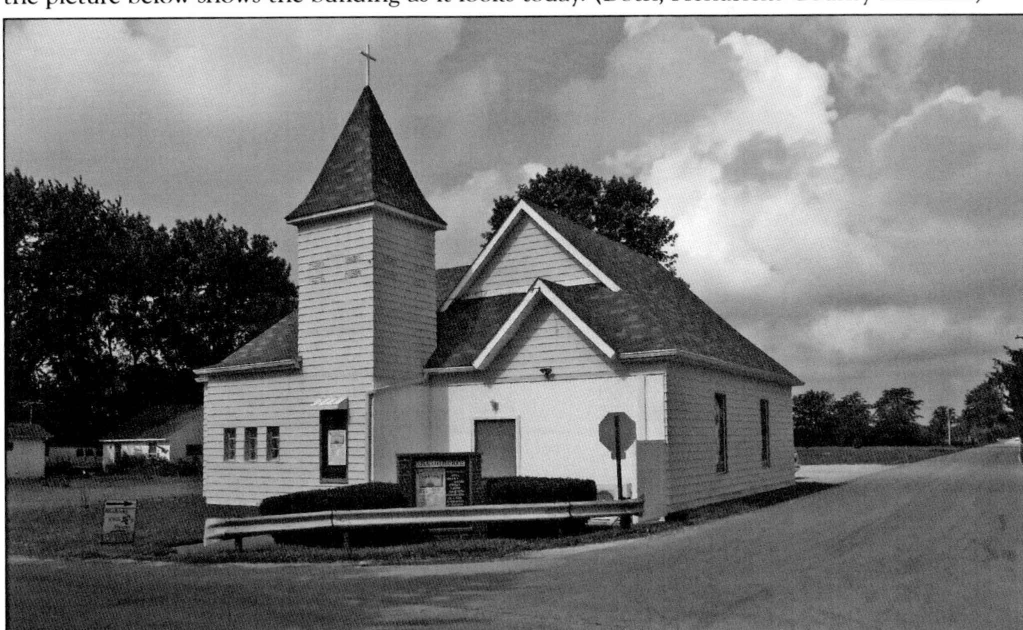

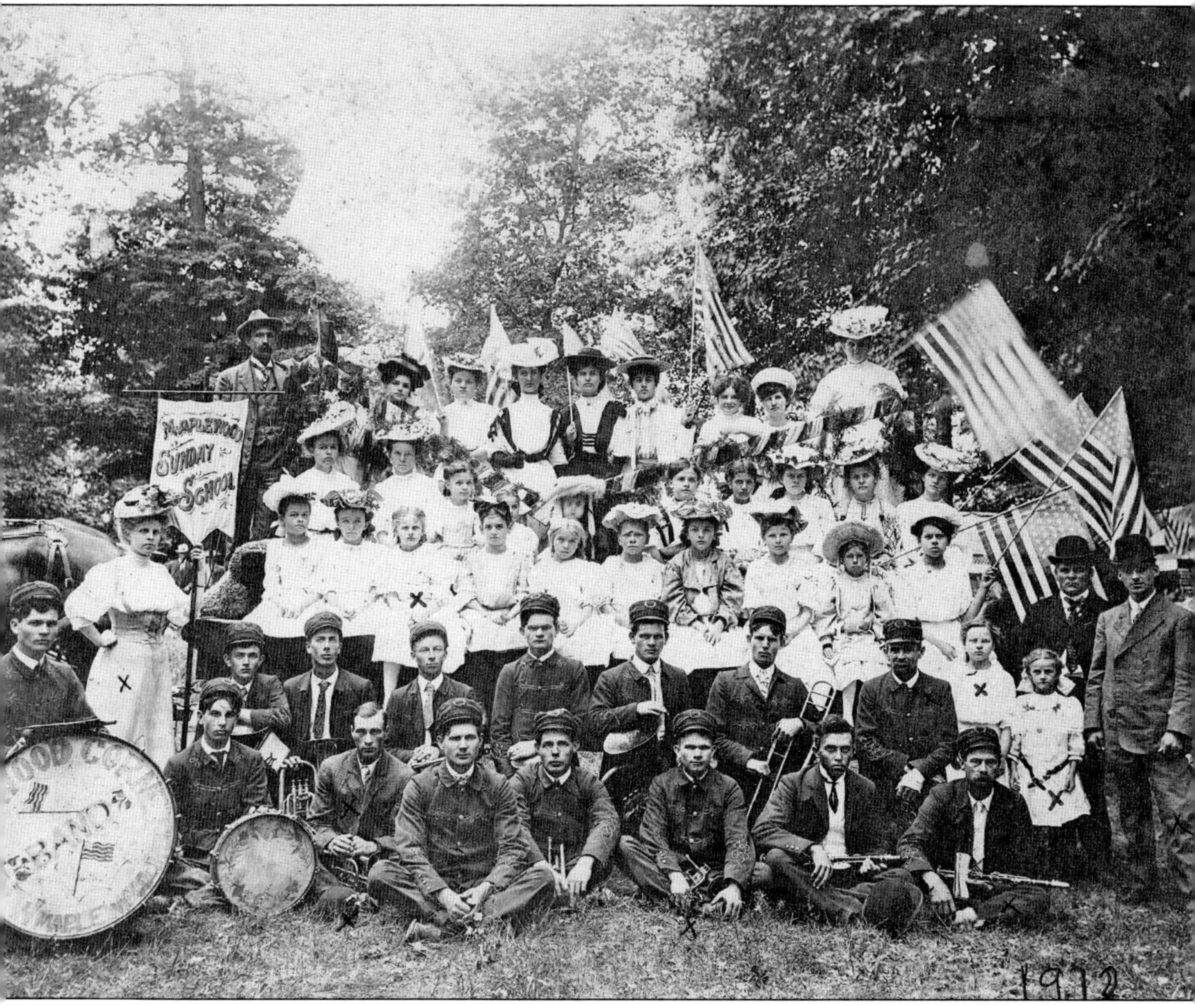

The Maplewood Sunday school band around 1912 included, from left to right, (first row) Russell Long (with drum), Lester Rounds, Porter Bryant, Arthur Strader, Raymond Thompson, Fred Parker, unidentified, Ora Bryant, and three unidentified; (second row) Mabel Parker Moore Bruner (standing), Virgil Hughes, Tom Swain, Clair Alexander, Hollis Long, Bert Long, Charlie Strader, John Hughes, Minnie Long Underwood, Edna Long Zimmerman, and Aubrey Moore; (third row) Edith Sears Wellman, Esta Rounds Sallee, Epha Parker Gray, Zoe Ray, unidentified, Hester Hughes, Goldie Hughes, Geraldine Long Kircher, Inez Long, Edna Clark, and John E. Parker; (fourth row) Ruth Long Thompson, Myrtle Long, unidentified, Stella Gentry, two unidentified, Nellie Strader, unidentified, Nellie Long Oldfield, and Grace Long Money; (fifth row) George Moore, unidentified, Fleda Moore Hughes, Bessie Long Clark, Anna Goodson, Opal Strader, Dale Alexander, Gertrude Gatson, Inez Strader Long, and unidentified. (Hendricks County Museum.)

Montclair is located in Union Township. It was originally named Singer Station. This community had two garages, a blacksmith, a wagon shop, a sawmill, a tile yard, and a railroad depot. The post office operated from 1880 to 1929. The Montclair No. 7 School building was reported in "fair" condition in 1878. At right is the school report that teacher Margaret Bailey kept in 1917. This once-bustling community is now a quiet rural area, consisting of several homes and a Christian church. The picture below shows the church building. (Right, Hendricks County Museum; below, Gail Tharp.)

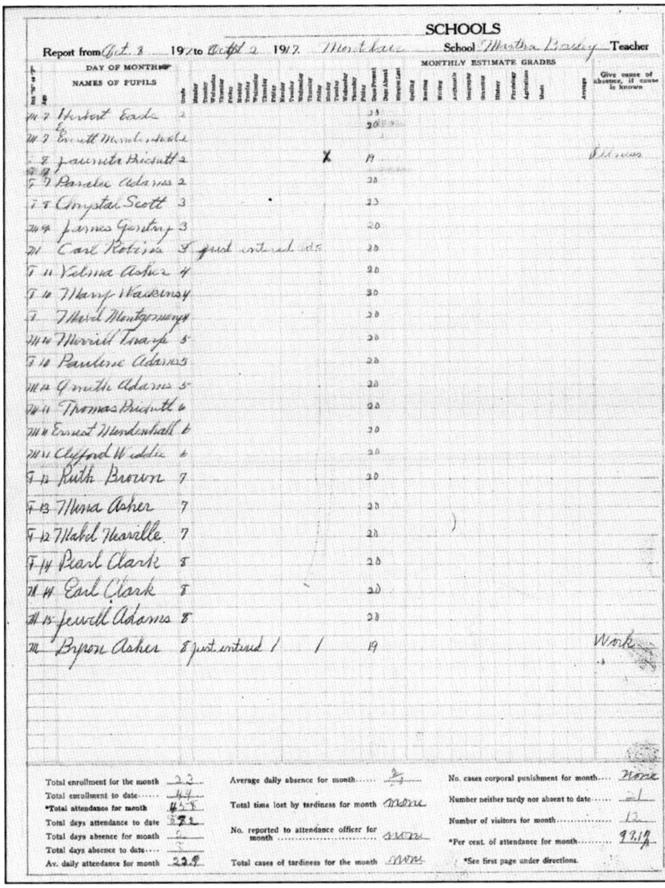

SCHOOLS

Report from Oct. 8 1917 to Nov. 2 1917 Montclair School ______ Teacher

DAY OF MONTH

NAMES OF PUPILS

MONTHLY ESTIMATE GRADES

Give cause of absence, if cause is known

Name	Grade	Days Present	Cause of absence
Herbert Eads	2	20	
Everett Mendenhall			
Jaunita Bicknell	2	19	Illness
Paralee Adams	2	20	
Crystal Scott	3	20	
James Gentry	3	20	
Carl Robison	5 just entered	20	
Velma Asher	4	20	
Mary Watkins	4	20	
Merel Montgomery	4	20	
Merrill Tharp	5	20	
Pauline Adams	5	20	
Gentle Adams	5	20	
Thomas Bicknell	6	20	
Ernest Mendenhall	6	20	
Clifford Weddle	6	20	
Ruth Brown	7	20	
Mina Asher	7	20	
Mabel Hanville	7	20	
Pearl Clark	8	20	
Earl Clark	8	20	
Jewell Adams	8	20	
Byron Asher	8 just entered	19	Work

Total enrollment for the month 22
Total enrollment to date 44
*Total attendance for month 458
Total days attendance to date 572
Total days absence for month 2
Total days absence to date 3
Av. daily attendance for month 22.9

Average daily absence for month ⅒
Total time lost by tardiness for month none
No. reported to attendance officer for month none
Total cases of tardiness for the month none

No. cases corporal punishment for month none
Number neither tardy nor absent to date 21
Number of visitors for month 12
*Per cent. of attendance for month 99.1%
*See first page under directions.

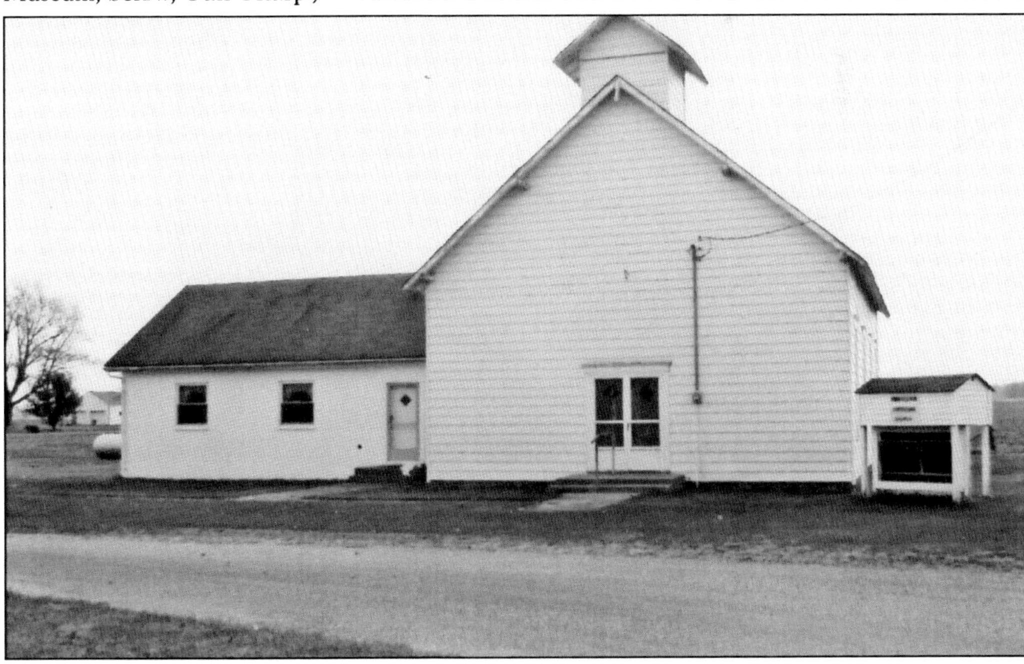

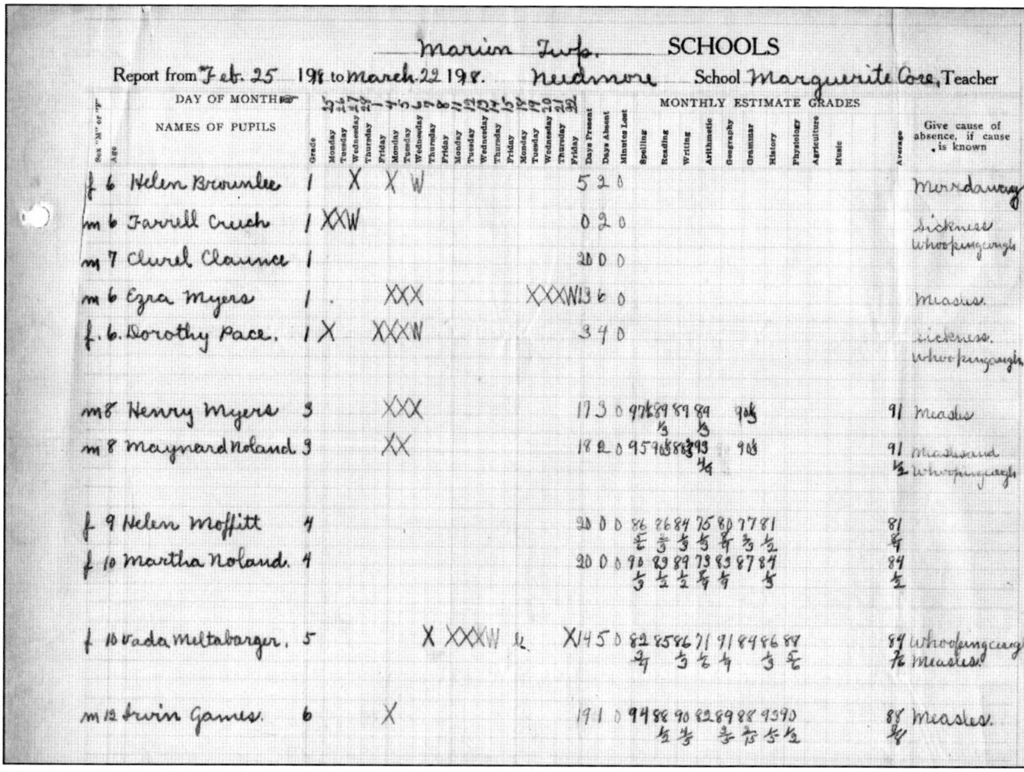

Marion Twp. SCHOOLS

Report from Feb. 25 1918 to March 22 1918. Needmore School Marguerite Core, Teacher

Sex "M" or "F"	Age	Names of Pupils	Grade	Days Present	Days Absent	Minutes Lost	Average	Give cause of absence, if cause is known
f	6	Helen Brownlee	1	5	2	0		[illegible]
m	6	Farrell Crouch	1	0	20	0		Sickness whooping cough
m	7	Clurel Claunce	1	20	0	0		
m	6	Ezra Myers	1	13	6	0		Measles.
f	6	Dorothy Pace.	1	3	4	0		sickness. whooping cough
m	8	Henry Myers	3	17	3	0	91	Measles
m	8	Maynard Noland	3	18	2	0	91½	Measles and whooping cough
f	9	Helen Moffitt	4	20	0	0	81	
f	10	Martha Noland.	4	20	0	0	84½	
f	10	Vada Meltabarger.	5	14	5	0	84	Whooping cough measles
m	12	Irwin Games.	6	19	1	0	88	Measles.

Needmore was located in Marion Township, six miles northwest of Danville. There was a post office (1868–1871), a blacksmith shop, a wagon shop, brick kiln, a Grange organization, a sawmill, and the Ramp Run Methodist Church. The Needmore School was established by 1843. In 1918, Marguerite Core was the teacher. Her report shows that measles, whooping cough, and other illnesses kept students home. The brick building was taken down in 1931. (Hendricks County Museum.)

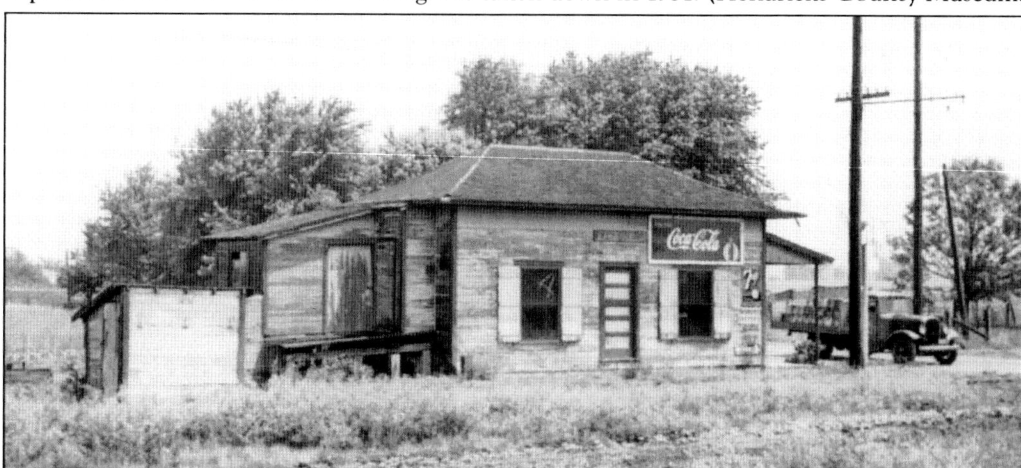

In Pecksburg, John Sheere ran a general store, and Abraham West owned the gristmill. The Vandalia Railroad line went through the community. Pictured years later, the former interurban depot at Pecksburg sits abandoned, with weeds growing between the rails. Coca-Cola and 7Up signs on the outside wall serve as reminders of busier days. The building sat on the northwest corner of CR 250W and CR 500S. (Guilford Township Collection–Plainfield Library.)

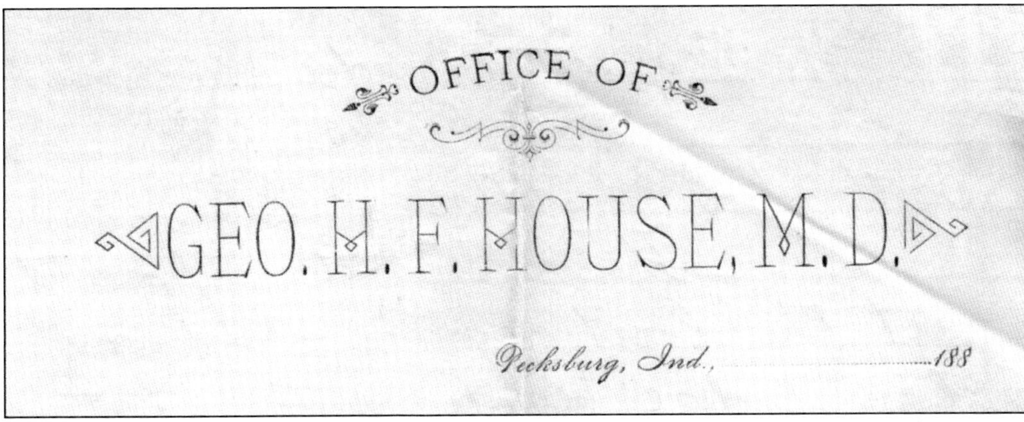
OFFICE OF

GEO. H. F. HOUSE, M. D.

Pecksburg, Ind., ...188

The 1884 Business Directory of Hendricks County lists George H.F. House as a physician in Pecksburg. Also listed are blacksmith Isaiah Archer, railroad agent Mr. Bowen, lawyer Robert Hallowell, Reverends Harvey and Truster, postmaster J.S. Marshall, painter and carpenter James Shirley, and the poultry breeders West & Whicker. Dr. House studied at the Medical College in Indianapolis. (Phyllis Parsons.)

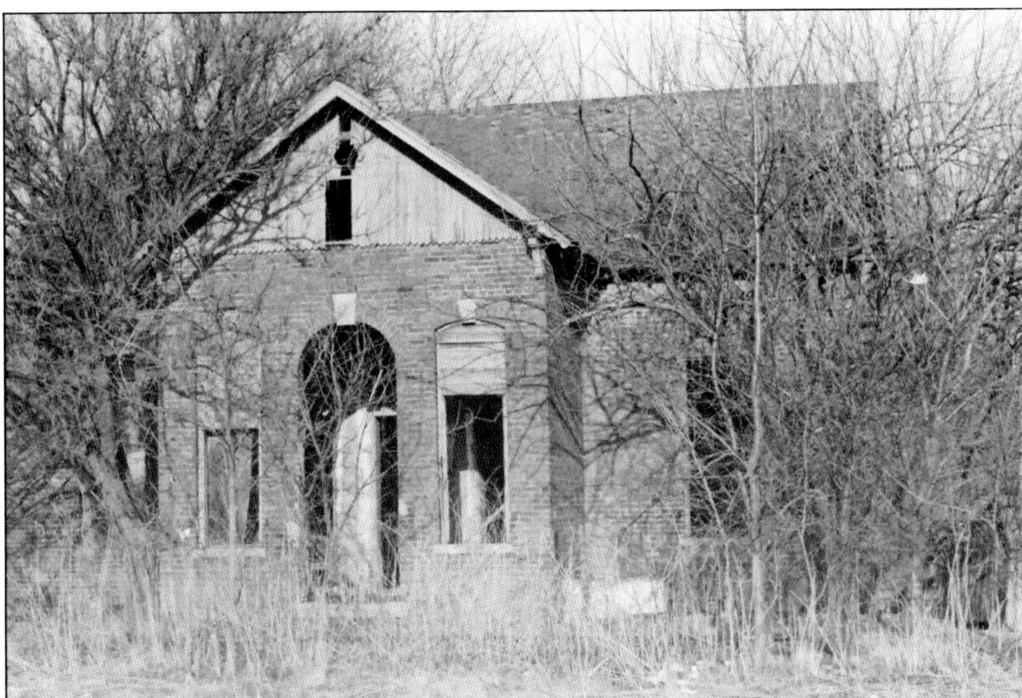

Pecksburg was located in the eastern portion of Clay Township. It was laid out in 1852 and named for Edwin Peck, the president of the railroad. It was once a thriving town, and this schoolhouse served the children there. After the school was closed, the building stood for some time as a lonely reminder of the past. (Guilford Township Collection–Plainfield Library.)

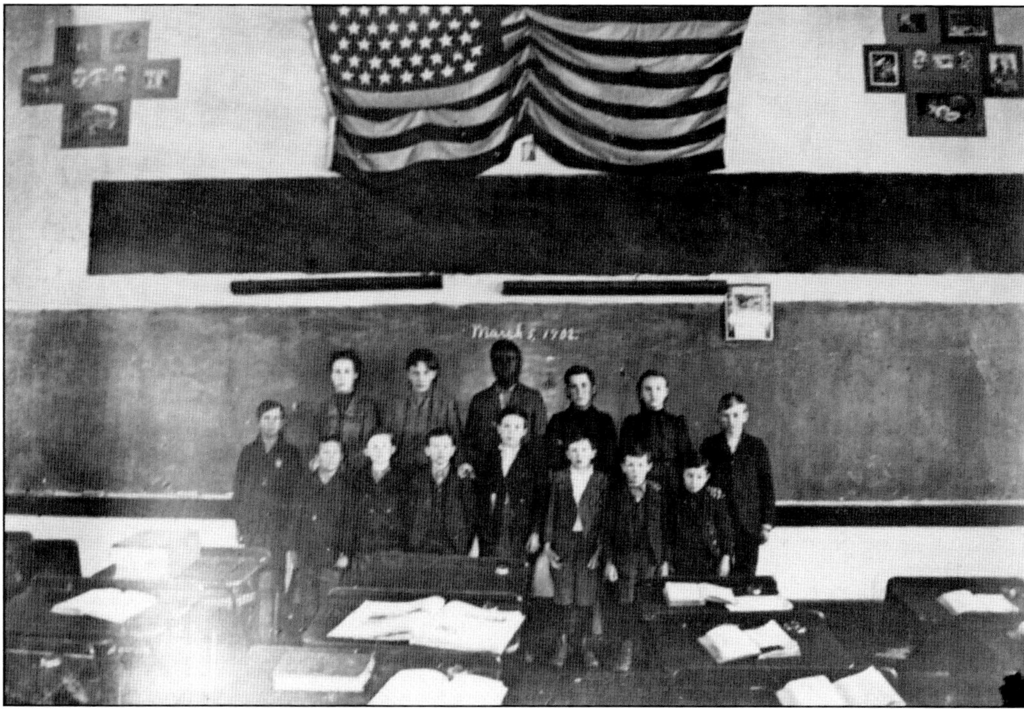

These pictures, taken on March 5, 1902, in Pecksburg, offer a rare look inside a one-room schoolhouse. Fourteen students are pictured standing in front of the blackboard, and from the looks of their clothes, it was known to all that it was picture day. The same unidentified students are seated at their desks below. The teacher has decorated the walls with homemade decorations. (Both, Guilford Township Collection–Plainfield Library.)

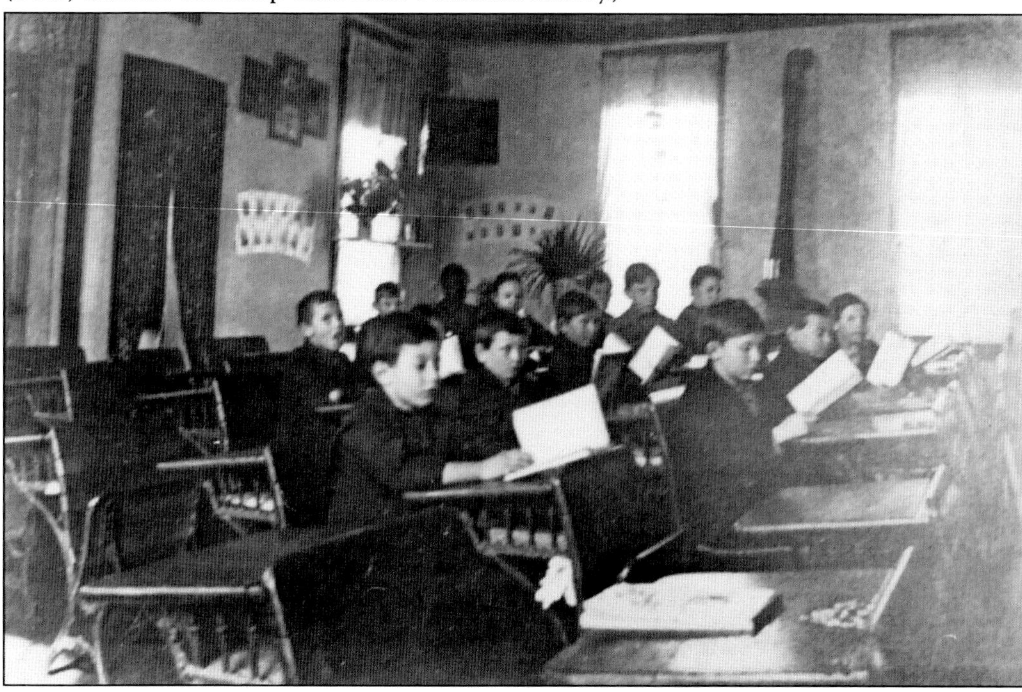

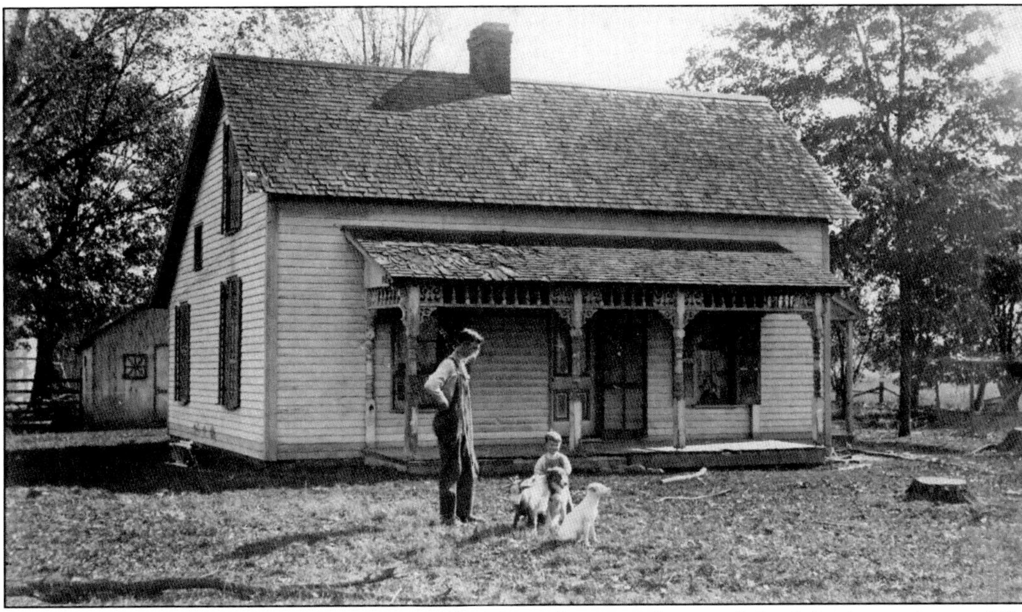

Quebec was a small community in Middle Township, southeast of the Maplewood area. The Christian church held services in 1878, but by 1926, most of the congregation had left Quebec to worship at Maplewood. The community essentially disappeared when the rail line was moved to another community. Grant Martin is pictured in the front lawn of his home in Quebec with his son Chester. (Judy Pingel.)

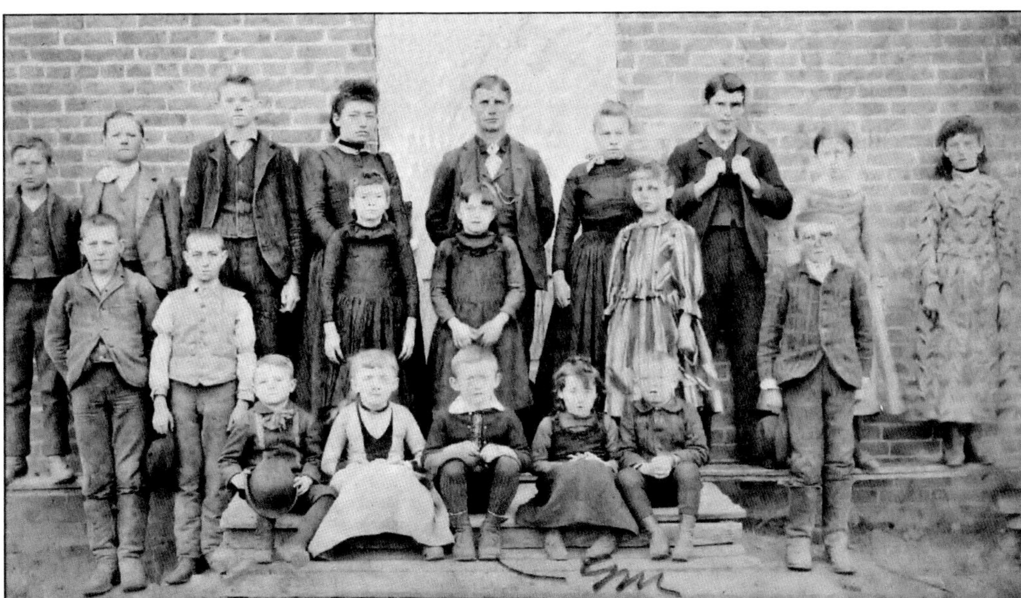

The Quebec school was located south on Parker Road. These are the students of Quebec in 1891, from left to right, (first row) Lester Holtsclaw, Esta Smith, Grant Martin, ? Hicks, and Walter Cox; (second row) two unidentified, ? Reed, Daisy Martin, Dell Warnock, and unidentified; (third row) N. Holtsclaw, unidentified, Ollie Hughes, Eunica Caterson, Ollie Flynn, Martha Hughes, Frank Flynn, Nellie Hughes, and Mayme Keenan. (Judy Pingel.)

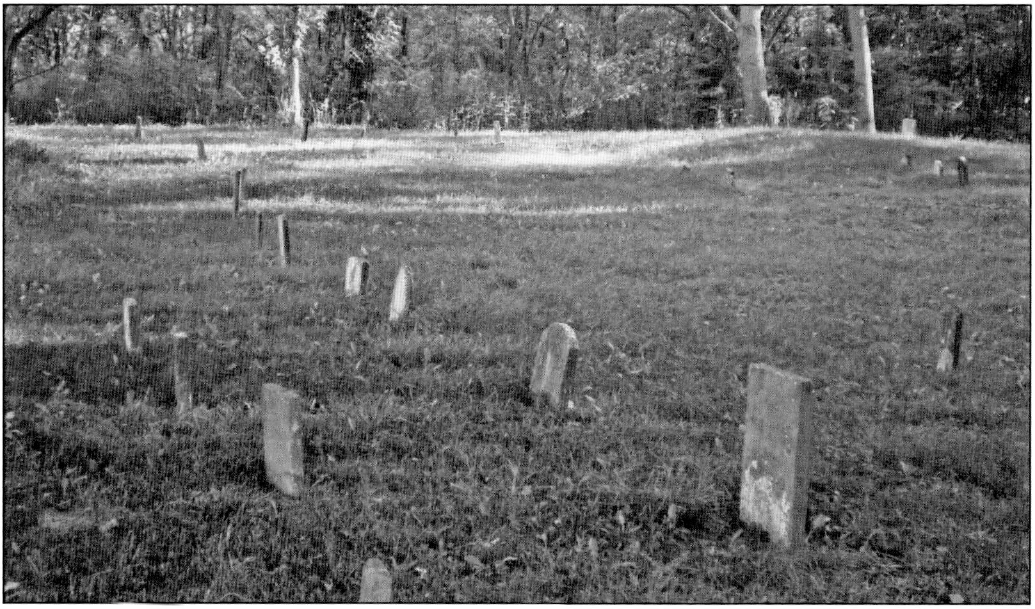

Springtown (formerly named Springfield) was laid out in 1836. At one time, there were three stores, two blacksmith shops, two shoe shops, and a gristmill. The Methodist Episcopal church was built about 1854. A post office was established in December 1843 and continued operation until November 1865. When the Vandalia Railroad was built a mile south, Amo became the flourishing community, and Springtown diminished. The Springtown Cemetery is the main reminder of that once-active community. The cemetery is well maintained. The gravestone below belongs to Rebecca, daughter of W.P. and E. Goolman. She was born on September 21, 1849, and died on September 2, 1850. (Both, Toni Waterman.)

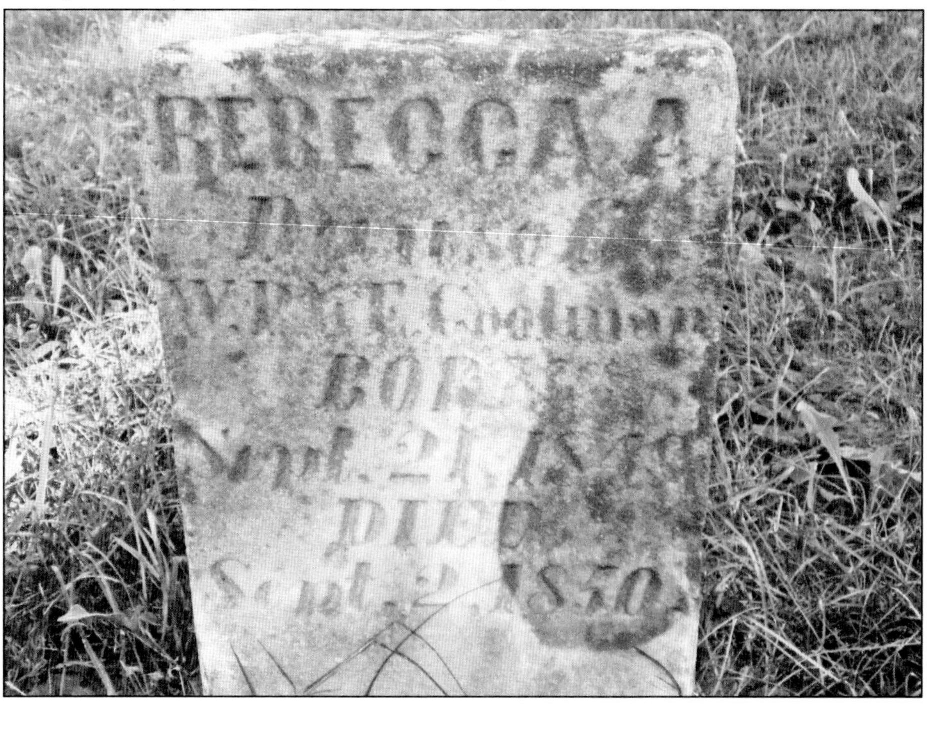

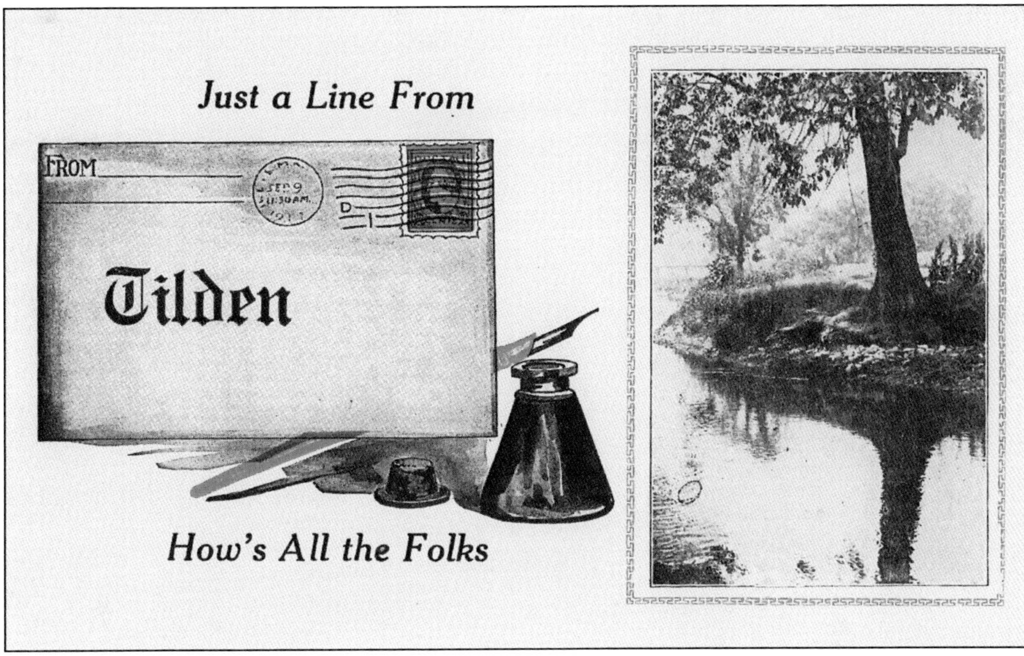

Tilden (formerly Oakley) is located west of Brownsburg on the Middle–Lincoln Township line. It was established in 1895 and is located on CR 500 East, between CR 350 North and CR 450 North. The community had a grocery store and a school and was a stop on the railroad line. The postcard is from Ancel to his mother, Mrs. Kate Jones, who lived in Montclair. Montclair is located in Union Township a few miles west of Tilden. (Both, Hendricks County Museum.)

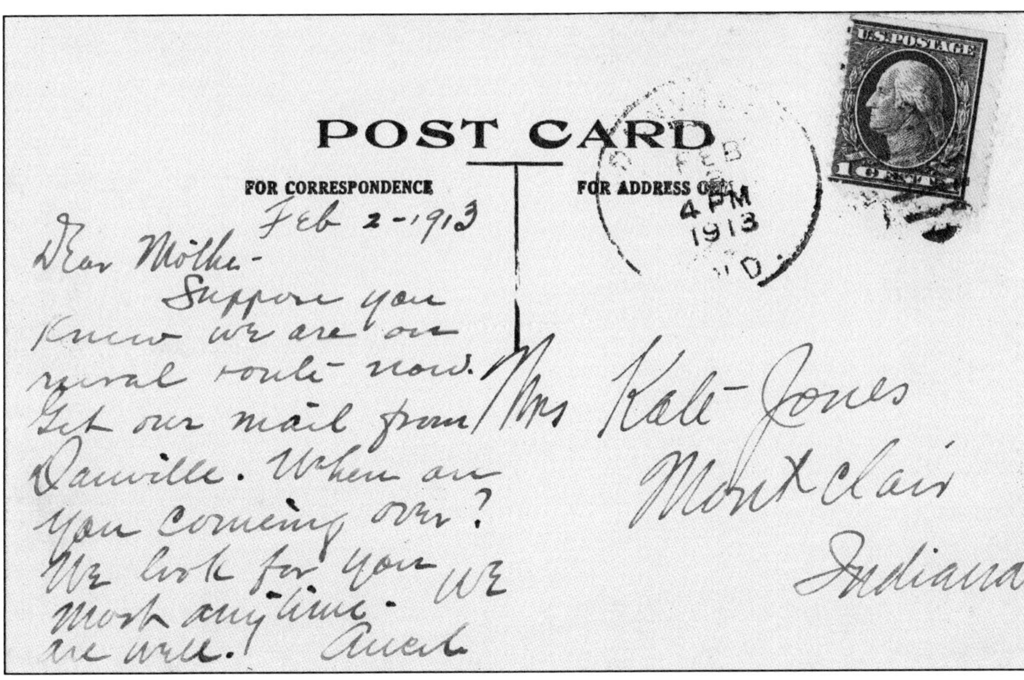

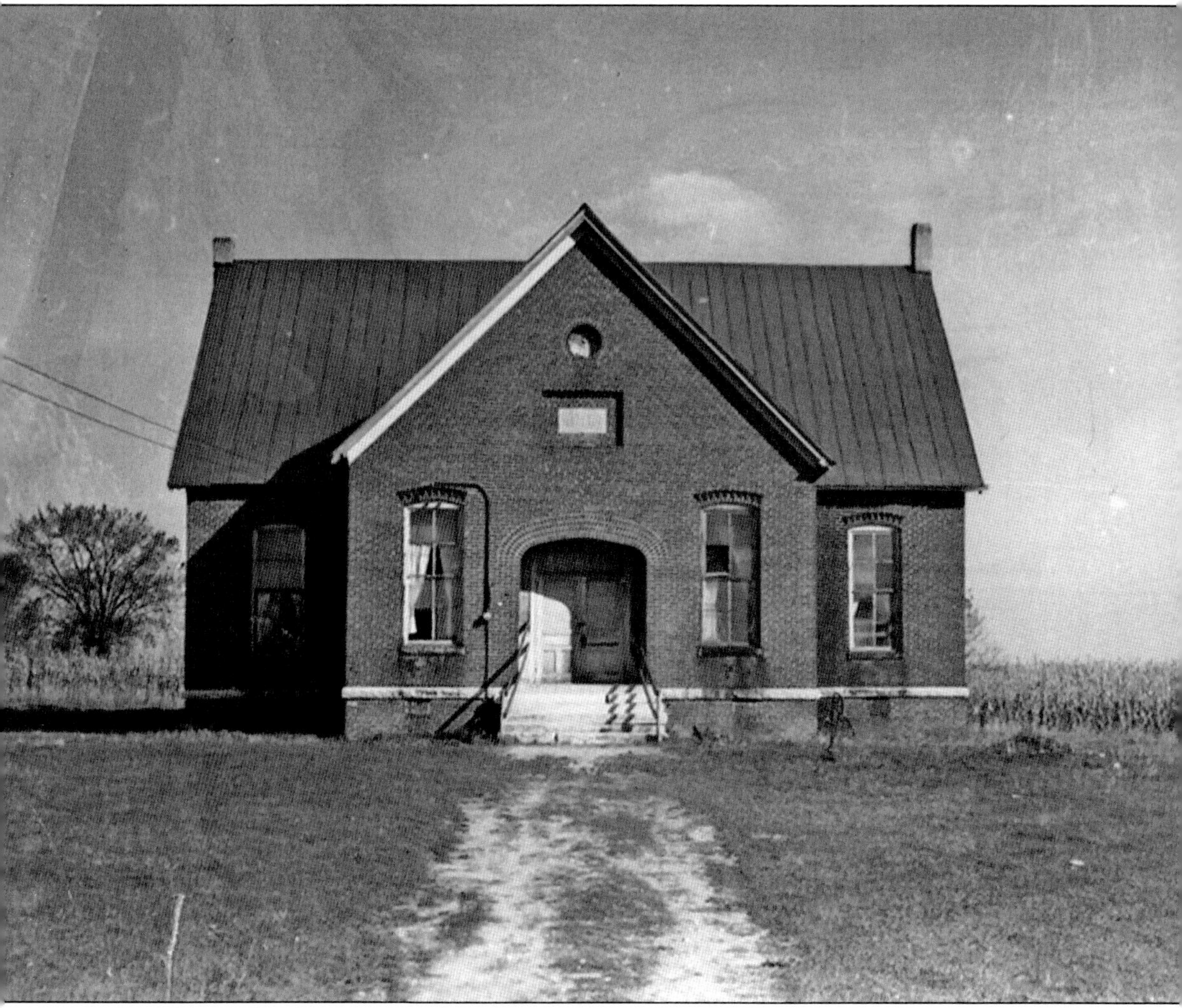

The Tilden School was a consolidation of the Barlow, Hughes, Crafton, and Blair schools. A room was used as a community building and was partitioned so that it could become a two-room schoolhouse. On the north side of the building were stalls for the students' horses. It was last used in the early 1900s. The building became a church, then a community center, and finally a residence. (Hendricks County Museum.)

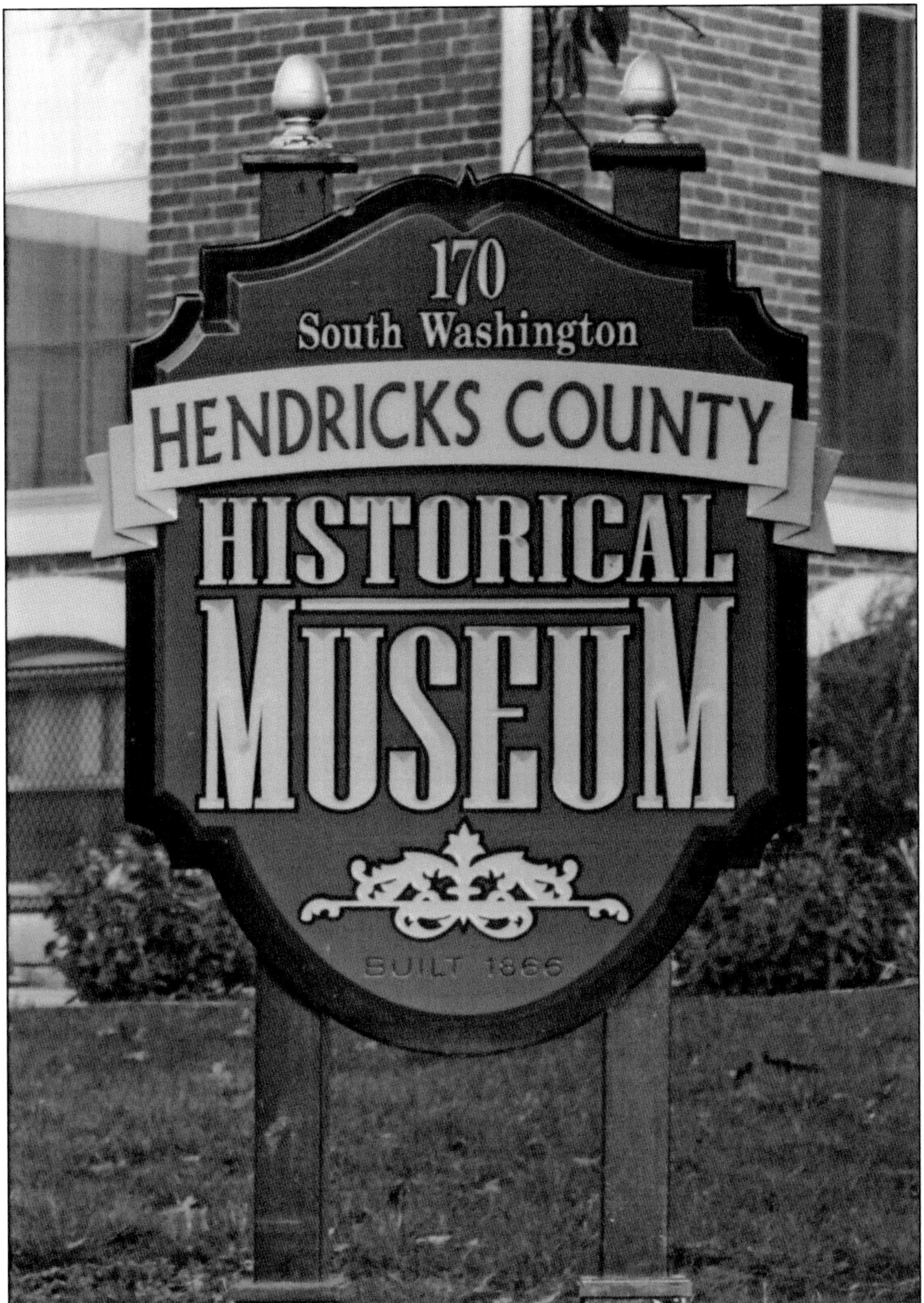

The Hendricks County Historical Museum houses a vast collection of items related to Hendricks County. The rooms throughout the house have been restored to reflect life through the years. Visitors can take a walk back in history and view artifacts from the various wars. The museum is operated by volunteers and is financially supported through memberships, donations, and grants. The authors are pleased to designate their portion of the proceeds of this book to help support the museum. (Phyllis Parsons.)